THE GOLEM REDUX

Golem mosaic (approx. 3.5 feet by 1.5 feet) set into the sidewalk in the former Jewish Quarter in Prague. Photograph taken in May 2007 by Elizabeth Baer.

THE
GOLEM
REDUX

From Prague
to Post-Holocaust Fiction

Elizabeth R. Baer

Wayne State University Press   Detroit

© 2012 by Wayne State University Press, Detroit, Michigan 48201. All rights reserved. No part of this book may be reproduced without formal permission. Manufactured in the United States of America.

16 15 14 13 12   5 4 3 2 1

Library of Congress Cataloging-in-Publication Data

Baer, Elizabeth Roberts.
The Golem redux : from Prague to post-Holocaust fiction / Elizabeth R. Baer.
p. cm.
Includes bibliographical references and index.
ISBN 978-0-8143-3626-7 (pbk. : alk. paper) — ISBN 978-0-8143-3627-4 (ebook)
1. Golem in literature. I. Title.
PN57.G56B34 2012
809'.93351—dc23
2011035239

Typeset by Maya Rhodes
Composed in Warnock Pro and Meta

This book is dedicated to my favorite golems,
my granddaughters,
DELLA RAE BAER and FLORA ESHATINE BAER,

and to my grandson
ANSEL REES BAER
who lives in my heart

Contents

Contents

Acknowledgments

I began reading post-Holocaust fiction and memoirs that incorporated fairy-tale motifs sporadically several years ago. As my exploration of these intertexts proceeded, I noticed a similar relationship between the golem legend and post-Holocaust literature. Eventually I chose that as my sole focus for this book. Along the way, I have received help and encouragement from many colleagues, friends, and strangers for which I am profoundly grateful. These include:

* Arnold Goldsmith, whom I have never met but whose book, *The Golem Remembered, 1901–1980,* has been invaluable in my own research

* The three people who read the initial proposal for the book and gave astute advice on revisions and on the manuscript in progress: Lou Roberts, professor of history at the University of Wisconsin (and my sister); Myrna Goldenberg, professor emeritus and my coeditor on an earlier book; and Hester Baer, associate professor of German and film studies at the University of Oklahoma (and my daughter)

* Scholars Stephen Feinstein of blessed memory, Simon Sibelman, Carol Rittner, Eric Carlson, and Lynn Higgins, who generously shared their knowledge of film, Holocaust studies, and German history, as well as their enthusiasm for the project

* Colleague Chris Johnson, who loaned me a crucial Marvel comic featuring the golem

* Hester Baer and Ryan Long, my son-in-law, who found other golem comics and presented me with the DVD of Paul Wegener's *Der Golem*

* The superheroic librarians who borrowed innumerable books and arti-

cles for me through interlibrary loan, Kathie Martin and Sonja Timmerman; Ginny Bakke, who supplied several key videos; and the remarkable library at the University of Oklahoma where I did research on Gustav Meyrink, Isaac Bashevis Singer, and Elie Wiesel

* The owner of Prairie Lights bookstore in Iowa City who introduced me to golem novels of which I was unaware

* The Anderson Center in Red Wing, Minnesota, a retreat center for scholars and artists, which provided quiet and an atmosphere for concentration and productivity

* Kathryn Peterson Wildfong, editor-in-chief of Wayne State University Press, who has been encouraging from our initial contact, understanding about delays caused by unforeseen problems along the way, and always forthcoming in our discussions; and Maya Rhodes, who gave invaluable assistance with illustrations in the text

* The outside readers of the manuscript who affirmed its value and made insightful suggestions for revision

* Gustavus Adolphus College, which provided a sabbatical that enabled me to write a substantial portion of the manuscript and gave me support to travel to Prague, where the golem resides

* The Gustavus students who have studied intertextuality with me in three senior seminars

* Janine Genelin, computer whiz extraordinaire, who is unfailingly helpful with manuscript formatting, preparation, and transmission, and Steve Vogt, who expertly assisted in the preparation of images for the text

* Clint, who evinces little interest in reading what I write yet is my strongest supporter

Introduction

One may recall the Golem, that rudimentary mass which received life and power from the letters which his creator mysteriously knew to inscribe on his forehead. But it is a mistake for the tradition to attribute to this being a permanent existence, similar to that of the living. The Golem was animated and lived with prodigious vitality, a life superior to all that we can conceive, but only during the ecstatic life, for he was himself nothing more than the instantaneous realization of an ecstatic consciousness. So he was at the origin, at least. Later, the Golem was changed into an ordinary magical work; he learned how to endure like all works and all things, and he became capable then of the turns and tricks that allowed him to enter into fame and legend, but also to pass out of the true secret of his art.

Maurice Blanchot, 1955

Intertextuality is perhaps the most global concept possible for signifying the modern experience of writing.

Julia Kristeva, 1985

The golem is back! In a May 2009 article in the *New York Times* titled "A New Heyday (and Many Spinoffs) for a Centuries-Old Giant, the Golem," Dan Bilefsky chronicles the many reincarnations of the golem in Prague. He quotes a Czech theater director as claiming: "The Golem starts wandering the streets at times of crisis, when people are worried. He is a projection of society's neuroses, a symbol of our fears and concerns. He is the ultimate crisis monster." Focusing on the same theme in the September

11, 2006, edition of the *New York Times,* Edward Rothstein endeavored to link together a review of a new collection of translated golem texts with the commemoration of 9/11 and sightseeing opportunities in Prague. Certainly any recent visitor to Prague has observed the crowds of tourists in the former Jewish Quarter eagerly seeking traces of the Jewish community who lived there before the Holocaust. And such tourists can purchase small clay figures of the golem, eat in a golem restaurant, and visit the Old-New Synagogue, built around 1270, where the golem, according to legend, lies at rest. Edward Rothstein headlined his article "A Legendary Protector Formed from a Lump of Clay and a Mound of Terror"; he declared: "But the Golem involves more than just legend. It also embodies a strategy: to meet irrational hatred head on, to undermine terror and mitigate its impact with resolve and persistence. Death is the threat; the Golem is the response . . . the Golem has taken on new metaphorical resonance."

I would argue that this metaphorical resonance is not new. In writing about the Holocaust and its legacy, Jewish novelists in the latter half of the twentieth century have embraced Jewish legends that reflect the long and treasured imaginative tradition in Jewish literature. In the United States over the past two decades, an astonishing number of novels that appropriate the golem legend have appeared. Many of these novels are post-Holocaust fiction: they deploy the golem legend as a vehicle for exploring the viability of narrative after the Shoah. Most, but not all, of these novels (which include graphic fiction) are written by Jewish American authors. Yet no recent scholarly monograph has brought together these novels and asked the question: Why this sudden spate of golem fiction?

The Golem Redux addresses this lacuna in scholarship about the golem. It includes an overview of the history of the golem legend; an analysis of two early twentieth-century German appropriations; late twentieth-century Jewish traditional retellings; and close textual readings of 1970s comics, seven post-Holocaust novels, and an *X-Files* episode. I address a highly controversial issue in Holocaust studies: I contend that the golem serves in several ways to provoke readers to consider the viability of *imaginative* works about the Shoah. T. W. Adorno famously said that "To write poetry after Auschwitz is barbaric,"[1] and this sentiment was echoed by Elie Wiesel's pronouncement that "A novel about Treblinka is either not a novel or not about Treblinka" (Wiesel et al., *Dimensions,* 7). Such statements seem to foreclose the possibility of post-Holocaust imaginative fiction. On the other hand, the renowned literary scholar Geoffrey Hartman, a Holocaust survivor, has written convincingly of the Jewish imagination as quintessentially "intertextual" because of the way in which the Torah is taught and studied. Hartman asserts: "The Jewish imagination has been dominated by a turn to the written word, and has developed within the orbit of the Hebrew Bible. The Jews are a People of the Book, and their mind is text dependent" (Hartman, 208). Thus I argue that the use of the golem is an intentional tribute to Jewish imagination and imaginative literature, as well as to the crucial importance of such imagination in the post-Holocaust period.

Who *Is* the Golem?

Although his incarnations and purposes have varied over the centuries, the most widely known story of the golem is as follows. The Jews in sixteenth-century Prague's Jewish Quarter were continually under threat from members of the surrounding non-Jewish community who, using many pretexts, would invade the ghetto and wreak havoc. Often the pretext was that of the blood libel: the accusation that Jews had stolen and killed a Christian baby to use its blood to make matzoh for the Passover seder. After repeated depredations, according to the legend, Rabbi Judah Loew, a real historical figure and the wise High Rabbi of Prague, directs a dream question to God, asking for help to stop the violence. God instructs Rabbi Loew to go with two trusted assistants to the banks of the Vltava River that bisects Prague. In the dark of night, they are to use the mud of the riverbank to fashion a humanoid figure and then perform a secret ritual to infuse the figure with life. Rabbi Loew names the figure Joseph/Yossele and provides him with clothing.[2] Rabbi Loew explains to the figure, now a golem and usually mute, that he will be a servant to the rabbi and do his bidding under all circumstances.

In the tales that follow his creation, the golem performs many feats of rescue and strength. Sometimes he patrols the streets of Prague at night; at other times he provides evidence regarding a Jew who has been arrested on blood libel charges so that the accused is exonerated. Eventually, either because the golem becomes destructive or because his heroic qualities are deemed no longer necessary, Rabbi Loew determines to withdraw his life, often in the attic of the Old-New Synagogue, the oldest operating synagogue in Europe. With his two assistants, Rabbi Loew reverses the ritual with which he created the golem and life seeps out of him. In most versions, Rabbi Loew then covers the inert clay figure with an old tallit or pages from discarded Torah scrolls and forbids anyone to enter the synagogue attic thereafter.

The golem has gone through long periods of quiescence in his history and then has been brought back to life, almost Rabbi Loew–style, at certain moments: as a key aspect of medieval Jewish mysticism; in the early 1800s when the golem legend was first attached to the historical figure of Rabbi Judah Loew; in the early twentieth century when pogroms based on the blood libel raged in eastern Europe; and now, in the post-Holocaust era. The golem has many images, for example, that of a monster (scholars have traced a direct line from early golem legends to Mary Shelley's *Frankenstein*)[3] and of a quixotic redeemer or savior figure. According to two Israeli writers, the golem even underlies much German philosophy and social science: "German thinkers—from Karl Marx through Ulrich Beck—continually write about the tremendous misfortunes that man-made Golems inflict upon humanity as a reprise for its vain Promethean effort to control nature. It shows that the basic narrative of a Golem rising over its master reappears in German historical interpretations of progress, capitalism and modernity."[4] Golem is also the name of a computer in Israel, a folk-punk klezmer band, a figure in the role-playing game Dungeons and Dragons, and an opera by John Casken. He has been featured in an *X-Files* episode and on *The Simpsons.* And many incarnations of the golem have been created for children: David Wisniewski's magnificent *Golem*, with haunting illustrations created from cut paper, is one of the most highly regarded. Barbara Rogasky's *The Golem* is enhanced with illustrations by Trina Schart Hyman; as with her many fairy-tale illustrations, Hyman has here researched the historical period (sixteenth-century Prague) and used the faces of real people to create compelling portraits. In a reverse of intertextuality, her painting of the golem on the book's cover is clearly influenced by filmic representations of Frankenstein. In addition, an odd twenty-five-minute film directed by Lewis Schoenbrun, titled *The Golem of L. A.* starring Ed Asner as Rabbi Judah Lowenstein, transplants the golem legend to 1990s urban America.[5]

Scholarship on the Golem

Four key contemporary texts stand as the cornerstone of scholarship on the golem: Gershom Scholem's masterful essay "The Idea of the Golem" (1960); Arnold Goldsmith's *The Golem Remembered, 1909–1980: Variations on a Jewish Legend* (1981); Byron Sherwin's *The Golem Legend: Origins and Implications* (1985); and Moshe Idel's *Golem: Jewish Magical and Mystical Tradition on the Artificial Android* (1990).

Gershom Scholem's essay appears in his book *On the Kabbalah and Its Symbolism* and this is indeed the focus of his golem essay. Beginning with an explication of Psalm 139, Scholem analyzes various versions of the creation story, Adam and Eve, their tellurian essence, and the parallels between these legends and that of the golem. Scholem traces the evolution of the golem story in the Talmud and in what he terms the "four main sources of instructions for golem making" (184): the commentaries of Eleazar of Worms and Pseudo-Saadya on the *Book Yetsirah* (also called *The Book of Creation,* written between the third and sixth centuries according to Scholem [167]) and explanations in two fourteenth-century manuscripts. Scholem notes that efforts at golem creation relied on "the letters of the alphabet—and how much more so those of the divine name or of the entire Torah, which was God's instrument of Creation—have secret magical power" (166). But he cautions the reader: "there is nothing in the instructions that have come down to us [from these four sources] to suggest that it was ever anything more than a mystical experience. . . . The motif of the magical servant or famulus is unknown to any of these texts" (184). The concept of the golem as an active figure "does not make its appearance until much later when, as we shall see, the golem becomes a figure in Kabbalistic legend" (184). Scholem draws from these early texts two important ideas: golem creation "is without practical purpose . . . [and] is dangerous" (190). But he hastens to add that the danger comes not from the golem but "lies in the tension which the creative process arouses in the creator himself" (191). The golem who "runs amok" represents a transformation of the early legend that occurs centuries later. Scholem also touches on the issues of golems and their inability to speak and golems and sexual urges. Scholem concludes his fifty-page essay by briefly mentioning sixteenth- to eighteenth-century German and Polish versions of the golem tale that include those of Rabbi Elijah Baal Shem of Chelm and Rabbi Loew of Prague, as well as the 1808 version published by Jacob Grimm. Characterizing Yudl Rosenberg's early twentieth-century tales as "tendentious modern fiction" (203), Scholem refuses to go there: "Since we have limited our investigation to the Jewish traditions of the golem up to the nineteenth century there is no need to go into the modern interpretations put forward in novels and tales, essays and plays. The golem has been interpreted as a symbol of the soul or of the Jewish people, and both theories can give rise, no doubt, to meaningful reflections. But the historian's task ends where the psychologist's begins" (204). Scholem has succeeded in giving his readers a deeply learned history of the golem, grounded in extensive research with ancient and original manuscripts and presented in the context of Jewish mystical tradition and the Kabbalah.

Two decades after Scholem's book appeared, Wayne State University Press published Arnold Goldsmith's *The Golem Remembered, 1901–1980,* the first book-length scholarly treatment of the golem legend and literature written in English. "In this book I am concerned with a single golem, the most famous one in modern times, the prototype of most of the golemim in twentieth century literature—the incredible Golem of Prague," he declares (15). Acknowledging his debt to Gershom Scholem, Goldsmith begins with a chapter on Rabbi Judah Loew, separating the historical figure from the legendary Rabbi Loew. He then devotes full or partial chapters to several of the golem texts included in my own analyses: those written by Yudl Rosenberg, Chayim Bloch, H. Leivick, and Gustav Meyrink. Goldsmith concludes with a chapter on Abraham Rothberg's *Sword of the Golem* (1970) and another on various popular culture manifestations of the legend. He notes that there is good reason for the resurgence of interest in the golem in the 1970s: "it is a legend combining all the ingredients of a popular film or television series: violence, the occult, religion, historical roots, supernaturalism, and even sex" (143). Goldsmith includes nineteen illustrations in his text—photographs from Prague, from theatrical and filmic productions of the legend, illustrations used in various editions, and a DC Comics golem—all of which enrich his text. In a real sense, my own text is a sequel to Goldsmith's fine book: the seven golem novels I treat in chapters 3, 4, and 5—by Frances Sherwood, James Sturm, Pete Hamill, Michael Chabon, Cynthia Ozick, Daniel Handler, and Thane Rosenbaum—have all been published since Goldsmith's study came out in 1981. Goldsmith, too, notes the links between golems and creativity: "The form changes, but the appeal of the golem in this century to the imagination of artists and their audience is undeniable" (15).

Byron Sherwin's modest fifty-five-page volume, *The Golem Legend: Origins and Implications,* is neatly divided into two areas of emphasis as indicated by his subtitle. In exploring the "origins" of the golem legend, Sherwin, by his own admission, relies "on the research of scholars such as Gershom Scholem and Joseph Dan who have consulted and who have utilized . . . largely inaccessible books" and manuscripts in which the golem legend is to be found (13). Sherwin's text is perhaps more readable for being a summary of earlier scholars' work; he introduces no radical new thesis but covers the primary features and variations of the legend. He concludes this section of his text with a very helpful twelve-point list of key ideas drawn from the classical literature of the golem (24–25). Sherwin then turns to the "implications" portion of his analysis: "Once a product of fantasy and of imagination, the Golem legend—its implications, its observations—is a matter of urgent relevance. The questions it engenders and the issues it evokes are matters of crushing contemporary concern" (25). As we now live in an era when genetic engineering has made it possible for humans to create "artificial life," Sherwin calls attention to the many ethical issues raised in golem tales that pertain to cloned animals, in vitro fertilization, surrogate motherhood, and machines and computers that take on human functions. He concludes on a moral note: "What the Golem legend can teach us is that the Golem, the machine, while not human, is nevertheless a reflection of the best and worst of that which makes us human. The potential harm and terror with which contemporary Golems can afflict us is but the reflection of our own penchant for self-harm and for self-destruction. . . . Ultimately, what distinguishes us from the Golem, from the machine, is our ability freely to choose the image of ourselves that we wish to become and can become" (48–49).

Moshe Idel is a professor of Jewish thought at the Hebrew University of Jerusalem and has published extensively on Kabbalah. His 1990 book on the golem, the last in the series of four influential texts outlined here, opens with an acknowledgment, as do the works by Goldsmith and Sherwin, of his debt to Gershom Scholem, whom he terms "the most important scholar who treated this subject" (xvi). But Idel sees Scholem as his starting point rather than as his source; Idel reexamined all of Scholem's manuscript and rare sources as well as several others to produce a three-hundred-page study that progresses chronologically from (as he has named his book's sections) "Ancient Traditions" to "Medieval Elaborations" to "Renaissance Period" to "Early-Modern and Modern Reverberations." Thus he both expands and in some cases endeavors to correct Scholem's analysis. "Whereas Scholem would assume that despite the magical aspects of the topic, the ultimate goal of the creation of an anthropoid was a mystical experience, I am inclined to stress more the technical part of the practice and its theological implications," Idel opines (xxv). He argues persuasively for *many* "ideas" of the golem, rather than the one idea implied by Scholem's title. Perhaps Idel's most provocative departure from Scholem is his suggestion that distinctions in conception and creation of the golem can be traced to differences in Ashkenazi and Sephardic traditions, as influenced by widely varied philosophies (see especially pages 269–81). Idel confines his study to Jewish mystical and magical texts and practices, and specifically excludes "the often discussed reverberations of the Golem theme in the legends of the late eighteenth and early nineteenth centuries" (xxix), except where their mention will elucidate the nature of the golem and the techniques for his creation.

I'll return to the scholarly histories and insights of these writers in the chapters to follow. In the years since Idel's book was published in 1990, new information about the legend and its various iterations has come to light and been published in articles or as part of anthologized collections. For example, Joachim Neugroschel published *The Golem: A New Translation of the Classic Play and Selected Short Stories* (2006), which includes a three-page introduction, and Curt Leviant brought out a new translation and edition of Yudl Rosenberg's *The Golem and the Wondrous Deeds of the Maharal of Prague* (2007), which carries an insightful twenty-page introduction.[6]

INTERTEXTUALITY AND POST-HOLOCAUST LITERATURE

If we lose our memory, we lose ourselves. Forgetting is one of the symptoms of death. Without memory, we cease to be human beings.

Ivan Klima, *The Spirit of Prague*

My argument in *The Golem Redux* focuses on the purposes of intertextuality in post-Holocaust fiction, specifically the purposes of appropriating the golem legend in this fiction. Julia Kristeva, the critic credited with coining the term, claims, "Intertextuality is perhaps the most global concept possible for signifying the modern experience of writing."[7] Intertextuality calls into question the viability of originality and stability in literary texts; in turn, it calls upon the reader to trace references, quotations, or allusions to other texts. Intertextuality allows for the re-vision and appropriation of older texts to suit new situations and meanings, and it presents the opportunity to critique outmoded assumptions. It is often seen as a specifically postmodern device in contemporary literature. By its very nature, intertextuality illuminates the act of storytelling: it makes us aware of the ways in which the author of the book we are reading is morphing an earlier text and creating a new one. It is a metafiction: a fiction about fiction.

In disrupting our sense of the text as a reflection of reality and positing instead the postmodern paradox that texts "both enshrine the past and question it" (Hutcheon, 6), intertextuality as a concept can be said to instantiate the disruption, induced by the Holocaust, of our notions of human nature, evil, and "history-as-progress," of meaning itself. I read intertextuality more broadly than simple influence; I read it as dialogue among a network of texts that at once destabilizes meaning and enables the writer to render ideological commentary. It is always a metafictional gesture.

Its central role in contemporary fiction has been explored by such critics as Graham Allen in *Intertextuality* (2000), Linda Hutcheon in *A Theory of Adaptation* (2006), and Julie Sanders in *Adaptation and Appropriation* (2006), to name just a few. We see manifestations of intertextuality everywhere, from the seemingly endless and enormously popular adaptations of Jane Austen's works (most recently revived in the best-selling *Pride and Prejudice and Zombies* by Seth Grahame-Smith) to sampling in hip-hop. Sue Vice, in her study of post-Holocaust fiction, claims that "Indeed, if there is one method that stands out among all the others used in Holocaust fiction, it is intertextuality deployed in very specific ways" (2). Her analysis, which focuses on the scandals and controversies surrounding novels about the Holocaust, attends to charges of plagiarism leveled at these fictions. Such charges often come from critics, reviewers, and readers who fail to understand the tropes and nuances of intertextuality. It is this deployment of intertextuality that I address in the book, attending to the evidence it provides of a belief in the importance of the imagination, of story for endeavoring to understand the Shoah.

Linda Hutcheon has proposed the term "historiographic metafiction" to describe the postmodern impulse to self-reflexivity and parodic intertextuality, that is, "fiction that is at once metafictional *and* historical in its echoes of the texts and contexts of the past" ("Historiographic Metafiction," 3). She defines it thus: "Historiographic fiction challenges both any naïve realist concept of representation and any equally naïve textualist or formalist assertions of the total separation of art from the world. The postmodern is self-consciously art 'within the archive' (Foucault), and that archive is both literary and historical" (6). Though Hutcheon does not use the term in reference to post-Holocaust literary texts, the term is, I believe, an apt one in that it recognizes the ineluctable hybridity of fiction about the Shoah. As we will see in chapter 5, Cynthia Ozick speaks fiercely to this issue.

It is within this postmodern literary and historical context that I will explore the intertextual appropriations of the golem legend in the chapters that follow, reading the books and films as reimagining text-centered Jewish traditions. I will emphasize how retellings of story—whether fairy tales or golem legends or the Faust myth—call attention to story itself and to the use of the imagination over the centuries as a tool for exploring human nature. By retelling or retooling golem stories, these novelists affirm the value of imaginative literature and thus rebuke Adorno's postwar prohibition that "To write poetry after Auschwitz is barbaric." At the same time, they acknowledge the instability of meaning after the Shoah. The golem is the perfect metaphor for such a plurality of images as he is often reincarnated as a servant, becomes a protector, and then, in some versions of the legend, morphs into a threat. His story is the story of human creativity and the *tension* of the creative process; he is at once a text and an intertext. No wonder he has been adopted, adapted, appropriated, and riffed upon in so many post-Holocaust fictions: intertextuality is an approach to writing devoted to instability, multiplicity, and correction.

As mentioned earlier, one of the most insightful studies of the concept of a Jewish imagination is an article by Geoffrey Hartman that appeared some time ago in *Prooftexts.* Hartman's essay opens by discussing the *ambivalent status* of imagination in medieval Jewish philosophy and by speculating about the anti-iconic second commandment "Thou shalt have no other gods before me. Thou shalt not make unto thee a graven image" (Exod. 20:3–4).[8] Hartman suggests that historically Jews "may have channeled imaginative energies into writing, into graphic rather than graven forms" (202). Of course, the whole issue of making a "graven image" is also at the heart of golem creation, suggesting an ongoing—and postmodern—ambivalence about the imagination. Hartman notes that "The Jewish imagination has been dominated by a turn to the written word, and has developed within the orbit of the Hebrew Bible. The Jews are a People of the Book, and their mind is text dependent" (208). He expands on this statement by claiming that such text dependency of the imagination means a respect for variant traditions in the Bible itself and a willingness to speak only in the name of older authorities. Further, Hartman envisions modern Jewish literature as "an involuntary or *insubordinate* midrash"; the emphasis, he states, is never on a newly developed tale but on "*the retold tale, the recycled motif . . .* and *a style composed of both explicit and inner quotations*" (210, italics mine). Hartman acknowledges the possibility that such a concept is essentialist yet his emphasis on ambivalence and insubordination is sufficient to prevent such a reading.

Thus Hartman asserts that intertextuality is at the center of the Jewish imaginative impulse, suggesting it would be predictable that writers as different as Cynthia Ozick and Lemony Snicket would appropriate golem legends. I have chosen to work with golem fiction that is largely realistic, except of course for the creation of the golem within these texts. Another monograph remains to be written about science fiction that has riffed on golem legends such as Marge Piercy's *He, She and It*. A whole strain of nonfiction analyses of the golem legend as a kind of precursor to cyborgs could also be included in such a study.

Representation and Post-Holocaust Literature

The issue of how (if at all) to represent the Holocaust and who has the authority to do so is fraught with difficulty and contentious debate among both writers and scholars in Holocaust studies. In the chapters that follow I explore this issue, particularly with regard to the golems created by Elie Wiesel (chapter 3), Michael Chabon (chapter 4), and Cynthia Ozick (chapter 5). Here I would like to offer a framework for this debate.

Sidra DeKoven Ezrahi has written extensively on the issue of Holocaust representation.[9] In her groundbreaking 1996 article, "Representing Auschwitz," Ezrahi opens by rehearsing the T. W. Adorno prohibition against "poetry after Auschwitz" and by quoting from the poetry of survivor Paul Celan. She then outlines what she perceives as the "two major clusters of attitudes" regarding representation in post-Holocaust literature:

> In the literature of testimony as well as of the imagination, in the theories of historiographical and of poetic representation, one can begin to discern a fundamental distinction between a static and a dynamic appropriation of history and its moral and social legacies. The static or absolutist approach locates a non-negotiable self in an unyielding place whose sign is Auschwitz; the dynamic or relativist position approaches the representation of memory of that place as a construction of strategies for an ongoing *re*negotiation of that historical reality. . . . In each case, the work of history or art is being performed in the aftermath, at a "safe" distance—but again it is distance itself which is at stake. (122, italics in original)

These "two clusters"—the absolutist and the relativist—are often defined as texts that purport to relate only the "facts" such as histories and survivors' memoirs (absolutist) and texts that are imaginative such as poetry and fiction (relativist).[10] Ezrahi notes that for writers such as T. W. Adorno and Tadeusz Borowski, the very possibility of metaphor in the post-Holocaust period has been foreclosed. Auschwitz is at once "the very center of evil" and yet is "located in a realm just beyond the borders of civilized speech and behavior" (121): it evacuates the possibility of representation and "obliterates the imagination as an agent of meaning" (123). By contrast, Ezrahi notes, Primo Levi affirms the possibility of imaginative literature by recounting in *Survival in Auschwitz* the moment in the camp when he shares with a comrade a passage from Dante's *The Divine Comedy*, which Levi quotes from memory.

Ezrahi's article goes on to analyze the work of Lawrence Langer, Claude Lanzmann, and Berel Lang as supportive of the position denying the possibility of metaphor, sometimes called the *mysterium tremendum* school of thought. And she delineates narrative strategies—for example, texts that provide "alternative histories" or "sideshadowing" such as Jurek Becker's novel *Jacob the Liar* and David Grossman's *See, Under Love*—that enable writers and readers to imagine "what ifs." Ultimately Ezrahi sees the issue of representation as a dialectic between the two poles: "the urgency of representation, then, unfolds in continual tension between desire and its limits" (145). She affirms intertextuality as "a postwar re-enactment of the continuity of storytelling as resistance to the black hole that would swallow the cultural forms along with the people who practiced them" (141). This, I believe, is exactly the role of the golem in post-Holocaust literature: to affirm the viability and authority of the imagination, of story, and of creativity.

A decade after Ezrahi's article appeared, Erin McGlothlin published a provocative essay on narrative transgression in Holocaust survivor Edgar Hilsenrath's novel *The Nazi and the Barber* (1971). Her analysis is also helpful in establishing a framework for the debate surrounding the viability of representing the Holocaust: "What sort of story does [Hilsenrath's] novel mediate about the process itself of representing the Holocaust?" (225), McGlothlin asks, thereby indicating her reading of the novel as a metafiction. She carefully delineates the debate among scholars, survivors, and writers by noting, among others, Saul Friedländer's anthology *Probing the Limits of Representation* (1992), the pronouncements of Elie Wiesel on this issue, and the searing claims of the novelist Leslie Epstein for the critical importance of imagination: "For Epstein, the Nazi attack on the Jewish imagination must be answered with an affirmation of that very same quality. . . . To affirm the role of the Jewish imagination with regard to the Holocaust would be to at least partially recover a history that was almost extinguished" (230). Like Ezrahi, McGlothlin reads much Holocaust literature as a "dialectic" in which writers "thematize . . . as transgression" their "ambivalence about their literary engagement with the Holocaust" (232). It is such transgressions in identity, narration, and history that she traces in Hilsenrath's novel.

Intertextuality, too, is a transgressive and dialectical strategy for addressing the debate surrounding representation in post-Holocaust fiction. Calling the reader's attention to the dynamic relationship between an earlier text and the reformulation revealed by the text in the reader's hands, intertextuality offers writers an opportunity to deploy imagination and yet acknowledge their understanding of the bravura of such deployment. The golem in particular allows such inherent metafictional commentary, representing as he does creativity, Jewish legend, mysticism, memory, ambivalent identity, and an actual intertext.

OVERVIEW OF THE TEXT

Chapter 1 of *The Golem Redux* traces the history of the legend from the first mention of the word "golem" in the Book of Psalms to careful consideration of medieval golem legends, to those surrounding Rabbi Judah Loew in Prague, and on to the versions by Yudl Rosenberg and Chayim Bloch in the early twentieth century. This historiography is critical to establishing the tropes with which contemporary writers play when they appropriate the legend. I also look at the history of the Josefov, the Jewish Quarter in Prague, where the legend of the golem reached its full flowering.

In chapter 2 I revisit two German texts in depth: Gustav Meyrink's *Der Golem* (1914), set in Prague in the late nineteenth century and often considered the ur-text from which later adaptations flow, and Paul Wegener's 1920 filmic adaptation, *Der Golem: Wie er in die Welt kam*. In connection with the latter, I also devote space to Wegener's earlier film, *Der Student von Prag* (1913), and the French-Czech film *Le Golem* (1936), directed by Julien Duvivier, which presents a sharp contrast to Wegener's classic film. I focus on Meyrink and Wegener's texts because they were largely responsible for the popularization of the golem legend in the early twentieth century and because they demonstrate how intertextuality can go badly wrong: these two texts have taken a Jewish legend and turned it on its head, making it perversely antisemitic in the process.

By contrast, chapter 3 presents three retellings of the legend by Jewish writers in which the golem is revered. Nonetheless, each writer brings his/her own idiosyncratic changes to the tale. Both Isaac Bashevis Singer and Elie Wiesel wrote their golem texts after emigration to the United States. Curiously, they published their English versions sequentially (Singer in 1982, Wiesel in 1983), and both texts were cast in a simplified form, with illustrations, appropriate for children as well as for adults. Both wrote the original story in Yiddish. And, sadly, both texts have been almost completely ignored by critics in studies of the opus of each man. While Singer's golem is an earthy and very human creature and the text is full of Singeresque invention, Wiesel's golem hews more closely to earlier versions and is a transcendent, philosophical creature. The last text studied in this chapter is Frances Sherwood's novel, *The Book of Splendor* (2002). In the author's acknowledgments at the end of the novel, she describes it as "a historical fantasy using fictional and non-fictional characters" (347). Set in Prague in 1601, the novel dwells on Rudolf II, the Holy Roman Emperor seated in Prague, his obsession with alchemy, and his fascination with the golem. Sherwood, the grandchild of Holocaust victims, draws on the tropes of traditional golem legends for this largely realistic novel.

In chapter 4 I begin to focus on contemporary post-Holocaust fiction. I look at the "comic golem," tracing the significant role that Jewish artists, writers, and entrepreneurs have had in the American comics industry and reading the appropriation of the golem as a superhero by Marvel Comics in the 1970s. James Sturm's graphic novel about baseball, *The Golem's Mighty Swing* (2001), continues this strain of golem stories with the integration of image and text found in comics. The Stars of David, a Jewish baseball team in the 1920s, bring a golem onboard to try for a winning season. In an intriguing intertextual gesture, Sturm draws the golem as he appears on the screen in Paul Wegener's 1920 film, then playing at the Criterion Theatre in

New York. I also include here Pete Hamill's *Snow in August* (1997), a novel by a non-Jew in which a young Christian boy living in Brooklyn in 1946 creates a golem. Michael, whose father died in World War II and who serves as a *shabbos goy* in the local synagogue, finds solace in the fantasies of power delivered by his beloved comic books.

Hamill acknowledges in an afterword that Michael is a rather autobiographical character and that he, Hamill, experienced a kind of epiphany in visiting Rabbi Loew's grave in the Jewish cemetery in Prague: "The golem is a triumphant symbol of the human imagination" (372). I conclude this chapter by showing how the tropes of the comics are imbricated in Michael Chabon's Pulitzer Prize–winning *The Amazing Adventures of Kavalier and Clay*, a novel that opens in Prague as the golem is smuggled out for safety during the Nazi occupation and continues as the Jewish immigrant characters find work and identity in the Manhattan comics industry. Thus, each of these texts tells of a yearning for superheroes, of the Jewish community's need to have a champion when danger and antisemitism threaten.

Finally, in chapter 5 I discuss three novels in which the golems are of (attempted) heroic stature as well as an episode from the television series *The X-Files*. Two of the novels take place in New York City: Cynthia Ozick's *The Puttermesser Papers* (1997) and Thane Rosenbaum's *The Golems of Gotham* (2002). Each novel depicts a post-Holocaust utopian impulse to create an urban paradise with golems as the tools for such a creation. Creation and creativity are certainly key themes in golem texts—historically, such texts tested the boundaries of what humans could create and what might tread on the prerogatives of the Creator; now the emphasis is on the creation of the golem as well as the creation of story. The third novel discussed in this chapter is Daniel Handler's *Watch Your Mouth* (2000), which explores creativity in yet another way: through sexuality. Handler, as a child of Holocaust survivors, is a member of the Second Generation and is better known as Lemony Snicket, author of the wildly popular children's books *A Series of Unfortunate Events*, which examine evil in many manifestations across thirteen volumes. In *Watch Your Mouth* (a reference to the use of a *shem* in the golem's mouth to activate and deactivate him, a trope in some of the legends), Handler has written a story that is avowedly sexual and avowedly adult. The narrator, Joseph, is a golem, and he tells a tale of creating golems and of performing a golem opera. Handler notes that he learned about the Holocaust at an early age and he sees his own books in the tradition of "Jewish literature [that] encompasses impending disaster."[11] Thus, a subtext of this chapter is the writing of the Second Generation, the children of Holocaust survivors.

The Second Generation is also the focus of *The X-Files* episode "Kaddish," which originally aired in 1997 and is included here in chapter 5. The episode revolves around a Holocaust survivor from Prague and his American daughter, Ariel, who creates a golem to serve as a substitute bridegroom when her fiancé is murdered shortly before their wedding.

Throughout *The Golem Redux* I argue that Jewish American writers have created golem stories as a reimagining of text-centered Jewish traditions by appropriating, adapting, revising, and riffing on golem legends, deploying the imagination to seek a better understanding of human nature. Understanding just what human nature is became a central focus of the humanities after World War II, when the question arose as to how human beings in a supposedly civilized country could have systematically and quite publicly done what the Nazis did. Ultimately the golem himself is a kind of text—created with rituals of words and having letters inscribed on his forehead in several versions of the tale. In this regard, I argue that intertextuality can be seen as a kind of *repository of literary memory:* by reprising old legends, we remember not only the value these tales had in earlier eras but also the importance of story to our humanity. If the gesture of intertextuality creates the memory, imagination is the magic elixir, the secret formula that effects transformation from one text to another.

1

The Golem Redux

Variations on the Golem Legend in Jewish Tradition

My being was not concealed from thee, when I was made
In secret, when I was (so to say) embroidered in the lowest
Parts of the earth. My undeveloped substance did thy eyes see;
And in thy book were all of them written down—the days
Which have been formed, while yet not one of them was here.

Psalm 139:15–16

"In the beginning . . . "

Most accounts of the history of the golem begin by mentioning that the first appearance of the word "golem" occurs in the Book of Psalms, as quoted above. Commentaries in the Talmud suggest that the speaker here is Adam and that he praises God for forming his "undeveloped substance" (i.e., *golem*) from the earth. The use of the word "golem" also implies the figure of man before he has acquired a soul (Bilski, 10). Of particular importance for this study of the appropriation of the golem legend in post-Holocaust fiction is the emphasis on *the book* and the *writing of the word* in this psalm. If intertexuality serves as a memory for literature, then this is the ur-text from which the golem legend arises. As Geoffrey Hartman declares, "The Jewish imagination has been dominated by a turn to the written word, and has developed within the orbit of the Hebrew Bible" (208).

In this chapter, we will look at several early manifestations of the golem legend that follow upon this verse from the Book of Psalms. This overview

17

is not intended to be exhaustive[1] but will provide the reader with a grasp of the key tropes of the legend that, in turn, will enhance appreciation and understanding of the post-Holocaust texts discussed in chapters 3, 4, and 5. I begin by presenting golem texts from the third and fourth centuries and from the medieval period. A much fuller exposition of Prague's golem legend, which is attached to the Maharal Rabbi Judah Loew, follows. Also important for context is the history of the Josefov, the Jewish ghetto in Prague, the site of the golem legend, and the setting for both filmic treatments and fiction in the twentieth century. Finally, attention is given to versions of the golem legend by Yudl Rosenberg and Chayim Bloch, which have informed and influenced late twentieth- and early twenty-first-century intertexts.

EARLY MANIFESTATIONS OF THE GOLEM LEGEND

References to a golem-like creature occur in several classical Jewish texts. In the tractate Sanhedrin 65b in the Talmud, we find legends about famous rabbis of the third and fourth centuries who succeeded in creating life. Despite the fact that the following passage does not use the word "golem," it "represents the first record of a creation of a Golem by a human being" (Sherwin, *The Golem Legend*, 4).

> Rava said: if the righteous wished, they could create a world, for it is written [Isa. 59:2]: "Your iniquities have separated between you and your God." The implication is that if a man is saintly without sins, his creative power is no longer "separated" from that of God. And the text continues as though its author wished to demonstrate this creative power: "For Rava created a man and sent him to Rabbi Zera. The rabbi spoke to him and he did not answer. Then he said: "You must have been made by the companions [members of the Talmudic Academy]; return to your dust." The Aramaic word here rendered by "companions" is ambiguous. According to some scholars Rabbi Zera's sentence should be interpreted to mean "You must come from the magicians." In the Talmud this passage is immediately followed by another story: "Rav Hanina and Rav Oshaya busied themselves on the eve of every Sabbath with the Book of Creation—or in another reading: with the instructions [*halakhoth*] concerning creation. They made a calf one-third the natural size and ate it." (quoted from Sanhedrin 65b in Scholem, *On the Kabbalah*, 166)

Several aspects of this passage are important for our purposes. First, we read the implication that human beings do have the power to create life and, second, that the creator of a golem must be as pure as possible. Sin, however, can hamper this ability: "Your iniquities have separated between you and your God." In some of the texts explored in the chapters to follow, such as those by Pete Hamill and Thane Rosenbaum, it is a child who creates the golem, one who is still innocent of evil. The passage also implies that some form of magic is employed to create the golem but, as Scholem notes, "This artificial or magical man is always lacking in some essential function" (166). Here it is clear that the golem is mute, which in turn suggests that he is not fully human. This is a trope that remains consistent until late twentieth-century golem tales when the golem sometimes does acquire the ability to talk, for example, in Isaac Bashevis Singer's and Cynthia Ozick's golem tales. Finally, this passage mentions the Book of Creation, another key text in the layering of golem texts.

The Book of Creation, as its name suggests, is interpreted by many scholars to be the source book for golem creation. Alternately called the Book Yetzirah or the Sefer Yetzirah, it is about two thousand words long and, "initially meant to be a speculative work, [it] . . . was later considered by Jewish mystics to be a manual to be used for the act of creation itself" (Sherwin, *The Golem Legend,* 5). Gershom Scholem notes that "the text that played so important a part in the development of the golem concept: the *Book Yetsirah* or *Book of Creation,*" may or may not be the same as the book referred to in the Sanhedrin passage above. The Book Yetzirah with which we are familiar, Scholem asserts, was written by a Jewish Neo-Pythagorean some time between the third and the sixth centuries (167).

Also crucial to understanding the development of the golem legend are commentaries on *The Book of Creation,* written subsequently by learned men and mystics. For example, Rabbi Eleazar of Worms, living in the twelfth and thirteenth centuries, actually enumerated instructions for the creation of a golem in his commentary (Kieval, *Languages,* 97).

The Book of Creation states:

> Twenty-two letter elements: He outlined them, hewed them out, weighted them, combined them, and exchanged them (i.e. He transformed them in accordance with certain laws), and through them (He) created the whole of all creation and everything else that would ever be created . . . it comes about that all creation and all language issue from one name (*Sefer Yetzirah* 2:2, 5). (Sherwin, *The Golem Legend,* 5)

Here, then, is the crucial importance of words and language in golem creation. As Scholem observes: "The letters of the alphabet—and how much more so those of the divine name or of the entire Torah, which was God's instrument of Creation—have secret, magical power" (166). In subsequent golem legends, we see the centrality of the Hebrew alphabet in the act of creation: whether it be the chanting of magical verses, the placing of the *shem* (a paper on which God's name is written) in the clay man's mouth, or the carving of the word *emeth* (life) in his forehead, the alphabet brings him to life.

Such words provide the ritual used by Rabbi Judah Loew of Prague in the creation of his golem, Joseph. They are rendered visually in the beautiful etchings by Mark Podwal that illustrate Elie Wiesel's golem story; the words of the Sunday edition of the *New York Times* are implicated in the creation of Cynthia Ozick's golem: "The notion that God creates the world by means of language—through words—is biblical. The idea that human beings can share in God's creative power by mastering formulae that combine and permutate letters of the alphabet is rabbinic in origin" (Sherwin, *The Golem Legend*, 5).

In these early manifestations of the golem legend, the emphasis is on the *act of creation* rather than the retention of the golem to perform duties of any kind. Scholem asserts that by "the twelfth century at the latest a set procedure for golem-making developed [but] this procedure was a ritual *representing* an act of creation by the adept and culminating in ecstasy . . . there is nothing in the instructions that have come down to us to suggest that it was ever anything more than a mystical experience" (184, italics in original). Such an emphasis on the creation of the golem as an end in itself is also a feature of German beliefs regarding the golem legend.

By contrast, an eleventh-century Spanish poet and philosopher, Solomon ibn Gabirol (1020–57), was said to have created a female golem to take care of household chores for him. As the story goes, Gabirol suffered from a severe skin disease that required him to isolate himself from other human beings. He created the golem not from earth/clay/dust as was the usual process but from wood and hinges. When questioned by the authorities, who suspected Gabirol might use the golem for "lewd activities," Gabirol willingly dismantled her (Sherwin, 16). Rabbi Eleazar of Worms provides one formula for the creation of a male golem and another for a female golem in his commentary on the Book Yetzirah. As we shall see, Cynthia Ozick writes of a female golem in her novel *The Puttermesser Papers*. But the key point here is that the golem is now created not as an end in itself but as a servant: "The intent of the golem creation had changed by the twelfth century: mystical and spiritual motives were replaced by utilitarian ends" (Krause, 126). This strand of the legend is one of the motives for Rabbi Loew's golem creation.

Before turning to Rabbi Loew, two more names deserve mention as we trace the variations in the golem legend: Rabbi Elijah Baal Shem and Jacob Grimm. Thus far, we have seen that the term "golem" is first used in the Book of Psalms, becomes the goal of a kabbalistic ritual that focuses on the act of creation, and then develops into a legend in which golems are created as household servants. Now, a new turn: "In the late forms of the legend, which arose in seventeenth-century Poland, a new element appears: the servant becomes dangerous" (Scholem, *Kabbalah*, 199). This legend is associated with Rabbi Elijah Baal Shem of Chelm (d. 1583), and about a century later, in 1674, we are given an account of his golem-making in a letter written by Christoph Arnold. Though many features of this account are familiar, the writing on the body of the golem is particularly noteworthy:

> After saying certain prayers and holding certain fast days, they make the figure of a man from clay, and when they have said the *shem hamephorash* over it, the image comes to life. And although the image itself cannot speak, it understands what is said to it and commanded; among the Polish Jews it does all kinds of housework, but is not allowed to leave the house. On the forehead of the image, they write: *emeth*, that is, truth. But an image of this kind grows each day; though very small at first, it ends by becoming larger than all those in the house. In order to take away his strength, which ultimately becomes a threat to all those in the house, they quickly erase the first letter *aleph* from the word *emeth* on his forehead, so that there remains only the word *meth*, that is, dead. When this is done, the golem collapses and dissolves into the clay or mud that he was. . . . They say that a baal shem in Poland, by the name of Rabbi Elias, made a golem who became so large that the rabbi could no longer reach his forehead to erase the letter *e.* He thought up a trick, namely that the golem, being a servant, should remove his boots, supposing that when the golem bent over, he would erase the letters. And so it happened, but when the golem became mud again, his whole weight fell on the rabbi, who was sitting on the bench, and crushed him. (Scholem, *Kabbalah*, 200–201)

This version of the legend was, in turn, published in a book by Johann Jakob Schudt in Frankfurt in 1714, which became the source for Jacob Grimm's version, published in the *Zeitung Für Einsiedler* (Journal for Hermits) on April 23, 1808. From Grimm, it passed into the tradition of German Romantic writers, including Ludwig Achim von Arnim in 1812 (Bilski, 13–14).

Some contemporary scholars have characterized the changes in the golem legend as an "evolution": from mystical experience for the sake of the experience, to a legend of golems who are mute but faithful servants, to the story of golems who protect the Jewish community from antisemitism, to an image of golems who turn destructive in some fashion, and, finally, to the comic or superhero golem. As the metaphor of evolution also suggests a sense of progression, I find it not only rather useless but also inappropriate. Several such metamorphoses often occur in one golem text in a specific time frame rather than over the centuries, nor do the metamorphoses move toward better "adaptation" in the Darwinian sense. More suitable is the literary idea of the *palimpsest:* texts layered upon texts through intertextual gestures that reveal and valorize various emphases at various times. This image of golem texts superimposed upon one another brings with it the notion that no one text is the "true" text and that all golem legends continue to exist and to serve as both sources and intertexts.

PRAGUE: RABBI JUDAH LOEW'S GOLEM AND THE JEWISH GHETTO, THE JOSEFOV

The most famous golem story, of course, is that created about the greatly admired rabbi of Prague, Rabbi Judah Bezalel Loew, sometimes called the Maharal (an acronym for **Morenu Ha-Rav** Loew, meaning Our Teacher Rabbi Loew). Despite the fact that Rabbi Loew is ineluctably linked with the golem in almost all nineteenth-, twentieth-, and twenty-first-century golem tales, ironically, he did not believe in magic or miracles, according to most sources. Indeed, the golem legend was not associated with the Maharal until a full century after his death, and another century elapsed before the legend linking the two appeared in print in 1841 (Kieval, *Languages*, 106). Another irony in the legends, potentially misleading, is that Rabbi Loew's ostensible reason for creating the golem was the need to protect the Jewish community from accusations of blood libel, yet no blood libels occurred during Loew's service as Prague's Chief Rabbi in the late sixteenth century (Leviant, xxix).[2] Indeed, the discrepancies between the legends surrounding Rabbi Loew and the facts we know about his life caused Arnold Goldsmith, whose book *The Golem Remembered, 1909–1980* is the first book-length scholarly study of literary golems, to title his first chapter "The Two Judah Loews: Historical and Legendary."

In his remarkable account of Jewish experience in Czech lands, Hillel Kieval estimates that Prague has been home to a Jewish community since at least the 1100s; that is the first century for which we have documentation. Prior to that, "Traveling Jewish merchants were doing business in the Prague and Bohemian regions in the ninth and tenth centuries—coming and going in caravans, selling spices, silk, and other luxury goods to barons, clerics of the upper hierarchy, and the court, and exporting from the Slavic east slaves, weapons, leather goods and beeswax to Mediterranean and Oriental countries" (Demetz, 40). Jewish fortunes in Prague waxed and waned during the centuries that followed, often in relationship to the attitudes of the current ruler toward the Jewish community. That community, whose primary language was Yiddish, quickly grew to be the largest in central Europe before 1800 (Kieval, *Languages,* 10). Jews were forced to wear a yellow badge; this requirement was not lifted until 1781 (Giustino, 154). Today, 1389 is remembered for one of the bloodiest and most tragic events the community in Prague endured. At Easter in that year, with the encouragement of the Prague clergy whose accusations against the Jews whipped non-Jewish citizens into a frenzy, a pogrom took place: an angry mob invaded the Jewish Quarter, killing dozens of Jews, burning and looting, and destroying much of the Jewish cemetery: "On the third day, three thousand corpses were buried" (Demetz, 116).

At other times, the Jewish community was threatened with expulsion from Prague, a fate that Jews in other areas in Bohemia and Moravia suffered as well. Both Goldsmith and Kieval label the period from the mid-1500s to the early 1600s as a Golden Age for Czech Jewry; these decades coincide with Rabbi Loew's professional life and his residence in Prague. By 1600 the Jewish Quarter sheltered approximately three thousand residents, having grown from a few dozen in the mid-1500s (Kieval, "Pursuing," 15); this remnant was the result of an expulsion order in 1541 that decimated the Jewish community (David, 44). By 1638, when the first official census was taken, the number had more than doubled to 7,815 (Kieval, "Pursuing," 19). In 1689 a devastating fire destroyed much of the quarter; another occurred in 1754, after which an ordinance was created forbidding the extensive use of wood in rebuilding.

Because this Jewish Quarter, often described as an overcrowded and dark neighborhood, figures so prominently in golem stories, a brief description of its history is useful here. The quarter was nestled between the Vltava River and the Old Town Square, a picturesque marketplace that functions today as it has for centuries; the quarter had been home to Jewish residents from almost their earliest days in Prague. The ghetto itself originated about 1400 (Giustino, 150); it was "an enclosed enclave . . . [with] six gates," the last of which "was torn down only in 1822" (Sedinova and Kosakova, 13). The area was alternately known as a ghetto and then as the Josefov after 1859, a year that saw the emancipation of Prague's Jews, who then could move outside the ghetto. Spaces that thus opened in the ghetto were quickly filled by impoverished non-Jews who could only afford the apartments in what has been described as a "foul-smelling . . . labyrinth of winding alleyways, closed-end courtyards, and crumbling walls" (Giustino, 6–7). For example, in a description of one multifamily apartment building given by Giustino, the reader learns that house 207-V had forty-three apartments, three hundred residents, and four toilets in 1886 (95).

But a visitor to the Josefov in the twenty-first century sees only traces of what once was. Radical change occurred in this part of Prague in the late 1800s and early 1900s as a result of a decision by Prague's city fathers to clear the ghetto, a project known as the Finis Ghetto plan (Giustino, 5). This was wholesale urban renewal: "of the 260 stone structures that had existed in Josefov in 1895, only roughly a dozen remained including six of the former nine free-standing, public synagogues, and the Jewish Town Hall" (Giustino, 7). To accomplish such destruction, dynamite was used steadily from 1896 to 1912. Luxury apartments and wide boulevards replaced the twisting streets of the ghetto where, according to legend, the golem had roamed. The city fathers justified such destruction as necessary to improve sanitation. In her book *Tearing down Prague's Jewish Town*, Cathleen Giustino asks whether this was indeed the real reason for clearing the Jewish ghetto. Was it part of the Europe-wide urban modernization trend at this time, similar to what was taking place in Paris and Vienna? Was there a genuine need to clear the part of the city where infectious diseases, and deaths due to these diseases, were the most rampant in Prague, according to the municipal health director? (Giustino, 86). Was it an antisemitic gesture, designed to eradicate Jewish history and presence in the center of Prague? Was the association of disease with Jews, so dominant in Nazi ideology, part of the rhetoric of Prague politicians?

Giustino's conclusion is careful and complex. She demonstrates that many Jews favored the demolition, anticipating the healthier living that would ensue. Unquestionably, some of the non-Jewish Czech politicians expressed their anti-Jewish hostility with this effort. Initial plans would have run three new streets directly through the Jewish cemetery; these plans were modified as were the plans that called for surrounding the Old-New Synagogue (on the preservation list) by tall buildings that would have obscured and diminished the thirteenth-century *shul*. Jews as well as non-Jews were affected by this demolition as the low-rent housing they had found in the Josefov disappeared and the town fathers did very little to provide alternatives for these displaced artisans and shopkeepers.

A related and intriguing question is why the golem legend resurfaced in Prague at precisely the time when the history and character of the Josefov were lost forever. Jirina Sedinova and Eva Kosakova offer this speculation: "Those [authors] like Jaroslav Vrchlicky or Alois Jirasek went back to the legend out of Romantic sentimentality with regret for the dying parts of Prague's history, while others—such as Gustav Meyrink—approached the question on the level of the symbolic and fantastic vision. The Golem stepped out of the Prague Sippurim [a collection of Jewish folktales] to become forever a part of the atmosphere of the old Jewish Town whose last traces were irretrievably disappeared" (28).[3] Gustav Meyrink will be treated in chapter 2, and the Prague ghetto has almost the force of a character in his strange novel. In any event, the loss experienced by Prague's Jewish community when the Josefov was torn down prompted the reappearance of the golem, and that might give us some clues as to the revival of the golem after the far more catastrophic losses of the Holocaust. In one of his guises, as a text, the golem serves to affirm the long history of Jewish legend and Jewish imagination in the face of lethal antisemitism and to create memory anew through intertextuality.

The golem legend is most profoundly associated with the oldest synagogue in Europe, which stands in the former Prague ghetto; it is reputedly the resting place of the golem, whose remains are said to be in the attic of the *shul*.[4] Completed in the 1270s and known as the Old-New Synagogue (or in German as the Altneu Synagogue and in Czech as the Staronova Synagoga), this venerable building still holds regular worship services for the Jewish community in Prague, the small remnant that remains after the Holocaust.[5] One enters by descending several steps into a capacious space enclosed by thick, stucco walls. There at the front of the room, to the right of the Holy Ark as one stands facing it, is Rabbi Loew's chair, a small wooden chair with a raised Star of David carved in its back. As Byron Sherwin has noted, "Though great scholars and mystics have been rabbis of Prague [since Rabbi Loew's tenure], none has presumed to sit upon that chair" (Sherwin, *Mystical Theology*, 14). Such reverence bespeaks the power of Rabbi Loew's presence in Prague today, four centuries after his death.

Uncertainty surrounds the date and place of Rabbi Loew's birth. While Arnold Goldsmith places it "around 1512" (23), Sherwin gives a broader time frame: "no earlier than 1512 and no later than 1526."[6] Rabbi Loew's ancestors had lived in Worms, Germany, in what is now Posen, Poland, and in Prague. Most accounts place his birth in Posen. We know little of his youth or his education, although we do know that his great-great-grandfather was a Talmud scholar and mystic and another ancestor, Avigdor ben Isaac Kara, served as Chief Rabbi of Prague in the early 1400s.

Loew married Pearl Reich, a native of Prague; a family legend suggests that their engagement was a long one due to Pearl's father's financial reverses and his inability to provide a proper dowry. Together they raised seven children, six daughters and a son, who became a rabbi and predeceased his father. Judah Loew served from 1553 to 1573 as Chief Rabbi in Moravia, where he did much to rationalize guidelines and regulations governing the Jewish community. He did not come to Prague until 1573, when he was approximately sixty years old; his reasons for relocation are unclear, but he did not assume the post of Chief Rabbi of Prague until 1598 or 1599. In the intervening years he served as director of the Klaus, a school supported by the wealthy Jewish financier Mordecai Maisel and attached to the synagogue Meisels had built. Loew had strong ideas about educational reform and this post enabled him to implement some of these ideas. Rabbi Loew also began to publish his writings during this time; Prague boasted an excellent press that could publish books in Hebrew. Records indicate that Loew departed from Prague for one, possibly two, stints as Chief Rabbi of Posen in the mid-1580s and again in 1592.

One of the most famous events in Judah Loew's life was a meeting with Emperor Rudolf II, which took place in February 1592, just prior to his departure for Posen. Historical sources conflict as to the matter the two discussed, one claiming that the emperor was interested in the rabbi's knowledge of Jewish mysticism and Kabbalah, others claiming that Rabbi Loew sought the intercession of the emperor to end the blood libel against the Jewish community. Two contemporaneous accounts of the meeting, one by Loew's student David Ganz and the other by his son-in-law, Isaac Katz, both claim that the subject of the meeting was secret and confidential. Kieval thus speculates that the topic the two men discussed may well have been "mysticism and the occult sciences" (Kieval "Pursuing the Golem of Prague," 7) and that this, in turn, may have led to the many legends surrounding the meeting that allege that Loew performed a feat of magic for the emperor. Certainly, Rudolf's interest in alchemy and kabbalism are well-documented historically, and we shall return to this topic in discussing Frances Sherwood's novel, *The Book of Splendor,* as well as the golem films by Duvivier and Wegener, all of which take place in sixteenth-century Prague. Rabbi Loew's term as Chief Rabbi of Prague was relatively short. He resigned in 1604, due to illness, and died on August 22, 1609.

The earliest published text linking Rabbi Loew and the golem appeared in 1841 in a Prague journal titled *Panorama des Universums;* its author was a non-Jewish journalist and folklorist named Franz Klutschak (1814–86) (Kieval, *Languages,* 106). Six years later, a colleague of Klutschak, Leopold Weisel (1804–73), a Jewish physician who had lived in the Josefov, contributed five stories to the collection of Jewish folklore known as *Sippurim: Eine Sammlung jüdischer Volkssagen.* One of these tales was that of Rabbi Loew and the golem, a somewhat briefer version than that of Klutschak, though similar in content (Kieval, *Languages*, 106–7). Here is the text of Weisel's story:

> During the reign of Rudolph II there lived among the Jews of Prague a man named Bezalel Löw, who because of his tall stature and great learning, was called "der Hohe" [the Great] Rabbi Löw. This rabbi was well-versed in all of the arts and sciences, especially in the Kabbalah. By means of this art he could bring to life figures formed out of clay or carved from wood, who, like real men, would perform whatever task was asked of them. Such homemade servants are very valuable: they do not eat, they do not drink, and they do not require any wages. They work untiringly; one can scold them, and they do not answer back.
>
> Rabbi Löw had fashioned for himself one such servant out of clay, placed in his mouth the Name (a magic formula), and thereby brought him to life. This artificial servant performed all of the menial tasks in the house throughout the week: chopping wood, carrying water, and so on. On the Sabbath, however, he was required to rest; therefore, before the day of rest had begun, his master removed the Name from his mouth and made him dead. Once, however, the rabbi forgot to do this and calamity ensued. The magic servant became enraged, tore down houses, threw rocks all around, pulled up trees, and carried on horribly in the streets. People hurried to the rabbi to tell him of the situation. But the difficulty was great; the Sabbath was already at hand, and all labor—whether to create or destroy— was strictly forbidden. How, then, to undo the magic? The rabbi's dilemma with his Golem was like that of the sorcerer's apprentice and his broom in Goethe's poems. Fortunately, the Sabbath had not yet been consecrated in the Altneu synagogue, and since this is the oldest and most honorable synagogue in Prague, everything is set according to it. There was still time to remove the Name from the crazy youth. The master hurried, tore the magic formula from the mouth of the Golem, and the lump of clay dropped and fell into a heap. Alarmed at this event, the rabbi did not wish to make such a dangerous servant again. Even today, pieces of the Golem are to be seen in the attic of the Altneu synagogue.[7]

The twenty-first-century reader who has previously encountered the golem legend can immediately identify elements of the legend missing in this foreshortened version: the description of the elaborate ritual by which the golem is created; the role of the golem to protect the Jewish community from pogroms; naming the golem "Joseph"; the blood libel and the anti-semitic priest Thaddeus. These are aspects of the legend that were subsequently added. Nonetheless, it is this simple tale of Weisel's that, according to Kieval, "appears to have served as the basis for subsequent borrowings" (*Languages*, 108).

Yudl Rosenberg and Chayim Bloch

To learn the details of the broader version of the golem legend, we must skip ahead to the early twentieth century and a pious Orthodox Polish rabbi named Yudl Rosenberg. In the words of Curt Leviant: "But then, in 1909, in Warsaw, a singular event occurred that changed the direction of the legend for the rest of the twentieth century and prompted the efflorescence of this story in so many branches of art. It was the appearance of *Niflo'es Maharal* (actual full title, *The Wondrous Deeds of the Maharal of Prague with the Golem*) by Yudl Rosenberg" (xvi–xvii). Yudl Rosenberg claimed in his preface to this collection of golem tales that he had purchased a three-hundred-year-old manuscript, written by Rabbi Loew's son-in-law, Rabbi Isaac Katz, and recently unearthed in an imperial library in the city of Metz. As if to provide "evidence" of the validity of this claim, Rosenberg includes in the text a "Bill of Sale" signed by one Chayim Scharfstein, attesting to Rosenberg's purchase of the manuscript; in turn, Rosenberg enjoins readers that "it is forbidden to reprint this book without my permission, for I purchased it at full value and I own it in perpetuity" (8). The irony of such an injunction is that not only is the bill of sale a forgery, but the entire book itself was composed by Rabbi Rosenberg. A further irony ensues when Rosenberg's text is indeed copied by subsequent writers, such as Chayim Bloch, and claimed as their own. There is no Chayim Scharfstein nor is there an imperial library in the city of Metz; no manuscript has ever been produced to prove Rosenberg's claim.

Leviant speculates that Rabbi Rosenberg's motivation for the forgery was his role as a respected religious figure "in a community that viewed fiction as frivolous and utterly outside the Jewish tradition of Torah study" (xvii) and that the assertion that the golem stories were written by the Maharal's son-in-law gave the book a certain authenticity that a text by a twentieth-century rabbi would not carry. Kieval notes that Rosenberg's narrative is "laced with historical inaccuracies, improbabilities, and terms and concepts that make sense only in a *Polish* context" (*Languages*, 111). Nonetheless, the forgery took hold of people's imaginations, and some still cling to this version of the golem legend as the "real" legend. As recently as

1980, Gershon Winkler, in his collection *The Golem of Prague,* described his rewriting of Rosenberg as "a new adaptation of the *documented* stories of the Golem of Prague" (Kieval, *Languages,* 111, italics in original).[8] The following year, 1981, when Arnold Goldsmith published his study of the golem legend, he was more cautious about the supposed forgery, stating that "a literary hoax *may* have been perpetrated on the Jewish reading public" (38, italics mine).

Rabbi Rosenberg's collection has recently become available in two new editions, with an intriguing and significant difference. Joachim Neugroschel's *The Golem: A New Translation of the Classic Play and Selected Short Stories* (2006) provides readers with an English translation of the *Yiddish version* of Rosenberg's golem tales, as well as other golem texts. Curt Leviant's *The Golem and the Wondrous Deeds of the Maharal of Prague* (2007), by contrast, presents us with the first English translation of the *Hebrew version* of Rosenberg's text. Leviant explains that the Yiddish version followed the Hebrew version and was created by Rosenberg for less well-educated readers: "We have translated this book into Yiddish to enable people of all classes to enjoy this illuminating work," wrote Rosenberg on the title page of the Yiddish edition (xx–xxi). Describing Rosenberg's style in the Hebrew edition as "a rabbinic Hebrew into which lines from the Bible, the Talmud, the liturgy, and occasionally, phrases from the kabbala blend seamlessly," Leviant helpfully includes in the notes to his text the sources of many of these intertextual references and borrowings for the contemporary reader who may be less familiar with these sources. A careful comparison of the translations by Neugroschel from the Yiddish and by Leviant from the Hebrew reveals that many of these biblical and Kabbalah references have been deleted from the Yiddish text by Rosenberg, presumably to make the story more direct and readable.

So, what are some of the additions to the golem legend introduced by Rabbi Rosenberg and why? As mentioned above, aspects of the legend familiar to twenty-first-century readers and missing from the Weisel text include: the ritual for the creation of the golem; the rationale for the golem as a protection for the Jewish community; naming the golem "Joseph"; and the blood libel and the viciously antisemitic priest Thaddeus. Let us look at each of these in turn, using Leviant's translation of Rosenberg from the Hebrew.

Chapter 8, "How the Maharal Created the Golem," opens with Rabbi Loew directing a question to God during a dream as to how he could fight against the antisemitic priest Thaddeus: "The answer came from heaven: 'you will create a golem made of clayey loam and order him to destroy the evil tormentors of the Jews'" (34). Suddenly, the narration switches from third person, which it has been in preceding chapters, to first person, a shift that adds "authenticity" to Rosenberg's claim that this manuscript was written by Rabbi Loew's son-in-law, as the narrator identifies himself as Yitzchok ben Shimshon Ha-Cohen, the son-in-law. Ha-Cohen continues:

> In the year 5340 (1580), on the 20th of Adar, at four hours after midnight the three of us left for the Moldau River[9] on the outskirts of Prague. By its banks we looked for and found an area with loam and clay, from which we made the form of a man, three cubits long, lying on his back, and then shaped a face, arms, and legs. Then all three of us stood at the golem's feet, staring at his face. The Maharal told me first to walk around the golem seven times, beginning on the right side, proceed to his head and circle around it to his legs on the left side. He told me what combinations of letters to recite as I walked around him. And thus I did seven times. When I completed the circuits, the body of the golem reddened like a glowing coal. (35)

Then Rabbi Loew's student, Rabbi Yaakov Sasson, completed seven circuits around the golem and hair and nails appeared. Finally, Rabbi Loew walked seven times around the golem and then "all three of us recited in unison the verse: 'He breathed into his nostrils the breath of life and the man became a living creature'" (36).

Suddenly, the golem opens his eyes and, responding to a command from Rabbi Loew, stands up. The trio dress him in clothes and shoes: "In short, he looked like the rest of us: he saw, heard, and understood, but he did not have the capacity for speech" (36). As the four return home at six in the morning, Rabbi Loew addresses the golem: "Know that we created you out of the dust of the earth to guard the Jews from all harm and from all the ills and troubles they suffer at the hands of their enemy and oppressors. Your name will be Yosuf" (36–37). Yosuf takes up his tasks as a servant to Rabbi Loew and as a protector of the Jewish community. Thirteen chapters ensue, recounting the golem's involvement in miracles, in catching fish for Rosh Hashana, and in battling with the priest Thaddeus, as well as recounting the accusations of ritual murder. Strikingly, no chapters are devoted to the golem's "running amok" such as the Weisel tale recounts.

Instead the Maharal determines that the golem is no longer needed. Since blood libels have ceased in Prague, as a result of Rabbi Loew's intercession with Rudolf and the ruler's subsequent edict banning blood libel trials, Rabbi Loew decides it is time to bring an end to the golem. Just as the ritual for creating the golem did not appear in Weisel's tale, the ritual by which he was "decommissioned" is an addition in the Rosenberg text. Again, Rabbi Loew's son-in-law narrates: "All three of us went up to the attic [of the Old-New Synagogue, where the golem had been sent to sleep the night before]. The golem was asleep on his bed. . . . All three of us stood by the golem's head. To bring about his demise all we had to do now was reverse what we had done then when the golem had been formed and brought to life" (183–84). So they walked the seven circuits in reverse and chanted the secret combination of letters in reverse: "Anyone who has an understanding of practical Kabbala and a thorough familiarity with *The Book of Creation* will grasp the secret of the creation process as well as the secret of annulling it" (184).

They wrapped the golem in two old prayer shawls and tied them together. "Then we took the golem's rigid body and, obeying the Maharal's instructions, hid him under a pile of tattered pages from the damaged books that were stored in the attic so that no one would see where the golem was hidden" (185). The legend persists that the golem's body still lies in the attic of the Altneu Synagogue. As we shall see, Michael Chabon's *The Amazing Adventures of Kavalier and Clay* includes a scene in which the golem's inert body is spirited out of the attic of the synagogue and whisked out of Prague in a casket in order to preserve it from Nazi depredations.

Finally, another feature of the Rosenberg 1909 collection of golem tales is the introduction of the "blood libel" or ritual murder accusation against the Jews in the Josefov and the creation of the golem to protect the community against such accusations. Rosenberg wastes no time in introducing this theme: it appears in the very first chapter following the specious bill of sale: "The Jews were then suffering from unrelenting persecution by the Christian nations, who claimed that the Jews needed Christian blood for their Passover matzas. Hardly a Passover festival occurred in the lands of Bohemia, Moravia, Hungary, and Spain without a dead Christian boy being thrown into a hidden corner of a rich Jew's property in order to accuse him of murdering the child and using his blood for ritual purposes" (10–11). To further dramatize this theme, Rosenberg connects it to Rabbi Loew's birth. A Christian carrying a dead child in a sack is caught by the police in the Josefov because he begins to flee when he sees people emerging from Rabbi Loew's parents' home running to fetch a midwife. The man confesses that he intended to bring a blood libel against Rabbi Bezalel, Rabbi Loew's father. "News of this salvation immediately spread through the entire city. Rabbi Bezalel prophesied regarding the newborn boy, saying: 'This one will comfort us and save us from the blood libel.' He named the boy Yehuda

Leib, after the verse: 'Judah is a lion's whelp; on prey, my son, have you grown'" (12). Two subsequent chapters identify specific dates when blood libels occurred—1585, 1589—and recount the story of Rabbi Loew's intervention and the assistance of Yossele (Joseph) the golem in restoring justice.

History, however, does not confirm Rosenberg's story. As mentioned above, there are no documented cases of blood libels occurring in Prague during Rabbi Loew's residence there. But blood libels did occur subsequently and a resurgence took place during Rosenberg's lifetime: "It was the Europe of Reb Yudel [Rosenberg], not of the Maharal, that witnessed a proliferation of accusations—and even formal, criminal trials—against Jews on the charge of ritual murder. Starting in 1882 in Hungary and continuing down to the eve of the First World War, central and Eastern Europe served up a half-dozen sensational murder trials, each prosecuted by agencies of the modern state, in which the case against the Jewish defendants hinged on a modern reworking of the canard that Jews require the blood of innocent Christians for their religious rites" (Kieval, *Languages*, 112). So Rabbi Yudl Rosenberg anachronistically injects demonstrations of antisemitism from his own period into his golem tales.

Ritual murder accusations have a very long history, one that is ineluctably intertwined with antisemitism. The first documented case of a blood libel accusation occurred in 1148, when an English boy, William of Norwich, was said to have been a victim of ritual murder. Such accusations became more widespread in the thirteenth century and reached their apex in the fifteenth and sixteenth centuries (Hsia, 2–3).[10] The most famous early such accusation took place in 1475 in the northern Italian city of Trent, where a two-year-old boy, Simon, went missing and his father accused local Jews of the kidnaping and murder. These Jews were promptly rounded up and tortured until they "confessed." Many, including the leader of the Jewish community, were executed. No fewer than three trials, presided over by clergy as well as secular authorities, followed. Simon was subsequently beatified as many miracles were attributed to the "martyr" (Hsia, 43). That accusations of killing Christian children to use their blood for matzoh were levied against Jews in Prague from the earliest days of the community there is demonstrated by the Statuta Judaeorum of 1262, decreed by King Otakar II of Bohemia. The Statuta "firmly defended Jews against blood libel and stated that Jews resident in royal lands could not be accused of using human blood, for, it said, Jews have no use for blood generally. . . . Six witnesses, three Christian and three Jewish, would be needed to sustain an accusation of that kind, but if they could not prove their allegation, the Christians would be punished and not without justification" (Demetz, 45).

Rabbi Rosenberg would have been aware of a number of blood libels in the period surrounding his publication of golem tales in 1909. In April 1899, in the eastern Bohemian town of Polna, Leopold Hilsner, a Jewish man, was accused of the murder of a nineteen-year-old seamstress for ritual purposes. What resulted was "the Hapsburg monarchy's most famous ritual murder trial" (Kieval, *Languages*, 183). Hilsner was found guilty and spent sixteen years in jail until he was pardoned by Emperor Charles (Giustino, 143). Rosenberg would also have been aware of notorious pogroms that took place in Russia in 1903 and 1905, further examples of antisemitism, in these cases organized by the government (Leviant, xxix).

It is little wonder, then, that Rosenberg's book, portraying as it does a wise, heroic rabbi and his superhuman golem helper, became a best-seller. As Hsia reflects: "In these legends about the life of Loew of Prague, the storm of persecutions is dispersed by piety and learning; rays of divine light break through the dark clouds of bigotry to illuminate the hope for the future. For the Jews of Eastern Europe, who had to endure the reality of anti-Jewish violence, these imaginary tales of a heroic age in a civilized Holy Roman Empire gave strength to the powerless and hope to the fearful" (225). Thus, in addition to nostalgia for golem tales engendered by the destruction of the Josefov, another reason for the revival of golem tales at the turn of the twentieth century is the threat that Jewish communities felt as ritual murder accusations resurfaced and pogroms were government sanctioned. Such threats and experiences—lethal anti-Jewish violence, the disappearance of whole Jewish communities—were intensified in the Holocaust and thus help us understand why the golem legend has been appropriated by so many post-Holocaust writers.

If, as the old saying goes, "Imitation is the sincerest form of flattery," then Rabbi Yudl Rosenberg is one of the most flattered authors, as his text has been imitated relentlessly, often without attribution. One of the earliest examples is the collection of golem legends published by Chayim Bloch (1881–?), first in a journal in 1917 and then in book form in German in 1919, ten years after Rosenberg's text. A subsequent edition by Bloch appeared in Vienna in 1925, in an English translation by Harry Schneiderman titled *The Golem: Legends of the Ghetto of Prague*. A reprint of this edition is widely available in the United States, published by Kessinger Publishing's Rare Mystical Reprints.[11] Bloch apparently felt the need, as had Rosenberg, to "document" his text and so, in addition to his own introductory remarks, he included an introduction by his translator as well as a prefatory note by Hans Ludwig Held.

The story put forth here is that Bloch was a rabbi and a soldier in World War I who collected these legends, in part, while serving in a POW camp in Hungary and encountering many Jews who shared their stories with him (Bloch, 13–17). Bloch verges on acknowledging his source: "Before me lies a manuscript in the Hebrew language and script, which bears the title 'Nifloet Mhrl' (The Miracles of Rabbi Loew). Redacted about three hundred years ago, it is rich in tragic episodes and enchanting tales" (31). From this we can deduce that he used the Hebrew version of Rosenberg's text, but it is unclear as to whether he simply accepts Rosenberg's claims regarding the text's origins or he passes it along to his own unsuspecting readers to enhance a sense of authenticity. In any event, nowhere does he mention Rabbi Rosenberg.

As with each successive version of golem tales, Bloch makes revisions and additions to the "original" he appropriated. Arnold Goldsmith gives a lengthy and detailed exposition of these changes, which I will only outline here (see Goldsmith, 51–72). Note, however, that Goldsmith is using the *Yiddish* version of Rosenberg, so some of his generalizations are incorrect when compared to the Hebrew version. For example, Goldsmith claims that chapter 28 in Bloch, "Rabbi Loew's Utterances on the Golem," is a Bloch addition: "It is as though Bloch takes all of the remaining statements about the golem which he could not incorporate into the stories and catalogues them in an appendix which he calls chapter 28" (58). But, in fact, this catalogue, while not in the Yiddish version, is included in the Hebrew version of Rosenberg and can thus be found in Leviant's edition of the tales. Close comparison of these two catalogues reveals that Bloch has omitted two of the seventeen items contained in Rosenberg (numbers 3 and 5), rearranged the order, and considerably simplified Rosenberg's language in many of the items.

Similarly, Goldsmith praises Bloch as "the more scholarly of the two, as he quotes from the Torah, other biblical sources, and the Talmud" (69). But, as we have seen, Rabbi Rosenberg intentionally simplified his Yiddish version of the golem tales in order to make them more accessible to all readers, particularly those without much formal education. Leviant's translation of the Hebrew version abounds in intertextual references.

However, in the most important distinction between Rosenberg's tales and Bloch's appropriation of Rosenberg, Goldsmith is correct: "In [Bloch's] stories, an element appears that was not evident in Rosenberg's: the increasing wildness of the robot and its potential destructiveness, an additional threat to the very Jewish community it was meant to serve" (53–54). We find this wildness culminating in Bloch's chapter 25, "The Golem Runs Amuck." In some versions, the rabbi neglected to remove the *shem* from the golem's mouth for the Sabbath, the usual practice which provided the golem with a day of rest. In Bloch's retelling, the rabbi forgot to give the golem his orders for the Sabbath and the golem "Like one mad, began running about the Jewish section of the city, threatening to destroy everything. The want of employment made him awkward and wild" (189). Rabbi Loew told his companions, "Now the golem has become superfluous, for the blood impeachment can by this time no longer occur in any country. This wrong needs no longer be feared. We will therefore destroy the Golem" (192). Telling the golem to sleep that night in the attic of the Old-New Synagogue, Rabbi Loew, accompanied again by his confidants, does everything in reverse of the order he used to create the golem, thus transforming him into the lump of clay. While this "wild" golem is not found in Rosenberg, he is, as we have seen, in the 1841 text by Leopold Weisel and earlier versions about Rabbi Elijah of Chelm. Such wildness remains a staple of twentieth- and twenty-first-century versions.

In his own introductory remarks to his volume, Bloch states that his golem stories were "originally printed in the year 1917 in the *Oester-reichischen Wochenschrift* [a journal] edited by my friend and Master Dr. Joseph S. Bloch" (12). He then includes two testimonials, quotations from letters he received upon this initial publication. These quotations (if we accept their veracity, an obvious question, given the other obfuscations of this text) may give us clues both to the reception of the stories by readers and, because Bloch includes them in this way, to his own motivation for telling golem stories in the 1920s. The first quotation comes from "the late Chief Rabbi of Vienna, Dr. Moritz Guedemann: 'I believe your work to be a most valuable one, because your legends will be very fitted for the enlightenment of *those non-Jewish circles who still believe in the use of blood by Jews*'" (12, italics mine). The second quotation comes from the "Chief-Rabbi of Jugo-Slavien, Dr. Isaac Alcalay in Belgrad: 'I think that the same longing for deliverance, which led our ancestors to the compiling of such beautiful tales, also transports us into a beautiful dream [and] makes us forget the terrible truth'" (12). Thus hinted at here are dual motivations: to disabuse non-Jewish readers of antisemitic stereotypes and to provide Jewish readers with tales of a time when Jewish heroes walked the earth.

We can conclude, then, by revisiting the ideas of the golem as we have done in this chapter, layered from the Book of Psalms through the third and fourth, medieval, and nineteenth and twentieth centuries, that considerable borrowing, adapting, and even copying have occurred. Prior to the post-Holocaust golem, the focus of this book, writers have morphed the legend to address issues of their era, to critique earlier representations, to glory in the story of human creativity, and to honor Jewish tradition. What emerges is a plurality of golems, a multiplicity of tropes, which provide a rich clay from which reimagined golems will awaken. But before meeting the post-Holocaust clay men (and women), we will look in-depth at two early twentieth-century German-language intertexts that demonstrate the damage done by careless and disrespectful appropriations.

2

German-Language Appropriations

The Golem Runs Amok

The supernatural is the most fascinating subject in the world.

Gustav Meyrink, *Der Golem*

The two primary texts we will consider in this chapter, Gustav Meyrink's novel *Der Golem* (1915) and Paul Wegener's film *Der Golem: Wie er in die Welt kam* (1920), are among the earliest popularizations of the golem legend for the general public beyond the Jewish community. Meyrink was born in Austria, lived for a period of time in Prague, and was residing in Germany when his novel was published there in German. Wegener was a German actor, writer, and film director whose 1920 film became a classic of German cinema. How the golem is represented in these texts, how the act of *creating* the golem is represented, and the depiction of the interaction between the Jewish and non-Jewish communities and between the Jewish community and Rudolf II, the Holy Roman Emperor, are all at issue. In approaching such representations, we must ask questions about the manner of appropriation: what levels of consciousness, fidelity, respect, disdain, revision, prejudice, misunderstanding, and malice were brought to the act of adapting the golem legend? In Gerard Genette's terms, to what extent has the early twentieth-century author, in creating an intertext, the *hypertext*, been faithful to, disregarded, rejected, or reimagined key aspects of the earlier text, the *hypotext*? Thus, we will also look briefly at an earlier Wegener film, *Der Student von Prag* (1913), as well as at Julien Duvivier's film *Le Golem: The Legend of Prague* (1936) by way of comparison. To what extent were Meyrink and Wegener's adaptations driven by a profit motive?

To what extent did they reflect the dominant attitudes toward Jews at that time? Why did they subvert the golem into a figure of evil?

It is the very manner in which the hypertext has changed up the hypotext that provides the writer the opportunity for critique, for satire, for acknowledging influence, for parody and humor, for homage, for achieving contemporaneity. The meaning emerges not solely from the "new" text but also from the relation of the two texts, or a whole network of texts. James Joyce's *Ulysses* can be read as both an homage to Homer and an effort to displace the journey of the hero trope from the classical era to contemporary time: the result provides both humor and chagrin, or *agenbite of inwit* in Joycean terms. Intertextuality also reflects the distinct historical context out of which it emerges. For example, considering Charlotte Brontë's *Jane Eyre* as the hypotext for Jean Rhys's *Wide Sargasso Sea*, readers see Jean Rhys "correcting" the image of Bertha, the madwoman in the attic in *Jane Eyre*. The greater consciousness about colonialism, capitalism, gender relations, and spousal abuse in the late twentieth century enabled Rhys to "re-vise" (in Adrienne Rich's term) an old classic—or to make explicit what Brontë left implicit in her text.

As it is always also a metafictional gesture, intertextuality signals attitudes toward story and the power of literature. When Charlie Kaufman decided to write a film script based on Susan Orlean's memoir *The Orchid Thief* (2000), the focus became not the hunt for rare orchids in the swamps of Florida but the challenges of adapting the plot line to cinema. Hence, the film is named *Adaptation* (2002), which carries the double entendre of the kinds of adaptation plants make to new environments as well. *Adaptation* is a film that enacts intertextuality.

Thus, at the outset of this study of appropriations of the golem legend, it is essential to focus on Meyrink's and Wegener's texts, which take up a Jewish legend, one that has already experienced intertextual metamorphoses, and revise it for popular consumption. These texts were among the first to disseminate the golem myth for a wider, non-Jewish public. What kind of transformations do we find in these fictional and filmic golems? What are audience and critical responses to the golem redux?

GUSTAV MEYRINK, *DER GOLEM* (1915)

Written with grace and an uncommon power to evoke eerie reactions by nebulous suggestion, [Der Golem is] apt to give one moments of what is vulgarly known as the creeps.

New York Times, 1928

The golem legend first received widespread attention in the non-Jewish community in Bohemia and Germany as a result of the publication of a novel titled *Der Golem,* written by the eccentric Viennese Gustav Meyrink and published initially in serial form in *Die Weissen Blätter* in 1913–14.[1] Meyrink's novel was published in book form in 1915 and became a best-seller; between 200,000 and 250,000 copies sold almost immediately (Bleiler, xi).

Der Golem seems almost a misnomer for this first popular retelling. Despite its reputation as the ur-text for subsequent golem fiction, the novel focuses very little on the clay man; the golem is at best a peripheral figure in the plot, causing one to wonder how many scholars who cite the book have actually read it. Told in the first person by a narrator who is at some points anonymous and at others named Athanasius Pernath, the story is set in the Jewish ghetto of Prague at the turn of the twentieth century. The first chapter, titled "Sleep," begins: "The moonlight is falling on to the foot of my bed. It lies there like a tremendous stone, flat and gleaming" (3).[2] This sets the tone for the entire narrative, which seems to drift in and out of wakefulness, sleeping, dreaming, and hallucinating. A sequential plot is barely discernible; rather, each chapter occurs as in a flash of light, illuminating a scene that may have only cursory links to the previous and following chapters. As one critic has commented: "Who is to say of this labyrinthine structure where fictional reality ends and dream begins? What is sanity and what madness? The hero has to experience both, he is forced to split and to double his ego and meet himself. By creating an all-pervading atmosphere of Kafkaesque mystery and uncertainty, Meyrink succeeds in suggesting inexhaustible depths and heights of meaning" (Rottensteiner, 224).[3]

The *New York Times Book Review,* responding to the first English edition of *Der Golem* in 1928, characterized the plot as "irritatingly muddled at intervals" with "all skeins . . . completely tangled" (December 30, 1928, p. 12). Indeed, providing any kind of plot summary here is a challenge. Perhaps the best way to begin is to say that the story proceeds from two seemingly unrelated events, involving a hat and a book: the narrator, an engraver of jewelry by trade who also restores books and antiques, mistakenly picks up a hat belonging to Athanasius Pernath and metamorphoses into that person (10); another doppelgänger is created when a stranger arrives in the narrator's rooms and hands him a mysterious book, *The Book of Ibbur.*[4] Thus, one thread that can be followed throughout the novel is the archetypal pattern of the quest for identity. In the opening chapter, the narrator asks: "'Who is this "I"?' That is the question I am suddenly beset with a desire to ask" (4). The third chapter is titled "I," and it is in this chapter that a stranger with a "fumbling" gait and "slanting eyes" arrives with a book, ostensibly to ask the narrator to repair it. The stranger points out a chapter titled "Ibbur, or the Fecundation of the Soul," in which the inlaid "I" had become separated from the page and is in need of restoration. As the narrator begins to read the book, "The book spoke to me as had my dreams, only clearer and more coherently" (11). As he gazes at the book, words begin to spin off the page, taking human form dressed in "shimmering garments" (11). Such power invested in the alphabet is reminiscent of the Kabbalah and of the deployment of words and letters in the creation of the golem. Indeed, it is gradually revealed that this mysterious stranger with the book *is* the golem (though the word "golem" is not used) and that the *Book of Ibbur* is a golemic text or a textual golem as well. As the narrator emerges from the trance induced by the flying words, he realizes he has become the stranger, that is, he has become the golem: "my eyes were slanting. . . . 'That is not my face!' I wanted to cry out" (14).

The most famous illustrations for *Der Golem* were done by Hugo Steiner-Prag, a Jew who was born in Prague, worked in Germany as a professor and artist until 1933, when he was dismissed from his post by the Nazis, and eventually emigrated to the United States, where he died in 1945.[5] The illustrations take their lead from the prose: "Always it happens that an apparition makes its appearance—an utterly strange man, clean shaven, of yellow complexion, Mongolian type, in antiquated clothes of a bygone day" (27). Steiner-Prag thus gave the golem a distinctly Orientalist mien. The slanting eyes are unmistakably Eastern, the nose and shape of the head rather apelike in most illustrations. Such an image of the golem seems to conflate stereotypes of *Ostjuden* and of other racial types viewed as strange and inferior. The lithographs are quintessentially Expressionist: black and gloomy, with huddled, looming buildings; often, the only illuminated object in the picture is surrounded by a frame of darkness. Steiner-Prag's twenty-five illustrations for *Der Golem* are considered his masterpiece. In a subsequent edition of *Der Golem*, published by Carl Schünemann Verlag in Bremen in the early 1930s, Steiner-Prag wrote an introduction addressed to "Lieber Herr Meyrink." He described his first reading of *Der Golem* while on an island in the North Sea in 1916 and the profound impact it had on him. The tone of nostalgia for their friendship at an earlier time in Prague and for the city itself is palpable: "Ihr Buch war das alte Prag" [Your book was the old Prague], he says (14).

Woven in and out of the story are appearances of the golem. He is first mentioned by the narrator in the fourth chapter, providing readers unfamiliar with the Jewish legend a brief summary: "Then, in mysterious fashion, comes into my mind the legend of the mysterious Golem, artificial man, whom once, long ago, here in the Ghetto, a rabbi learned in the Kabbala shaped from the elements, investing it with an unreasoning, automatic life when he placed a magical formula behind its teeth. And . . . that same Golem stiffened into clay the instant that mysterious phrase was removed from its lips" (16). But in a curious twist that is not part of the original golem legend, Meyrink's golem returns every thirty-three years to wreak havoc on the ghetto. One cannot help noting the Christian connotations: Jesus Christ is said to have lived for thirty-three years until his crucifixion.[6] As characters recall their encounters with the golem from thirty-three or sixty-six years previously, it is always with a note of horror. Gone is any sense of the golem as a faithful servant or heroic protector; here he is a figure engendering terror, alternately described as a fiend, as a giant, as the "mass-soul" of the ghetto (29), or as an astral "projection" of thought (30). For one woman, "what she had seen was her own soul divested of its body . . . a part of her innermost self" (30). Yet another character claims that "the Golem signifies the awakening of the dead through the innermost life of the spirit" (46).

As the story continues to unfold, the reader learns that Pernath, the narrator, now forty-five years old, has endured a period of madness earlier in his life, perhaps resulting from a trauma, and has been treated in an asylum with hypnosis. The effect has been to permanently block the memory of the trauma from his conscious mind. As the narrator struggles to regain memory of his earlier life, he travels, in a very Gothic scene, through underground tunnels in the Josefov and arrives in a mysterious room with only a barred window and no external door; here he discovers a pack of Tarot cards and the golem, again perceived as his doppelgänger, staring back at him with his own face. Paralyzed with a "deepset horror . . . frigid lips . . . [and a] heart that began to contract convulsively" (66), Pernath realizes that he has found the room where the golem hides between periods of reincarnation.

The plot meanders along: Pernath becomes embroiled in conflicts with various characters in the Prague ghetto, and he falls in love. The reader is confronted with symbols of mysticism and spiritualism, including mysterious seeds, the god Osiris, somnambulism, prophetic dreams, and images of hermaphrodites. Eventually Pernath is arrested, falsely accused of murder, and spends months languishing in jail. These jail passages are among the most vivid in the novel, reflecting, no doubt, Meyrink's own experiences in prison in Prague. One Amadeus Laponder (yet another doppelgänger?), accused of rape and murder, joins Pernath in his cell and becomes a kind of spiritual mentor, telling Pernath, "You bear within yourself the *spiritual vestiges* of thousands of your forebears" (166). Meyrink brings his novel to a close as Pernath, after several months' incarceration, is released from prison. He finds "The whole Jewish quarter was one waste of earth and rubbish" (177), and his own room is in ruins. The "urban renewal" of the Josefov, discussed in the previous chapter, has begun during his absence. In the final chapter, appropriately titled "End" (all the chapters have one-word titles), the narrator wakes up: "My name is not Pernath at all. Has it all been just a dream?" (182). We are brought full circle to the sense of dreaming in the first chapter. The narrator muses: "the whole world, in fact, seems enchanted, seen through a haze of dreamy recognition, as though I had lived already at many times, and in many places, simultaneously" (188), an apt description of the novel itself. Meyrink gives us no final word on the fate of the golem.

Who was Gustav Meyrink? Born Gustav Meyer in Vienna in 1868, he lived in Munich and Hamburg during his "helter-skelter childhood" (Bleiler, iv) before relocating to Prague in 1883 to attend a commercial college and open a bank. Bleiler tells the reader in his introduction to the novel that there were actually "three" Meyrinks: banker Meyer, Meyer the "aggressive playboy," and Meyer "the occultist, dreamer, mystic, and magician" (iv). It is clearly the latter Meyer who was at work writing *Der Golem.* According to Meyrink lore, when he was in his twenties he was in the act of committing suicide in his apartment when an advertisement for occult books was slipped under his door.[7] "He interpreted this as a warning and as an invitation" (Bleiler, iv) and began to explore the occult, including alchemy (which figures in tales of Rudolf II and Rabbi Loew in Prague), Kabbalah, and Sufism.

Meyrink frequented coffee houses, meeting Max Brod, Oscar Kokoschka, and others in a circle that was "avant-garde, liberal, internationally minded and very largely Jewish" (Bleiler, viii). Max Brod is, of course, the confidant of Franz Kafka (b. in Prague in 1883) who singlehandedly and against Kafka's wishes saved his manuscripts after Kafka's death from tuberculosis in 1924. Although Meyrink was a favorite writer of Max Brod, Kafka found him "'farfetched and much too blatant. [Kafka] rejected anything that seemed contrived for effect, intellectual, synthetic'. In other words, too Prague" (Gilman, 39–40).[8] He adopted his nom de plume— Gustav Meyrink—when he published his first story, "Der Heisse Soldat" (The Ardent Soldier), in October 1901. His new role as author came about during confinement in a sanatorium where the writer Oskar Schmitz encouraged Meyrink to try his hand at writing. A young writer in his circle, Paul Leppin, described his Prague apartment during this period: "He had a terrarium with two African mice he had given the names of characters from Maeterlinck, a genuine confessional he had dug up God knows where, pictures of Madame Blavatsky, the sculpture of a ghost disappearing into the wall and lots of other things that had no place in the home of a banker" (Mitchell, *Vivo*, 38).

In January 1902 Meyer was charged with fraud in his dealings in the bank and was jailed for several months during the ensuing investigation. Cleared of the charges and released in April 1902, he was diagnosed with tuberculosis of the spine. His reputation ruined despite his exoneration, Meyrink turned to writing and translating. Sometime between 1902 and 1904 he left Prague for good, relocating initially in Vienna, then in Montreux, Munich, and finally settling in Starnberg, south of Munich, by 1911, where he lived until his death. He published several books before taking up *Der Golem* in 1906; between 1909 and 1914 he translated *sixteen* volumes of Charles Dickens from English into German.[9] Undoubtedly this work was undertaken for financial reasons, but it is interesting to speculate about the intertextual impact all that Dickens might have had on *Der Golem,* being drafted simultaneously. Mitchell suggests: "the way the brooding, menacing city of Prague becomes an almost animate presence in *The Golem* seems to owe something to Dickens's London, especially its portrayal in *Bleak House*" (*Vivo*, 124).

While one scholar identifies Meyrink as the "illegitimate son of Baron Karl von Varnbüler . . . and Maria Meyer, a Bavarian Jewish actress" (Irwin, n.p.), and another describes him as a "Jewish writer from Prague who wrote in German" (Rottensteiner, 219), Arnold Goldsmith declares emphatically that Meyrink "was not a Jew" (Goldsmith, 91), as does Sander Gilman (Gilman, 39). In a recent biography of Meyrink, Mike Mitchell, a translator of much of Meyrink's work, clarifies the confusion: Meyrink's mother is often mistaken for another actress, Clara Meyer, who was Jewish. Meyrink himself was baptized shortly after his birth (*Vivo*, 13) and raised as a Christian, although he later rejected Christianity in favor of various occult pursuits and roundly satirized clergy and aspects of Christianity in his stories. Contributing to the perception of Meyrink as Jewish during his lifetime were other factors: his birth name, Meyer, was a common Jewish name in Germany; he wrote about Jewish topics; and he was the victim of specific antisemitic attacks that identified him as Jewish made by Albert Zimmerman, in German publications, in 1917.[10] Following upon these attacks, "Adolf Bartels, a right-wing nationalist who was an early member of the National Socialist Party, joining in 1925, said in his three-volume [1921] *Deutsche Dichtung der Gegenwart* (German Literature of the Present): 'Meyrink has denied he is Jewish, however from his literary physiognomy and the slant of his writings he is Jewish'" (Mitchell, *Vivo*, 159). Meyrink spent almost a decade and a considerable amount of money trying to get this sentence expunged from the encyclopedia; he was eventually successful in getting a favorable court settlement. Perhaps such an expenditure of effort portends his own antisemitism; just as likely, he was concerned about the impact the perception of his ethnicity had on book sales. Meyrink died just three months before Hitler came to power; had he lived, his success at getting this sentence expunged would have taken on new importance.

Meyrink's identity is of concern when we turn to the depiction of Jewish characters, Judaism, and the Josefov in *Der Golem*. As mentioned above, the novel takes place in the Jewish Quarter in Prague around 1890, just as the destruction of the ghetto is getting underway. Here we find prominent and distasteful stereotypes of Jews embodied in Meyrink's characters and voiced by the narrator. Such statements begin already on page six of the novel, when the narrator declares: "I find it easy to pick out the divers breeds of Jew among all those faces that crowd the Hahnpassgasse every day." The narrator goes on to claim that these "varied types loathe one another" (6) but keep this hatred secret from "the eyes of the outer world" (6). Aaron Wassertrum, a junk dealer and a Jewish resident of the Josefov, is described as looking like "a human spider" with "goggle fish eyes and sagging hare-lip" (6) and his daughter/ward, Rosina, as lascivious (with the implication that she is a prostitute). Bestial terms are used as yet more characters are introduced: one is "strangely reminiscent of a frog" (15); twin brothers involved in a weird, unconsummated triangle with Rosina are respectively described as "a hungry wolf" (7) and "a wild beast, half crazed with jealousy and suspicion" (8). A Dr. Wassory, said to take unscrupulous financial advantage of his patients, is described by another character as a "degenerate beast of prey" (19). He is not the only character accused of greed; so, too, is Wassertrum: "The only driving force within him is the acquisitive instinct" (84).

Generalizations about Jews as parasites are made by the narrator— "Lurking and waiting . . . waiting and lurking . . . the terrible, perpetual motto of the Ghetto. Never are its inhabitants seen in the act of work" (16)—and by one character about another: "None but a man born and brought up in the Ghetto could have gone on successfully perpetrating such atrocities for such a length of time; a man who has learnt from childhood upwards to lurk like a spider in its web, forever on the watch" (21). Such stereotypes of Jews as subhuman, as shirkers, and as parasites will, of course, be echoed by the Nazis, as will those relating to blood, a stereotype that also figures in the novel. The medical student, Charousek, accuses Wassertrum of having raped his mother: "*Hatred*? That's not the word for it. The word has yet to be invented that would serve to express my feelings against him. It's not him I hate. It's his blood. Can you understand that? I can scent it in a minute—like a wild beast of the woods—if a single drop of that blood runs in a man's veins, and . . . that happens in the Ghetto once too often" (81). The image of Jewish men as rapists reappears in the Nazi propaganda film *Jud Süss* (1940).

When we turn to a consideration of the setting of the novel, we find the noxious antisemitic stereotypes outlined above to be attributed to the Josefov; indeed, the Prague Josefov becomes a character in the novel. In 1900 about twenty-five thousand residents of Prague were Jewish (roughly 7 percent of the population); newspaper headlines frequently referred to the "Jewish Problem" and carried accusations of the "blood libel," the anti-semitic myth that Jews murdered Christian babies to use their blood in religious rituals (Gilman, 28–31). This is the period when the ghetto in Prague, the Josefov, was torn down by order of the government. Today the only remnants of the old ghetto are the famous Old Jewish Cemetery, the burial place of Rabbi Judah Loew, the Jewish Town Hall, and the surrounding synagogues, including the Old-New Synagogue, the putative burial place of the golem.[11] It is this atmosphere of Prague that figures centrally in *Der Golem*.

In 1935 Hugo Steiner-Prag created a book of pen and ink drawings for his fiancée that depicted the area around her apartment in the Josefov as it looked in the late 1800s, before the destruction of the ghetto began. Included is a brief history of the ghetto in which Steiner-Prag acknowledged the decadent atmosphere of the actual Josefov and yet redeemed its image:

> Once it was the ghetto and it had its own secluded existence until the end of the eighteenth century. After that Jews were permitted to live outside the ghetto walls. Those who were wealthy moved, while the poor and the poorer stayed . . . in the vicinity of their house of worship. But gradually all types of people moved there: the destitute, the dissolute and finally criminals. The streets were crowded with pubs of the foulest sort, dark hideouts and infamous bordellos. . . .
>
> It was picturesque, hazardous and dreary at the same time. It smelled of corruption and misery, disease and crime. The people fit the setting. But side by side with this misery lived peaceful lower-class people and pious Jews. On Friday evenings one could hear their monotone of prayers mingling with the bickering of whores and the loud tumult of the drunken. . . . Around 1895 the demolition was begun. Hundreds of buildings and numerous alleys were destroyed. It was an unbelievable sight . . . but for one who knew this district as it once was, in spite of its seeming ugliness, it remains immortal. (Bilski, 59)

But in Meyrink's depiction of the Josefov, no such contextualization or redemption occurs. The very air of the Jewish Quarter is depicted as menacing: "may it not be that the whole mass of stagnant thought infecting the air of the Ghetto needs clearing" (28). Indeed, the Prague Jewish Quarter becomes a forceful character in this novel, and some of the most brilliant passages evoke, in the manner of German Expressionism, buildings as if they are alive: "the discolored buildings, standing there side by side in the rain like a herd of derelict, dripping animals. . . . Beneath this dreary sky they seemed to be standing in their sleep, without a trace revealed of that something hostile, something malicious, that at times seemed to permeate the very bricks of which they were composed" (14). This sense of the bestial, of the diseased air, exacerbates the antisemitic descriptions of the characters in the novel. It anticipates the description of the Jewish "home life" in *Der ewige Jude* (1940), a profoundly vicious Nazi propaganda film in which footage taken in a Nazi ghetto—of crowded, dirty, and insect-ridden dwellings—is said to represent the way Jews normally lived.

Despite Meyrink's reputation as a biting satirist, especially in his short stories—his objects of ridicule most often being the military, physicians, and government authorities—the reading experience of *Der Golem* does not include larger issues of the empire, and these stereotypical depictions of Jews in the Prague ghetto are never interrogated. Such holds true for the depiction of the golem as well who, in his flitting appearances, is described as a murderer rather than as the traditional image of a servant or heroic savior of the ghetto. The initial description of the golem, as mentioned above, is expanded in the following chapter when a puppeteer by the name of Zwakh recounts for a small audience what he knows of the legend: "The original story harks back, so they say, to the sixteenth century" (26), and Zwakh gives a credible rehearsal of the rabbi who created the golem and the golem's destruction after he runs amok. But then Zwakh veers from the traditional story:

> [T]here is something here in this quarter of the town . . . something that cannot die, and has its being within our midst. . . . More or less every three and thirty years something takes place in our streets, not so out-of-the-way or startling in itself, yet the terror of it is too strong for either explanation or excuse. Always it happens that an apparition makes its appearance—an utterly strange man, clean shaven, of yellow complexion, Mongolian type, in antiquated clothes of a bygone day; it comes from the direction of the Altschulgasse [*sic*; the street where the Old-New Synagogue is located], stalks through the

ghetto with a queer groping, stumbling kind of gait, as if afraid of falling over, and quite suddenly—is gone. (26–27)

Thus the golem is racialized and established as a kind of criminal stalking the ghetto in this account.

Gershom Scholem has aptly criticized Meyrink's *Der Golem* in the opening pages of his essay "The Idea of the Golem," although he stops short of characterizing it as antisemitic:

By taking up a figure of Kabbalistic legend and transforming it in a very peculiar way, Meyrink tried to draw a kind of symbolic picture of the way to redemption. Such literary adaptations and transformations of the golem legend have been frequent. . . . Meyrink's work, however, far outdoes the rest. In it everything is fantastic to the point of grotesque . . . Indian rather than Jewish ideas of redemption are expounded. The alleged Kabbalah that pervades the book suffers from an overdose of Madame Blavatsky's turbid theosophy. . . . *This literary figure, which has achieved considerable fame, owes very little to the Jewish tradition even in its corrupt, legendary form* (*On the Kabbalah*, 158–59, italics mine).

It is intriguing to learn that Gershom Scholem actually visited Meyrink in his home in Starnberg on more than one occasion in 1921. Scholem was at this time a student at the University of Munich and an expert in Kabbalah, and had yet to publish his first book, which came out in 1923. In his memoir *From Berlin to Jerusalem: Memories of My Youth* (originally published in 1977), Scholem recalls the antisemitic posters already appearing on the campus: "There was no disregarding the huge, blood-red posters with their no less bloodthirsty text, inviting people to attend Hitler's speeches: 'Fellow Germans are welcome; Jews will not be admitted'" (135). In describing his visit to Meyrink, Scholem characterizes him as "a man in whom deep-rooted mystical convictions and literarily exploited charlatanry were almost inextricably amalgamated" (133). Acknowledging that he had read both *Der Golem* and Meyrink's subsequent novel, *The Green Face*, Scholem confesses that "[I] had to shake my head over the pseudo-Kabbala presented there" (133). Scholem found it strange that Meyrink asked him to explain passages in *Der Golem;* Meyrink said that although he wrote these passages, he did not understand them. Scholem provides an example from chapter 4 of *Der Golem*, in which Meyrink had employed a Latin phrase he wanted explained; Scholem speculates the phrase must have been "incorrectly transcribed by some ignoramus in an English book in Meyrink's library" (134). Meyrink also astonished Scholem by informing him that God is located in the spine. (This obsession of Meyrink's occurred after he came to believe he had cured his tuberculosis of the spine with the practice of yoga.) Scholem says that his meetings with Meyrink "opened my eyes to how an author could score points with pseudo-mysticism" (133).

Bleiler also raises the question of antisemitism in his introduction to the widely available Dover edition of *Der Golem:*

> How was Aaron Wassertrum to be taken? Or how Rosina? Are these to be read as anti-Semitism in Meyrink? Do Meyrink's comments about the horror-soul in the Ghetto indicate hatred in his mind? It is quite conceivable that these questions should be raised. Yet the answer is obvious and clear: no. Meyrink portrayed saints as well as villains, and he said no more about the Ghetto than has been said about ghettos of all sorts by generations of sociologists. (xvii)

This strikes me as a lame justification for the virulent stereotypes recounted above. Given such stereotypes, one might be surprised to learn that Meyrink's books were among the first to be burned by the Nazis. But it was Meyrink's satires of the military (he was a pacifist during World War I), of fervent nationalism, and of totalitarianism that the Nazis found offensive, as well as his valorization of mysticism as a kind of freedom.

Finally, let us turn to Arnold Goldsmith for his observations on *Der Golem.* Noting that "Meyrink's novel does not give the golem a central role despite its title . . . [and] the legendary figure actually appears in no more than one-fifth of the pages" (96), Goldsmith renders a largely Freudian interpretation of the novel: "Pernath must undergo an intensely psychological experience in which he confronts his frightening alter ego in order to discover his true identity" (96). Emphasizing the appearances of the golem as Pernath's double and the repression of Pernath's past trauma, Goldsmith traces the evidence in the novel of "the growing popularity of Freudian theory in European literary circles at this time" (101). As Freud declared, there is always a return of the repressed, and Pernath must, according to Goldsmith, recover his unhappy memories if he "is to find true mental health" (100). Though Goldsmith does not specifically mention Carl Jung and Joseph Campbell, he describes Pernath's quest in terms of the motif of the journey of the hero and quotes descriptions of "the Archetype Woman," both the temptress and the saintly woman, which appear (Meyrink, 50; Goldsmith, 95–110 passim). Pernath must go literally underground, through the tunnels that lead to the golem's room, to meet the "dragon," do battle, and secure his boon. Likewise, Goldsmith also sees

Pernath's descent into sensuality and sexuality as a figurative underground portion of his archetypal quest.

Goldsmith devotes considerable attention in his analysis to Hillel, a character I have not yet mentioned. Hillel is another resident of the Josefov and a kind of mentor in mysticism to Pernath. Goldsmith describes him as representing love in the novel, a "Jewish sage [who] is a saintly altruist who gives his salary away despite his poverty" (108) and who represents the opposite of the character Charousek, a materialist whose outlook is suffused with hatred. Goldsmith concludes his analysis with an upbeat, psychological interpretation:

> Here is the key to Meyrink's novel. The golem ultimately symbolizes all those "unruly ghosts and warring elements" deep within each man. They must be overcome, tamed, in the individual's quest for immortality, to attain that perfect state which is the redemption of the soul, that discovery of the ideal self made real. This is the true mystical (some would say religious) experience. (115)

While a valid Freudian/Jungian reading of the novel, Goldsmith's analysis finally fails to engage the antisemitic descriptions of characters, the menacing air of the Josefov, the depiction of the golem as a monster completely wrested from Jewish tradition, and the conflation of Kabbalah with myriad other mystical traditions.

In conclusion, then, we can justifiably read *Der Golem* as intertextuality gone awry. In his depiction of characters in antisemitic terms, Meyrink has failed to critique or interrogate these age-old stereotypes. In using the Josefov as a setting associated with the bestial and the decadent without clarifying as Steiner-Prag does that the evil influences were often outsiders, he further maligns the Jewish community of early twentieth-century Prague. In conflating Judaism with the occult, with vague mystical ideas from other cultures and religions, he manifests a disdain for Judaism itself. As we have seen, Meyrink's own relationship with Judaism was vexed at best. Thus, in a real sense, Meyrink has taken a Jewish legend and stood it on its head. If, as other scholars have done, one shrinks back from labeling the novel itself antisemitic, we must at least acknowledge that this is a disrespectful intertextual appropriation.

Such a conclusion should not, however, be interpreted to suggest that intertextuality must be unidirectional or largely faithful to the original—as we will see in James Sturm's graphic novel, *The Golem's Mighty Swing*, the golem is an African American baseball player in a golem disguise. Nor should this conclusion be taken to imply that only the Jewish community can appropriate the legend—Pete Hamill, who is non-Jewish, imagines a Catholic boy as the adept who creates a golem in *Snow in August*. Marvel Comics creates a cartoon golem. Yet in each of these hypertexts, the golem legend retains the storyline of the struggles of a minority against a hostile majority rather than demonizing the minority. By contrast, in *Der Golem*, readers may find affirmation of antisemitic stereotypes and profound misunderstanding of the history of the Josefov, of the golem legend itself, and of the practice of Judaism. As we shall see, these are the serious concerns we will also find with Paul Wegener's film *Der Golem: Wie er in die Welt kam*.

PAUL WEGENER, *DER GOLEM: WIE ER IN DIE WELT KAM* (1920)

> The affinity between [the golem] legend and the very act of filmmaking is both obvious and elemental, and the influence that this connection has exerted over artists, visual and otherwise, is inestimable. For it not only invites reflection on the act of aesthetic production—particularly on the art of cinema—but allows for exploration of the golem as a kind of artist's double, an analogous process to the Divine creation of human beings.
>
> Noah Isenberg, *Weimar Cinema*

Contributing to the popularity of the golem legend after Gustav Meyrink were a series of early German films by Paul Wegener, the first of which appeared in 1915 and the third in 1920.[12] It is this latter version that has survived, is available in restored format on DVD, and is described on the DVD jacket as "one of the greatest achievements of the legendary UFA Studios and . . . an undeniable landmark in the evolution of the horror film."

In his filmography Dietrich Scheunemann notes that the screenplay for the 1920 film *Der Golem* was written by "Paul Wegener, Henrik Galeen, adapted from Gustav Meyrink" (273). Emily Bilski also mentions that "The opening credits in many versions of *Der Golem: Wie er in die Welt kam* claim that the film is based on Gustav Meyrink's novel *Der Golem*" (56). Goldsmith comments upon this, too, asserting that the claim is "a mystery as the film has no resemblance to the novel" (145). This attribution to Meyrink is *not* included in the most easily available edition of the film on the DVD mentioned above.

By contrast, Cathy Gelbin recounts this commonplace attribution to Meyrink and claims the opposite is probably true: "However, it is much more likely the case that Wegener's *Der Student von Prag* and his first *Golem* film, both released before the publication of Meyrink's novel, inspired Meyrink's novel. The latter certainly bears some interesting similarities with Wegener's *Student von Prag*, with Prague providing the scenery for the uncanny doppelgänger motif in both works" ("Narrative"). Both views may be correct and the intertextuality may have worked in both directions: the early Wegener film influenced Meyrink, who began writing his novel around 1906, and Meyrink in turn influenced the 1920 *Der Golem*, as by that time Meyrink's novel had been published in hardcover (1915) and become a best-seller. Elfi Ledig observes that the film and the novel both borrowed from a variety of other sources. Sources for Meyrink include "the Prague golem legend (told by the old puppeteer Zwakh, a friend of the protagonist), folk legends (Loew as the inventor of the camera obscura), themes of occultism and spiritualism, Kabbalistic aspects (*Sefer Yetsirah*), [and] Egyptian mythology (Isis and Osiris)" (38).

Wegener divided his silent film into five "chapters"; the total running time of the film is eighty-six minutes. The setting is sixteenth-century Prague, alternating between the walled Jewish ghetto and the court of Rudolf II. The film opens to reveal Rabbi Löw reading the stars, which predict trouble will come to the Jewish community ("Löw" is a variant spelling and used in the film's intertitles). At the court, Rudolf signs a decree declaring that the Jews are "Christ-killers" and must be exiled from Prague.[13] This decree is entrusted to a rather fey Knight Florian to carry to the ghetto. We see Rabbi Löw beginning to massage clay into a humanoid shape and, as the chapter closes, his daughter Miriam can be seen primping. The opening intertitle for chapter 2 tells us that "The position of the stars is favorable to the spell" as Rabbi Löw struggles to bring the golem to life. Florian initiates a flirtation with the vain Miriam, brazenly groping her. In a lengthy scene, Rabbi Löw consults his "Necromancie" book as he and his assistant, Famulus, call upon evil spirits to jumpstart the clay figure; they succeed when they put the magic word "shem" into the star embedded in his chest. This scene involves considerable special effects, including smoke, fire, and lightning.[14] In chapter 3, the viewer sees the golem performing as a servant for Rabbi Löw and then accompanying him to the royal court for the Rose Festival celebration. At the court, the golem causes considerable consternation by virtue of his size; when one of the maidens offers him a rose, he appears to take on a new consciousness. Members of the court sit down to watch a magic lantern film of "the Wandering Jews"; when one of the characters appears to emerge from the screen, pandemonium ensues and Rabbi Löw calls upon the golem to save the day. Meanwhile, back at the ghetto, Florian and Miriam are reunited as Florian has used the distraction of the Rose Festival to steal away for a rendezvous. As chapter 4 opens, we see Rabbi Löw and the golem returning to the ghetto, followed by a shot of Florian and Miriam in bed together. News reaches the ghetto that "The King has pardoned the Jews" in gratitude for the golem's help, and much gaiety ensues followed by the ghetto residents gathering in the synagogue to give thanks for their pardon. Miriam tells Florian to escape while the community is praying but Famulus, carrying a torch for Miriam, discovers Florian in her room and sets the golem on him, who manages to throw Florian to his death. In the final chapter, a scene in the synagogue is shown; Rabbi Löw is informed that his house is on fire and dashes out. By this time the golem is pulling Miriam by her hair through the flaming streets of the ghetto: Wegener colorized these frames in red. As a strain of klezmer music rises, the golem escapes from the ghetto and picks up a very blond little girl who offers him an apple and playfully removes the star from his chest, causing him to collapse. A group of Jews carries the golem back into the ghetto, the Star of David appears onscreen, and the film comes to a close.

Critical opinion is sharply divided regarding whether the 1920 *Der Golem* is antisemitic. What I would like to argue here is that, as with Gustav Meyrink's appropriation of the Jewish legend, Paul Wegener's film represents intertextuality gone awry, and it definitely reveals distortions of and disrespect toward Judaism and the golem legend that can be read as antisemitism. Early analyses by Lotte Eisner and Siegfried Kracauer are silent on the matter. Elfi Ledig finds "a latent anti-semitism" in a novel Paul Wegener wrote about the golem but asserts that such "implications . . . cannot be found in the film" (41).[15] In the other column, however, is an impressive list of scholars who find persuasive evidence of varying kinds that Wegener's film exemplifies the pervasive, "every day" antisemitism of Germany in the early days of the Weimar Republic. These scholars include Omer Bartov, Paul Cooke, Klaus Davidowicz, Lester Friedman, Cathy Gelbin, and Noah Isenberg. Indeed, Paul Wegener's *Der Golem: Wie er in die Welt kam* would strike many present-day viewers as an antisemitic twist on a Jewish legend. In this regard, Wegener's golem film is prescient: the Nazi feature film *Jud Süss* (1940) took a best-selling novel written in 1925 by a Jewish man, Lion Feuchtwanger, and turned it into a virulently antisemitic story.[16] As we turn to consideration of Wegener's film, let us begin by consulting the two founding texts of film criticism for the Weimar era, Siegfried Kracauer's *From Caligari to Hitler* (1947) and Lotte Eisner's *The Haunted Screen* (1952). Perhaps not so coincidentally, both of these film critics were Jewish refugees from Nazi Germany and both fled to Paris in 1933. Kracauer went on to emigrate to America in 1941; Eisner remained in Paris and spent some time in the concentration camp Gurs after the Nazi occupation of France in 1940.

The preface of Kracauer's book is revealing, dated as it is "May, 1946," just a year after the end of World War II in the European theater:

> This book is not concerned with German films merely for their own sake; rather, it aims at increasing our knowledge of pre-Hitler Germany in a specific way.
>
> It is my contention that through an analysis of the German films deep psychological dispositions predominant in Germany from 1918 to 1933 can be exposed—dispositions which influenced the course of events during that time and which will have to be reckoned with in the post-Hitler era.
>
> I have reason to believe that the use made here of films as a medium of research can profitably be extended to studies of current mass behavior in the United States and elsewhere. I also believe that studies of this kind may help in the planning of films—not to mention other media of communication—which will effectively implement the cultural aims of the United Nations. (v)

An ambitious aspiration for his volume, as well as an inspiring faith in the potential impact of the medium of film. Eschewing the formalism that was fashionable at this time, Kracauer uses a psychological framework to make sweeping claims that films "provide clues to hidden mental processes" and are "more or less characteristic of the inner life of the nation" (7).

Despite Kracauer's avowed purpose to study film with the goal of "increasing our knowledge of pre-Hitler Germany," he does not comment on the antisemitism in *Der Golem: Wie er in die Welt kam.* Having devoted about three pages to Wegener's earlier films, *Der Student von Prag* and *Der Golem* (1915), Kracauer provides only two paragraphs of analysis of the 1920 golem film. He is here writing of the various trends in German film following *Das Cabinet des Dr. Caligari,* trends that reveal a German desire to "discover a *modus vivendi,* a tenable pattern of inner existence" (107) with which to confront the chaos of the post–World War I period. Kracauer identifies four such trends: the adoption of romantic fairy-tale motifs, the deployment of "Christlike love" (108), the mountain films, and, finally, the effort to implement reason, "endowing rational thinking with executive powers" (112). It is into this latter category that Kracauer places Wegener's 1920 golem film. Because Kracauer's treatment of this film is so short and so curious, I quote it here in full:

> Professor Pölzig had devised the settings for this enlarged version of the old prewar film. In it the Hapsburg emperor issues an order that

the Jews are to be expelled from their ghetto, a dreamlike maze of crooked streets and stooped houses. To soothe the emperor's mind, Rabbi Loew, by means of magic, conjures up a procession of Biblical figures—among them Ahasuerus, who proceeds to trespass on the domain of reality, starting to destroy the imperial palace. The emperor, panic-stricken, agrees to withdraw his order of expulsion if the rabbi will avert the danger; thereupon the latter directs the Golem, his servant, to prevent walls and ceilings from falling down. The Golem obeys with the automatic promptness of a robot. *Here reason avails itself of brute force as a tool to liberate the oppressed.* But instead of following up this motif, the film concentrates upon the Golem's emancipation from his master, and becomes increasingly entangled in half-truths. (112–13, italics mine)

Given that Wegener has ineluctably linked Rabbi Löw with the occult, evil spirits, and astrology, Kracauer's assertion that the film demonstrates the use of reason to address oppression seems misguided. Also telling is Kracauer's omission of any reference to the antisemitic subplot of the Jewish woman, Miriam, who seduces Florian, precipitating his fall to his death.

Kracauer insists that his book is "not concerned with establishing some national character pattern allegedly elevated above history, but it is concerned with the psychological pattern of a particular people at a particular time" (8). Lotte Eisner, too, reflects the era in which she wrote in her analysis of Weimar films, but her approach more obviously describes the national character. Her generalizations may seem to the twenty-first-century reader somewhat essentialist: "The German soul instinctively prefers twilight to daylight" (51) and "Nordic man's Faustian soul is committed to gloom, whereas Reinhardt—we should remember that he is Jewish—created his magical world with light, darkness serving only as a foil to the light. This was the twofold heritage of the German film" (56). Here, Eisner suggests a difference in German Jewish and non-Jewish approaches to film-making but hints in only the most delicate way that the darkness of the non-Jewish films may, to close analysis, yield up antisemitism.

The subtitle of Eisner's book provides a clue to her focus: *The Haunted Screen: Expressionism in the German Cinema and the Influence of Max Reinhardt*. It is in this context that she further comments on the German national character and the centrality of German Expressionism in films of this period:

Mysticism and magic, the dark forces to which Germans have always been more than willing to commit themselves, had flourished in the face of death on the battlefields [of World War I]. The hecatombs of young men fallen in the flower of their youth seemed to nourish the grim nostalgia of the survivors. And the ghosts which had haunted the German Romantics revived, like the shades of Hades after draughts of blood. A new stimulus was thus given to the eternal attraction towards all that is obscure and undetermined, towards the kind of brooding speculative reflection called *Grübelei* which culminated in the apocalyptic doctrine of Expressionism. (9)

And, indeed, this is her emphasis in her three-page analysis of the 1920 Wegener golem film, which focuses almost exclusively on its technical aspects. She includes a lengthy quote from Paul Wegener on the origins of his idea for the golem films that affirms her own focus on light and dark. Wegener opines: "Everything depends on the image, on a certain vagueness of outline where the fantastic world of the past meets the world of today. I realized that photographic technique was going to determine the destiny of the cinema. Light and darkness in the cinema play the same role as rhythm and cadence in music" (40). Eisner documents Wegener's appropriation of "every one of Reinhardt's lightning effects" (56) in a list two paragraphs long and talks about the interaction of the Expressionist sets created by Hans Poelzig and the crowds inhabiting the ghetto: "The narrow gables are somehow echoed in the pointed hats and wind-blown goatees of the Jews, the excited fluttering of their hands, their raised arms clutching at the empty yet restricted space" (58). Yet she never comments on the fact that those very hats were a marker of Jewishness, required garb for Jews in the ghetto. Instead, she goes on to compare the "alternately terrified and exultant crowd" to "a painting by El Greco" (58–59). Thus, neither of these early critics of Weimar cinema, despite their own Jewishness and their flight from their native Germany to France, finds overt antisemitism in the film.

Frances Guerin, whose 2005 analysis of Weimar films is entitled *A Culture of Light* and thus follows Eisner's lead in its focus, treats *Der Golem: Wie er in die Welt kam* in about a dozen pages of analysis. She is primarily interested in the metacinematic aspects of the film, in which "Rabbi Loew will assume the role of the diegetic 'director' of events [and] . . . the ersatz director of Wegener's film" (126). Guerin presents a complex argument for the attitude toward technology and cinema instantiated in the film: on the one hand, the film appears to valorize technology as a possible solution to the German-Jewish question of the 1920s, and on the other hand, Rabbi Loew, in essence, destroys the film in the "film with a film" scene at the court, thus suggesting that Jewish history is more crucial to the Jewish community than technology. Finally, Guerin refuses to choose:

"Rather than bemoaning the irresolution of *Der Golem*'s relationship to modernity, the film's openness can be understood as being at the heart of its innovation" (135). While her analysis shows a sensitivity to both the Jewish German context in which the film was produced and to the Jewish themes depicted therein, had Guerin more carefully questioned key scenes, she might have come to a definitive conclusion. Her bland and inaccurate description of the golem's creation leads to a misguided conclusion. She states that "Rabbi Loew heeds the stars' warning and turns to the Cabala. From the Cabala, he learns . . . Astaroth can be summoned [to] . . . utter the magic word to be placed in the Golem's heart" (128). But it is a book on "Necromancie" that Rabbi Löw reads and the Kabbalah does not suggest summoning a devil figure to perform magic. Guerin goes on to claim "In contradistinction to *Faust*, the coming together of magic and cinema in this first scene of conjuring in *Der Golem* is not associated with evil and immoral temptations" (128), while I make exactly the opposite argument, based on both the historical understanding of the figure of Astaroth and on Wegener's earlier film, *Der Student von Prag* (1913).

If we begin thinking about Wegener's *Der Golem* by going back seven years to *Der Student von Prag* (1913), a film in which Wegener acted in the role of the student Balduin and which he also co-wrote, we find indications of the antisemitism to follow. *Der Student von Prag*, directed by Stellan Rye, is the story of a mendacious young man, described on an intertitle as "Prague's finest swordsman and wildest student." He is in love with the Countess Margit but unable to act upon his love due to his penury. Approached by one Scapinelli, Balduin agrees that Scapinelli may "take from this room whatever he chooseth for his own use as he desires for which privilege he shall pay me one hundred thousand pieces of gold." From Balduin's perspective, there is precious little in his sparse room to take, but Scapinelli unexpectedly summons from the mirror Balduin's double and leaves with him. Balduin pursues the Countess, who is betrothed to another man, and with his newfound wealth he purchases fine clothing and living quarters. But at key moments in the film, his double suddenly materializes to thwart his plans, his love, and his honor. In the final scene, Balduin contemplates suicide: he writes a note and removes his pistol from safekeeping. Once again, the double suddenly appears; Balduin shoots him, enjoys a moment of joyful relief, and then notes that he is himself bleeding from his chest; he falls over dead and Scapinelli arrives to exult, shredding the contract over Balduin's body.

With intertextual references to Goethe's *Faust*, E. T. A. Hoffmann's "The Story of the Lost Reflection," and Edgar Allan Poe's "William Wilson," Scapinelli is clearly a stand-in for the devil who, metaphorically, buys Balduin's soul; thereafter, Balduin has no reflection in the mirror. Scapinelli, with his Italian name, represents the racialized other in this film, and it is not a stretch to think of him as a specific racialized other, the Jew. Not only does he play the role of the devil, a figure often associated with Jews in antisemitic stereotypes that depict Jews with horns and cloven feet, but he is also described as "an adventurer" and "a sorcerer" in the credits for the film. Furthermore, Scapinelli is a kind of moneylender, pouring a seemingly unending stream of gold onto Balduin's table as he tempts him to sign the contract that Balduin misunderstands. The association of Jews with usury is a longstanding stereotype, grounded in an era when Jews were not allowed to own property or to enter many professions and so indeed did serve as moneylenders. Paul Cooke notes that Scapinelli "is decidedly Semitic looking" (22), a view echoed by Heide Schlüpmann, who describes Scapinelli as "a thin grey man with a top hat and *pointed nose. . . .* He sits down opposite Balduin: the uncanny has arrived" (21, italics mine). Finally, as if all these stereotypical "markers of Jewishness" were not enough, the 1926 remake of *Der Student von Prag* (in which Wegener was not involved) explicitly depicts Scapinelli in antisemitic fashion. It is worth noting that Hanns Heinz Ewers, who coauthored with Wegener the screenplay for the 1913 version and wrote the 1926 version of the film, also wrote the novel *Horst Wessel,* which he subsequently adapted to the film *Hans Westmar.*[17] This 1933 film was "one of three explicit propaganda feature films made in the year of Hitler's rise to power depicting National Socialism's revolutionary phase" (Schlüpmann, 9–10). Wegener, too, became engaged in Nazi cinema, "making propaganda films for the Nazi regime, which reciprocated by naming him 'Actor of the State'" (Bartov, 3).

In a curious way, *Der Student von Prag* has a very similar theme to *Der Golem: Wie er in die Welt kam,* yet the theme is realized in diametric opposition. In the former, a caricature of a "Jewish" sorcerer figure takes the soul (and, ultimately, life) from a man; in the latter, a Jewish rabbi, depicted as a sorcerer, infuses life into a clay figure and, by the end of the film, the golem seems to possess a soul (although in the Jewish tradition of the golem legend, this is debated but rarely the case). Further, both films are set in Prague, although *Der Student* was actually filmed in Prague while *Der Golem* was filmed in a studio in which an intensely Expressionist set of the Jewish ghetto in Prague had been constructed. *Der Student* does have one constructed set in which a significant scene occurs: it is a reconstructed Jewish cemetery (as the Jewish community in Prague understandably refused to allow the film crew to use the real Jewish cemetery in the Josefov). Large gravestones with Hebrew letters are set up in a forest where Balduin's tryst with the Countess is interrupted by his double (see Eisner, 42, for a sharply reproduced still of this tryst). Cooke observes that the film sets up a number of dichotomies: not only the obvious doppelgänger theme already discussed but also a "good/bad split . . . symbolised in the opposition in the film between 'rational' Christianity (again symbolized in the Komtesse who in one sequence looks for guidance from the church) and 'irrational' Judaism. . . . [W]hen Balduin sets up a tryst with the Komtesse where should he choose to meet her but in a Jewish graveyard, thus bringing together most clearly his death and sex drives unlocked by his pact with Scapinelli" (22). Yet another dichotomy in the film exists between the Countess and Lyduschka, a gypsy woman with a crush on Balduin; these two women form a good/bad split in which Lyduschka embodies the stereotype of the racialized other woman, that is, a whore. We will see that Rabbi Löw's daughter, Miriam, in *Der Golem* has a similar function.

Wegener's 1920 *Der Golem* opens with a view of the night sky and several brightly lit circular stars. An intertitle announces: "The learned Rabbi Löw reads in the stars that misfortune threatens the Jews." Thus, before the viewer even sees an actor on the screen, Rabbi Löw is linked with astrology and reading the stars as omens. This impression is confirmed with our first view of the rabbi: seated on the roof of a high stone tower, he peers through a telescope and alternately consults a book on alchemy. This association of the rabbi and by implication, of Judaism, with astrology, the occult, and evil spirits is consistent throughout the film; the partner of this malevolent depiction of Judaism is the consistent misrepresentation of various Judaic symbols and practices. Together, these strands in the film serve to, at once, demonstrate disdain for Judaism and Jews and to associate Jews with demons, as we saw in *Der Student von Prag*. A contemporaneous reviewer in the *New York Times* got it right: "The black magic of the Middle Ages, sorcery, astrology . . . have been brought to the screen of the Criterion in 'the Golem.' . . . The story is said to be based on an old Jewish legend, but it is no part of an orthodox Jewish tradition surely" (June 20, 1920, p. 20).

As the film unfolds, the audience learns that the threat to the Jews, supposedly foretold by the stars, will come from Rudolf II, the king of Bohemia and the Holy Roman Emperor, who, in the film, draws up an edict expelling the Jews from Prague. To be sure, such edicts did exist, but Rudolf II never issued one.[18] In fact, his reign was considered to be a "golden age" for Jews in Prague and, indeed, in 1577 he confirmed the *revocation* of all expulsion orders that his father, Maximilian II, had declared in 1567. In turn, Rudolf II's brother Matthias confirmed Jewish privileges in Prague when he came to the throne in 1611. Rudolf also extended various other legal protections to the Jewish community during his reign (1575–1611) that overlapped entirely with Rabbi Loew's tenure as Chief Rabbi in Prague.[19] This anachronism, upon which all the action of the film is premised, is just the first of many such inaccuracies in the film that combine to depict a poisonous atmosphere in the ghetto.

The plot of *Der Golem* runs along two geographically and visually divided tracks: scenes set in the Jewish ghetto, a remarkable set created by Hans Poelzig, and scenes set at the court of Rudolf II. In the ghetto, the action revolves around the creation of the golem and the illicit affair between Rabbi Löw's daughter, Miriam, and a knight from the Court named Florian. In the court scenes, we see Rudolf issuing his antisemitic edict, inviting Rabbi Löw to bring the golem to the court, and the golem saving the court from destruction, for which the grateful Rudolf rescinds his expulsion edict. The two locations in the film stand in sharp contrast to one another: the ghetto set, often described as quintessentially Expressionist, is dark and gloomy; misshapen houses are topped with roofs reminiscent of the hats the Jews must wear to identify themselves as Jews; the interiors are largely cast in shadows and are often cavelike and sinister; and many of the Jews appear unkempt and barefoot, wearing not only identifying hats (the pileus) but also circular badges (rondelles). The court is a much brighter and livelier atmosphere, filled with well-heeled, light-hearted young people who are laughing and dancing.

The action begins in earnest when the king signs the edict of expulsion. The audience reads the text onscreen:

> Decreed against the Jews. We can no longer neglect the popular complaints against the Jews. They despise the Holy Christian ceremonies. They endanger the lives and property of their fellow-men; they practice black magic. We decree that all Jews shall leave the city and all territory in sight of the city before the month is ended.

In a real sense, the action to follow confirms this accusation: Rabbi Löw is depicted as practicing black magic and so the expulsion seems justified. Florian serves as the court's messenger, delivering the edict to the ghetto. He bears this devastating news in the most ingratiating manner, mincing around with a rose in his teeth and a supercilious sneer on his face as he deals with the watchman at the gate to the ghetto. Rabbi Löw is already busy in his secret chamber, molding the clay into a golem and reading from a text titled "Necromancie: The Art of Bringing the Dead to Life." The film then offers a series of jump cuts, in which the audience alternately sees lovemaking between Florian and Miriam, and golem-making by Rabbi Löw and his assistant, Famulus (whose name means "servant"). Miriam (played by Lyda Salmonova, Paul Wegener's wife) is every bit the seductress, wearing off-the-shoulder dresses and heavy makeup (another anachronism), and serving unmistakably as the stereotype of the Jewish vamp luring innocent non-Jews to their destruction (and Florian will pay with his life for his dalliance with Miriam). That they consummate their relationship, which starts out with very visible breast grappling, is made explicit in the film. Meanwhile, in Rabbi Löw's secret chamber, set up as an alchemy laboratory, progress is being made toward creation of the golem. The rabbi reads instructions that tell him he must summon Astaroth, who can give him the secret code word which, when placed in the golem's chest cavity, will infuse him with life. In a very dramatic scene, Rabbi Löw creates a ring of fire around himself and Astaroth arrives in the form of an enormous mask that breathes smoke.[20] In demonology, Astaroth is alternately identified as male, a prince of Hell, and as female, Beelzebub's granddaughter.[21] So in either case, Astaroth is associated with the devil, further strengthening the link being made in the film between Jews and the devil, a link we have already seen in *Der Student von Prag*. As Omer Bartov has aptly noted: "Here we find Rabbi Loew doing what can only be described as witchcraft, black magic, and wizardry. The books he consults, the demons he calls forth, the secret formulas he recites, all evoke the images of evil consorting with the powers of the devil. The Jews may be threatened, but the forces they arouse are greater than any the gentiles can muster" (4).

While in this circle of fire, Rabbi Löw wears a wizard's hat inscribed with the six-pointed Star of David. But he also has a "magic wand" that ends in a five-pointed star. The star that covers the golem's chest cavity, where the code word will go, is also a five-pointed star, though it is often mistakenly referred to as a "Star of David" in critical articles about the film.[22] Thus one of the most widely recognized symbols of Judaism is carelessly bungled in the film. Such misrepresentation occurs in many other instances, for example, the inaccurate ways in which Jews are depicted worshiping in the synagogue. Such errors serve as a synecdoche for the disdain shown toward Judaism in general in Wegener's film.

The word that Astaroth breathes out is "Aemaet." This word is part of the golem legend: some versions of the legend state that this word, meaning "life," is carved on the golem's forehead to bring him to life and when Rabbi Loew wished to withdraw his life he had only to erase the first letter, leaving the word "Meth," which meant death. But a *crucial difference* must be emphasized between the traditional versions of the legend and Wegener's film, and this goes to the heart of the matter of antisemitism in the film: in traditional Jewish versions of the legend, the secret of bringing the golem to life is contained in sacred books and a strong sense prevails that God himself is involved in the formula. For example, in some texts such as that by Chayim Bloch, Rabbi Loew falls asleep and directs a dream question to God for the best method by which to protect the Jews. God's answer is to go to the banks of the Vltava River and create the mud man. Often the creation of the golem involves the use of incantations, rituals, Hebrew letters, or numerology, but always there is a sense of God's involvement, too, in the divine plan that is recorded in the Kabbalah and other books with these formulas. By contrast, in Wegener's film, the secret comes from the devil himself, and thus Rabbi Löw, the supposed man of God, is depicted as consorting with the devil, as making pacts with the devil, as a master of the occult, all things anathema to Jewish religious tradition but also things that have been levied as accusations against Jews for centuries.

When Rabbi Löw inserts the code word into the clay figure's chest, the golem does indeed flicker to life. Paul Wegener himself plays the golem: his face, which looks Orientalist in the manner of Steiner-Prag's illustrations for Meyrink's novel, is burnished in such a way as to make it appear clay-like; Wegener was a tall man, six feet six inches, and so his golem towers over most of the other actors; he walks with a stiff-legged gait on boots with thick soles, a detail borrowed by makers of early Frankenstein films. Perhaps most remarkable is his "hair"—prominent bangs and an inert, carved pageboy style that frames his face. After a few scenes depicting the golem's function as a servant—chopping wood, shopping—Rabbi Löw takes him to the court for the Rose Festival. As the golem lumbers into the gaily decorated court, he strikes fear into the courtiers, who fall back in amazement. The king directs a questioning glance at Rabbi Löw, who replies in an intertitle: "He is my creature, called Golem. More I cannot tell you." The king then inquires: "What manner of miracle will you show us today, strange magician?" And Rabbi Löw promises: "I will show you our people's history and our patriarchs. And if you value your lives, let no one speak or laugh." What ensues is a kind of film within a film: Rabbi Löw magically projects onto a wall a scene depicting desert sands and a crowd of people moving from left to right. Richard Byrne, in his shot analysis, describes the figures who next appear as "Three patriarchs, a woman on a donkey's back, and a young boy with two lines of people in the background" (74). Roger Manvell, writing seven years later, infers something more specific: "We see the three Wise Kings, Mary on the donkey's back with the Christ child, and the wandering tribes of Israel" (41).[23] The audience, despite the rabbi's warning, begins to snicker and then to laugh outright, another sign of disdain for Judaism and its history. Then a flash of light on the "screen" and, as Byrne describes it, a "patriarch . . . walks rapidly toward camera leaning on staff" (75) while Manvell identifies this approaching figure as Moses, who "walks towards the mocking guests, his staff threatening them" (41). Preceding both of these suggestions was Kracauer's identification of the figure as Ahasuerus (113). Ahasuerus served as the king of Persia from 486 to 464 B.C. and is also called Xerxes. He issued an order for all Jews in his kingdom to be killed and was persuaded to rescind the order by his Jewish wife, Esther.[24] Given the context of the Wegener film, where an edict to evict the Jews is at stake, it seems Kracauer's speculation is most likely.[25] It is worth noting that this scene in the film is based on an old Czech legend in which Rabbi Loew is summoned to Rudolf's palace to provide entertainment for the guests. Though not accompanied by the golem in this legend, Rabbi Loew does admonish the guests not to laugh. The figures in the procession that Loew magically creates are identified as "a gigantic old man, the patriarch Abraham. . . . He paced slowly and graciously across the hall . . . [followed by] figures of Isaac, Jacob, and Jacob's sons, the Jewish forefathers" (Petiska, 36–37).

As this patriarchal figure looms larger and larger on Rabbi Löw's improvised screen in *Der Golem,* the laughter of the screen audience gets louder and suddenly, the ceiling of the palace begins to collapse. In a panic, the king pleads with Rabbi Löw to intervene and the golem comes to the rescue, holding up the walls and ceiling. The king rescinds the eviction order and Rabbi Löw returns triumphantly to the ghetto with the golem. Alas, in his absence, Miriam has been cavorting with Florian in her bed, her sexual availability mirroring that of Rosina in Meyrink's novel, another antisemitic stereotype. With various plot twists and turns, the golem pursues Florian, who is attempting to sneak away. They grapple on the rooftop and the golem pitches Florian to the ground several stories below. The message: blood mixing between Jews and non-Jews carries a terrible price. The golem, whose interest in Miriam has been aroused, now pursues her, placing her on a table and caressing her body in an imitation of the caresses bestowed by Florian earlier in the film. Famulus attempts to intervene, and in the scuffle Rabbi Löw's home is set on fire. Now the golem has truly "gone berserk," dragging the hapless Miriam through the streets by her long braids. Rabbi Löw is summoned from the synagogue with the cry "The demon has carried Miriam away," thus ineluctably linking the golem with the devil. Eventually Miriam is saved and the golem escapes the confines of the ghetto into a light-filled scene of blond (read: non-Jewish) children playing. One of them offers the golem an apple to eat. The golem lifts her up and she fiddles with the star on the golem's chest, withdrawing the code word. The golem suddenly goes slack, drops the little girl, and falls over, lifeless. In a memorial gesture, the children gather around, sit on the golem, and cover him with flowers. The Jews rejoice at their rescue and the film ends.

In his study of antisemitic imagery in twentieth-century film, Omer Bartov begins with an analysis of Wegener's *Der Golem*. Using this film as the ur-text for demonstrating European images of Jews, Bartov observes: "But what is most important to recognize about this early venture into cinematic stereotypes is the extent to which it reflected existing notions about Jews, further popularized them among ever-larger audiences, and provided models for their depiction that generations of filmmakers with very different goals and agendas have employed or have tried to avoid until the present day" (3). While noting that *Der Golem* is not "overtly antisemitic" (3), Bartov outlines "three main motifs" in the film that will continue to be used for the next century. These include: the notion of the " 'Jew' as malevolent outsider"; the "anxiety about Jewish transformation, accompanied by an insistence on the unchanging Jewish essence"; and "the obsession with sexual relations between Jews and gentiles" (3). We see two of these themes in *Der Student von Prag*: Scapinelli, the Italian moneylender, certainly represents the "malevolent outsider"; he also undergoes transformation, seeming at first to be offering aid to Balduin to enable him to win his sweetheart and then clearly acting as Mephistopheles, stealing his soul.

We see all three themes in *Der Golem: Wie er in die Welt kam. A*s we have noted, the Jews are defined as outsiders in many ways. They are secluded in a ghetto that, though such a ghetto existed in Prague in reality, is represented in the film as strange and weird, as are the Jews themselves: "The strangeness of the Jews is depicted through dress, beards, facial expressions, gesticulations, modes of living, sites of habitation, and language, which is understandable yet apparently distorted, and sometimes comical or menacing. . . . The synagogue . . . reveals itself as the heart of darkness, the very center of all that is weird and ominous about the Jews" (Bartov, 4). As for the theme of the essentialized Jew who also can fool the gentile world by transformation, Bartov reads the "film with a film" scene as an image of the Eternal Jew (rather than Moses or Ahasuerus), "who bears a disturbing physical resemblance to the figure popularized a few years later in Nazi posters and subsequently in the most notorious 'documentary' produced in the Third Reich [i.e., *Der ewige Jude* (1940)]" (5). As for a further image of transformation in the film, Bartov describes the golem as "an ambiguous creature" (5), supposedly the protector of the Jews yet transformed into a marauder within the ghetto and then "a gentle ogre" once he has escaped the clutches of the Jews into the outside world of children, flowers, and sunshine at the close of the film. Miriam, too, undergoes transformation: on the one hand, she portrays "the lecherous Jewish woman" (6), and on the other hand, claims Bartov, she is used as bait by her father to wangle an invitation to the court. She is also the source of the golem's sexual awakening, which in turn unleashes his destructive streak. Thus, she is at the nexus of the third motif Bartov traces, the obsession with sex between Jews and non-Jews, in this case, between Miriam and Florian: "Sex and the Jews, the threat posed by Jewish women and men to the natural order of things and the transformation that sexual intercourse with gentiles entails, are at the center of the cinematic imagination from its very cradle" (6).

Noah Isenberg has included essays on *Der Golem* in two books, *Between Redemption and Doom: The Strains of German-Jewish Modernism* (1999) and his 2009 anthology, *Weimar Cinema: An Essential Guide to Classic Films of the Era*. The essay in the latter is an abridgement of the earlier essay. Like Guerin, Isenberg endeavors to establish a context for the film; for Isenberg, the large migration of Jews from eastern Europe into Germany, particularly Berlin, after World War I is a key to understanding *Der Golem*. Approximately seventy thousand new immigrants nearly doubled the existing eastern European Jewish immigrant population in Germany (*Cinema*, 45). Isenberg notes the film's enormous popularity, running for two months after its premiere on October 29, 1920 (*Cinema*, 36), a popularity comparable to that of Meyrink's novel. Isenberg astutely links aspects of the film to attitudes held by non-Jewish audiences. For example, he provides the text from the intertitle for the "Decree against the Jews" issued early in the film: "The many serious charges against the Jews can no longer be disregarded, being that they crucified our Lord, wrongfully ignore the holy Christian holidays, thirst after the goods and lives of their fellow men, and practice the black arts. Hence, we decree that all Jews must evacuate their quarter, known as the ghetto, before the new moon" (*Cinema*, 36–37). Noting that the golem legend serves as "a modern allegory of invasion—one of horror's time-honored subjects and a subject that had enormous potential to resonate with Weimar audiences" (*Cinema*, 37), Isenberg implies that prejudices against Jews, particularly against the immigrant *Ostjuden*, fueled the popularity of Wegener's film. In a subsection of the essay titled "The Architecture of the Jew," Isenberg speaks to the film's "predilection for myth based, caricatured constructions of Jewishness" (*Cinema*, 44) and the fact that the depiction of Rabbi Löw as using the black arts fulfills the "Decree against the Jews" issued by Rudolf in the film. The stereotypical Jewish figures in the film "paradoxically evoke at once capitalistic dominance, political prowess, and scientific insight on the one hand and stifling swarthiness, exotic practices, and ghetto sensibilities on the other" (*Cinema*, 46). These are, of course, the contradictory stereotypes that the Nazis will impugn to Jews within months after the release of *Der Golem*. Hitler's meetings with his early followers in the beer halls of Munich resulted in the Beer Hall Putsch in 1923.

Considering all this evidence, then, it is clear that the impact of Wegener's *Der Golem* was to propose that the Jews were a *virulent threat* to the German nation rather than the message of the original golem legend, which was that the golem is created as *a response to the threat posed to Jews.* Like Meyrink's *Der Golem,* Wegener's film is truly intertextuality gone awry, a Jewish legend turned on its head and used against the Jewish community.

Julien Duvivier, *Le Golem* (1935–36)

When considering Meyrink's and Wegener's appropriations of a Jewish legend and reading them as antisemitic precursors of what was to come in Nazi Germany, it is instructive to turn to a golem film made in this period by a French director, Julien Duvivier. Duvivier began making films in the silent era and completed over seventy-five films before his demise in 1967 at the age of seventy-one. He is often considered to be one of the most important directors in the history of French cinema but one who is overlooked, in part, perhaps, because his work is of uneven quality. Many of his films have Jewish themes or topics, such as *David Golder,* a film based on the controversial novella by the Russian French Jew Irene Nemirovsky, who died in Auschwitz in 1942. Duvivier's *The Golem: The Legend of Prague* (the film's American title) was released in 1936 and is credited with being the first golem "talkie." The film was made in Prague, with the sets designed by Andrej Andrejew, who collaborated on *The Cabinet of Dr. Caligari;* the sets were described by the *New York Times* reviewer Frank Nugent in 1937 as "weird—almost futuristic street architecture."

The film opens with two text introductions: one that recounts the golem legend as it is associated with Rabbi Loew, and another that sets up the plot:

> Medieval Prague was a city of great luxury and license, and also a city of squalor, misery, and plagues. The Emperor Rudolph II, a half crazy tyrant, vacillated under the oppressive influence of his mistress Countess Strada and his ruthless Chancellor, Lang. Thus was Prague kept in a perpetual state of terror.

The camera then zeroes in on the statue of Rabbi Loew that stands to this day next to the Prague Town Hall. The statue was sculpted by Czech native Ladislav Jan Saloun (1870–1946) and probably put in place around 1917. Thus the film begins with an anachronism and contains many other similar inaccuracies and misrepresentations of history as well as of the golem legend itself. The camera tracks to a fairly faithful set of the Old-New Synagogue in which the congregation, enslaved to the emperor, have gathered to pray. The rabbi, Jacob, urges the congregation to maintain their faith in God, despite their sufferings as "Liberty will come." The viewer learns that Rabbi Loew has already died and promised on his deathbed that the golem, "asleep" in the *shul* attic, would return at the moment of crisis to save the Jewish community. And the crisis is upon the community at this moment, in the form of a cholera plague and starvation.

Suddenly the synagogue is overrun by Emperor Rudolph II's soldiers; they are searching the attic on orders from Rudolph to take the "magic statue" as the emperor "is afraid of it." The emperor's chancellor, identified as a Jew who has left the community to seek power and fame, encourages Rudolph in his search for the golem. The scene changes to the emperor's palace, where we see a clearly obsessed and crazed Rudolph monitoring experiments in a Frankenstein-like lab where a homunculus has been created. Rabbi Jacob, anticipating his arrest by the emperor, confides in his very capable wife, Rachel, the secret formula for waking the golem and instructs her: "When the golem awakes, tell him 'Revolt is the right of slaves.'" Jacob's subsequent imprisonment gives Rachel agency to provide leadership to save her community. She warns the congregation: "You will all be destroyed and yet you do nothing—Listen! Your brothers are in the hands of murderers." Given the years when the film was in production—1935–36—this might be read as code, urging European Jews, about to be enslaved by Hitler, to rise up and resist. Rachel subsequently arms herself, goes to the palace to intercede with Chancellor Lang, is thrown into the dungeon, walks bravely through a cell with lions in it to reach the golem who has also been taken captive, and writes on his forehead "Revolt is the right of slaves."

By the time the golem thus appears, an hour of the ninety-six-minute film has already elapsed. Duvivier's golem, played by Ferdinand Hart, is dressed in a long wool cape and a rough approximation of a "superhero" style suit underneath the cape that is tied with a rope. He is balding, has prominent eyebrows, and his face has been bronzed to a high gloss, giving something of the impression of a metal robot. The golem knocks down some walls and ceilings in the palace and then proceeds to the Jewish Quarter, where he breaks open the gates. Jacob praises him: "Golem—your mission is fulfilled. Return to the dust from which you came," and the golem obediently collapses into a pile of dust and clothes.

A messenger announces: "Chancellor Lang is dead. The emperor has abdicated." Thus, the menace in this film is clearly Lang and the emperor, not the golem; the emperor has enslaved the Jews and displays a paranoid and vengeful personality that results in unpredictable behavior, that is, he represents the erratic and evil dictator Adolph Hitler. The golem is the Jews' secret weapon, to be deployed at the moment of crisis as instructed by the revered Rabbi Loew before his death. With the abdication of Rudolf, the Jews are freed, largely through the efforts of Rachel, who has successfully urged her fellow Jews to action. It is notable in this context that Duvivier himself left France in 1940 to live in the United States, returning only after the war.[26]

As Emily Bilski notes: "The spread of fascism led to a renewed interest in a golem as redeemer. Julien Duvivier's film, *Le Golem* (1936), a Franco-Czech co-production, was shot in Prague after Hitler's Nuremberg Laws had gone into effect in 1935. It focused on the golem as a rescuer of Jews, and was both germane and prescient" (70). Simon Sibelman is somewhat less sanguine about the film, finding it reifies certain stereotypes of Jews already current in French cinema of the first decades of the twentieth century. Although acknowledging that "no direct evidence arises from his notes, letters or personal papers that would indicate that Duvivier himself maintained anti-Semitic beliefs" (81) and that the film provides "authentic portrayals of Jewish life" (91), Sibelman does note that "Duvivier nevertheless resorts to stereotyping shorthand in order to advance the narrative" (91). The most prominent uses of such shorthand include the "apostate Jew" Lang, who "symbolizes an extreme menace to the state" (91), and the scene of a cabal: a "malevolent surreal ballet [that] produces an impression of Jews as maniacal demons capable of calling upon the forces of Evil in order to obtain the appropriate kabbalistic formulae necessary to achieve victory over their enemies" (92).

To be sure, these aspects of the film are unsavory and mirror aspects of Wegener's film that we have found objectionable. Nonetheless, it can be argued that Duvivier's film's prevailing impact on its audiences is to present the emperor, who has enslaved the Jewish community, as an evil dictator who fails to attend to the plague and starvation that have left the community in the ghetto in a weakened state. We also see a Jewish woman who bravely carries the secret of reviving the golem through danger and acts collaboratively with him to destroy the palace, the seat of oppression. This is radically different from the portraits of conniving, lascivious Jewish women we have seen in Meyrink and Wegener. The golem, too, is a figure of rescue in Duvivier's film and, rather than running amok, simply lapses into listlessness when, his act of redemption complete, the letters are erased from his forehead. Overall, one can read the film as an allegorical warning to all Europeans about their impending fate as Hitler greedily overtakes the continent and subjugates the Jews.

In conclusion, then, we have examined two texts from the early twentieth century that appropriate the golem legend inappropriately. Rather than creating a hypertext that pays homage to the legend, overtly interrogates or critiques it, or endeavors to give it contemporary meaning, these texts—by Meyrink and Wegener—crassly exploit the golem legend for its occult and financial potential. Recalling Gershom Scholem's observation upon meeting Gustav Meyrink that his eyes were opened as to "how an author could score points with pseudo-mysticism" (*Jerusalem*, 133), we see that both Meyrink and Wegener produced best-selling works by astutely sizing up audience hunger for the mystical and titillating. While we might grant that neither engaged in antisemitic characterizations, themes, and stereotypes in an intentionally malevolent manner, nonetheless, such adoption of societal prejudices is, obviously, harmful. The disdain for Judaism demonstrated by misrepresentation of its major symbols, worship practices, and beliefs as well as the conflation of Judaism with astrology are seriously detrimental to Jews and their religion. The subversion of the golem into a figure of evil turns him into an exotic other, a synecdoche for the "evil" of Judaism and Jews. Considering that these works were sent forth into a society that already harbored serious antisemitism and would in a few short years elect a leader who could imagine the heretofore unimaginable idea of a "Final Solution" to the Jewish question, the impact of such intertextuality gone awry is immeasurable. How sharp the contrast as we turn now to the work of Isaac Bashevis Singer, Elie Wiesel, and Frances Sherwood, who also transmogrify the golem legend but do so in a manner that is creative, life-giving, affirming of Judaic beliefs, respectful, and even humorous.

Traditional Retellings of the Golem Legend

Few post-biblical Jewish legends—if any—have evoked the interest or have provoked the imagination of Jews and of non-Jews as has the legend of the Golem.

Byron Sherwin, *The Golem Legend*

In this chapter we will encounter the golem in three stories that hew closely to traditional Jewish legends of the clay man. Two of these retellings were published in 1982 and 1983 and were written by Isaac Bashevis Singer, who fled Poland for America in 1935, and by the Holocaust survivor Elie Wiesel. Both books were marketed for children and have been neglected by the literary critics and biographers of the two authors. The third is more contemporary: Frances Sherwood's full-length novel *The Book of Splendor* (2002). These intertexts are all set in sixteenth-century Prague and follow closely the tropes of golem stories established by the early 1800s, as we saw in chapter 1. Yet the modest changes that have been introduced by each author create a palimpsest; in the resulting layers of old and new, tradition and change, the reader can discern something of the author's purposes. Further, such layers reveal the malleability of the golem legend in various historical periods. Finally, these traditional retellings help affirm the plots, characters, imagery, narration, and impulses of the usual legend and thus set the stage for understanding the significant intertextual variations we will see in chapters 4 and 5.

The reader will note immediately a stark contrast with the malevolent golems we have seen in Meyrink and Wegener. In these much more gentle tales, homage is being paid to the golem legend and hence to Judaism and Jewish texts. Intertextuality as a literary strategy is deployed as a tribute to the power of the Jewish imagination over the centuries, despite threats and persecution. The golem serves as a text, providing continuity for the Jewish people and a memory for their literature. In effect, intertextuality is the *shem* put into the golem's mouth to effect a transformation of one text into another, and imagination is the instrument of intertextuality. It permits literature to continue to serve its crucial cultural purposes: helping readers find identity, understand human nature, discern what we can of divinity, and achieve social justice.

Isaac Bashevis Singer

All we have done here is to illuminate a few aspects of Yiddish literature in Poland and the conditions under which it existed. For the Yiddish writer who comes from there, the very ground from which he derived literary sustenance has been destroyed along with Jewish Poland. His characters are dead. Their language has been silenced. All that he has to draw from are memories.

Isaac Bashevis Singer, 1943

These lines, the final sentences of an article Singer contributed to an American publication, *Di tsukunft* (*Yiddish Literature*), are a wrenching acknowledgment that the world he left behind when he immigrated to America in 1935 was forever destroyed by the Holocaust. Yet these are not the first lines in which Singer expressed a sense of profound loss. The move to America had already created in him a sense that he had irrevocably yielded up contact with the wellspring of his creativity. His transition to New York City caused a writer's block that lasted several years. Because Yiddish was his mother tongue, opportunities to publish in America were severely limited; he contributed a weekly column to *Forverts* (*The Jewish Daily Forward*), then being published in Yiddish, and occasional articles elsewhere, but such meager appearances in print did not provide a living wage. The epigraph above, then, expresses a central dilemma for Singer: how to express his identity and his beliefs, "his inner landscape" (Hadda, 104), when the source of those ideals has been ruthlessly destroyed by the Nazis. Singer lived "between a dead past and an impossible future" (Hadda, 105).

Singer liked to say that the first word he learned in English was "delicious." Attending a Hadassah luncheon shortly after his arrival, where he expected to hear Yiddish spoken, he was surprised to hear the seated women repeating "delicious, delicious" as he entered the room.[1] While he eagerly began to learn English, he recognized that Yiddish would always be the tongue in which he wrote. It was beyond his wildest imaginings that anyone would want to translate his work into English. Though his older, and initially more famous, brother Israel Joshua Singer, who had preceded him to the United States, had arranged for his own best-seller, *Yoshe Kalb* (*Yasha the Loon*),[2] to be translated into English, Isaac did not envision a reading audience for himself in America:

> As a writer in Yiddish, I felt like a has-been. . . . Abe Cahan, the editor of *The Jewish Daily Forward*, kept repeating in his editorials that Yiddish had only one mission: to help bring Socialism and then disappear forever. Even the Yiddish journalists and writers I met in the Royal Café on Second Avenue contended that my writings had no relevance in America, neither for the Jews nor for the Gentiles.
>
> Who was going to be interested in a false Messiah who lived some 300 years ago? Who would believe in the lore of the cabala, in such superstitions as reincarnation, dybbuks, haunted houses, girls seduced by demons, corpses rising from their graves and other such balderdash? The world was moving forward, not backward. I agreed with them. I seemed to have been born an anachronism. (Stavans, 27)

The first appearance of Singer's golem story in 1969 was in Yiddish. By now, despite his gloomy expectations, he had indeed established a following in the United States. The English translation of *The Golem* did not appear until 1982. Despite the Nobel Prize awarded to Singer in the intervening years (1978) and the literary fame and critical attention that followed, very little mention is made of *The Golem*. Neither Janet Hadda's well-regarded biography of Singer nor Florence Noiville's more recent biography nor the Library of America volume on Singer's life and work even acknowledge this publication. Yet careful examination of both what Singer maintains from earlier versions of the legend and what he rings in the story that is uniquely Singer reveal much about the influence of his life on his golem tale as well as about the malleability of the golem.

Isaac Singer's Life and Work

Isaac Bashevis Singer was born on July 14, 1904, in Leoncin, Poland, which is located in the Lublin area of eastern Poland; he was steeped "in Jewish folk culture of the villages and market towns" in which "traditional forms of Jewish life persisted well into the twentieth century" (Stavans, 9). On his father's side were seven generations of rabbis "belonging to a long-standing Hasidic tradition," and his maternal grandfather was also a rabbi (Noiville, 6–7). A commonplace of Singer scholarship tells of the conflicted environment in the Singer household: his mother was eminently rational and practical, as well as intellectual, while his father was "a mystically inclined rabbi, who literally predicted the Messiah would come on a certain date" (Stavans, 96). This sharp contrast in parental perspective is well illustrated by the anecdote of the screaming geese Singer retells in *In My Father's Court*, his autobiographical volume about his early life in Poland. As the story goes, a woman who had just slaughtered two geese for the Sabbath meal arrived at the Singers' home to consult with the rabbi: the geese "shrieked" when thrown against one another, despite having been beheaded and eviscerated. Singer describes his father's reaction: "In his blue eyes could be seen a mixture of fear and vindication. For my father this was a sign that . . . omens were sent from heaven. But perhaps this was a sign from the Evil One, from Satan himself?" (18). By contrast, "Mother's face was growing sullen, smaller, sharper" (19). Ever the pragmatist, Singer's mother grabs the geese, removes their windpipes, and demonstrates that they thus no longer "shriek." Singer comments: "I stood trembling, aghast at my mother's courage. Her hands had become bloodied. On her face could be seen the wrath of the rationalist whom someone has tried to frighten in broad daylight" (20). This conflict between the rational and the spiritual is a conflict played out, as we shall see, in Singer's golem tale.

When Isaac was four years old, his parents relocated to Warsaw, where his father presided over a *beth din*, a kind of unofficial court to which the Jewish neighbors appealed when disputes, matters of Jewish law, or religious or marital concerns arose (or when geese seemed to shriek). Warsaw offered a sharp contrast to the sleepy little villages where Isaac had previously lived. The streets rang with vendors; theatrical performances beckoned; petty crime was everywhere. Singer's father was "scandalized by girls dressed in the latest fashions, [and] warned against 'salacious females who uncovered their flesh to arouse men to evil thoughts'" (Stavans, 12). This section of Warsaw, destroyed forever by the Nazis, also supported sex workers: "The neighborhood had a seedy side as well, as streetwalkers and pickpockets mingled with pious Jews on Krochmalna Street and shopkeepers paid protection money to gang leaders" (Stavans, 13–15), a fact that undoubtedly contributes to the strands of the earthy and fleshly in Singer's work and to the warnings about the danger of the flesh in his golem tale.

His home was 10 Krochmalna Street. For Singer, "everything started on Krochmalna Street and everything brought him back to it. When he won the Nobel Prize, he said, 'I keep going back to 10 Krochmalna Street in my writing. I remember every little corner and every person there. I say to myself that just as other people are digging gold which God has created billions of years ago, my literary goldmine is this street'" (Noiville, 17). At the age of ten Singer encountered Dostoevsky's *Crime and Punishment*, the first secular book he read, borrowed from his older brother Israel. This, too, was an important influence as were the books by Hamsun, Zweig, and Thomas Mann that he translated into Yiddish a decade later.

In 1925 Singer published his first story in a Yiddish literary magazine in Warsaw. His first novel, *Satan in Goray*, came out in Poland in 1935, the year he immigrated to the United States. Almost twenty years would elapse before his most famous short story, "Gimpel the Fool," translated by Saul Bellow, appeared in *Partisan Review* in 1953 and Singer's audience widened to include non-Jews. Though he made occasional return trips to Europe, Singer's literal home was now New York City and later Miami, though his virtual home continued to be Krochmalna Street and the small Jewish towns he came to know as a boy.

Singer's immediate family did not die in the Holocaust. His father died in Poland, shortly before Isaac's departure for America in 1935. Singer's beloved brother Israel Joshua died suddenly of a heart attack at age fifty in New York in 1944. Singer lost contact with his mother and younger brother, Moishe, after the invasion of Poland by the Nazis in 1939. "He was told sometime after the war's end that they were deported by the Soviets to Kazakhstan, where they were reported to have frozen to death" (Stavans, 43).[3] His sister, Hinde Esther, who had married and moved to London, died there in 1954.

Isaac Bashevis Singer, *The Golem* (1982)

Arnold Goldsmith has commented that "It comes as no surprise that America's foremost Yiddish author with his extensive knowledge of the folklore and legends of seventeenth century Poland and his love of and belief in the supernatural, should turn to the remarkable golem of Prague as the subject of a short novel for adolescents" ("Singer," 39). That, indeed, Singer knew well the history of the golem legend is demonstrated by an article he contributed to the *New York Times* upon the occasion of the New York Shakespeare Festival's production of H. Leivick's famous play *The Golem*. Appearing in 1984, two years after Singer's own golem tale was published, this article endeavors to respond to the query "why the myth of the golem . . . has interested so many creative people in the past and continues to do so even today in our epoch of science and technology." Tracing the word "golem" from its first mention in the Book of Psalms to *The Book of Creation* through the belief in female golems, Singer comes to the legends surrounding Rabbi Loew, those he uses for his own tale. Alluding to the work of Leivick, Gustav Meyrink, and other authors of golem tales such as Arthur Holitscher and Johannes Hess, Singer approaches a response to the query he has posed: "I am convinced that these writers felt in the legend of the golem a profound kinship to artistic creativity. Each work of art has the elements of miracle. The golem maker was, essentially, an artist. . . . The golem makers were actually the fiction masters of their time."

After this emphasis on creativity and storytelling, Singer goes on to discuss the golem legend in the context of both science and religion. Threaded through his account are frequent references to connections among the golem legend, the erotic, and free will. Noting that Rabbi Loew's golem became rebellious, Singer compares that danger to the danger "of our nuclear age and [our] more destructive golems." He concludes on this ominous note: "According to the Cabbalistic thinker, bloody wars are always fought by golems. The real and most important war is the one between the lure of the flesh and the aspirations of the soul; between the sublime sense of freedom and the deadly slavery of being and behaving like a golem." This is a "war" he had seen played out on Krochmalna Street so many years ago. Singer's astute comments on the history and malleability of the golem legend provide a lens for us as we read backward to the golem tale he had already written, which is both an intentional tribute to the Jewish imagination and imaginative literature and a uniquely Singeresque exploration of the temptations of the flesh.

Singer revised and expanded this article to serve as the introduction to Emily D. Bilski's *Golem! Danger, Deliverance, and Art,* the catalogue for an exhibition by the same name at the Jewish Museum of New York in 1988. Singer added these significant autobiographical paragraphs, reaffirming the link between golems and creating story:

> I was interested in the golem legend from my early childhood. I was brought up in the home of a rabbi, and his sermons often spoke of miracles, by the Baal Shem Tov and other wonder rabbis—the human potential for rescue and salvation. . . . Whenever I tried to write or create a story, I always felt as if I was witnessing a miracle. It was a miracle that I took part in. In my own way, I too was creating little golems.[4]
>
> In writing the story of the golem, I tried to express my philosophy of God and Being both for children and for adults. I felt that the children of our epoch should grow up with the idea that the desire

for creativity is both a desire for miracles and a desire to be like God, a creator. . . .

     I consider the golem legend to be the very essence of Jewish folklore. It is rich in mysticism, in the lore of the Kabbalah and potentiality of human creativity. It tells us, in a way, that under certain circumstances man can create something in his own form and his own image just as he himself was created in God's image and God's form. (Bilski, 9)

Singer thus calls attention to the metafictional aspects of the golem legend and quite boldly claims, "I too was creating little golems." He sees this as an act that is neither a transgression of the commandment against making graven images nor the appropriation of godlike powers but a loving tribute to God, as the exercise of a human power endowed by God: creativity.

    Arnold Goldsmith, whose important book *The Golem Remembered* had already appeared when Singer's version of the golem was published, subsequently wrote a careful comparison between Singer's golem and that of Yudl Rosenberg and Chayim Bloch, Singer's primary sources.[5] Because Singer turned to Rosenberg, an early twentieth-century source, Singer opens his tale with the anachronism of the blood libel as the motivation for the creation of the golem. Though it is true that the blood libel had been a persistent accusation against Jews since the Middle Ages, no such accusations occurred in Prague during Rabbi Loew's tenure there.[6] Almost immediately Singer introduces new characters not found in earlier versions: Count Jan Bratislawski, "who had been immensely rich, with many estates and hundreds of serfs, but he had lost his fortune in gambling, drinking, and private wars with other landlords" (4), and Reb Eliezer Polner, "a well-known banker . . . also known for his charity in helping both Jews and Christians . . . [and] a scholar in his own way" (5). Though Singer locates his story in Prague, the count's name, not surprisingly, is Polish. Predictably, the count drinks heavily during a card game, loses an enormous amount of money, and comes to Reb Polner for a loan, which the banker refuses as the count is already greatly indebted. It is interesting to note that Singer here introduces alcoholism and gambling, two human failings not commonly found in golem tales; thus, Singer strikes a note of fleshly temptations at the outset of his tale, echoes of his experiences at 10 Krochmalna Street. The count then schemes to raise money in another way: devising "a devilish plan" (8), he conspires with two servants to hide his young daughter, Hanka, in order to abscond with her considerable fortune in jewels, inherited from her deceased mother. Then he blames her "death" on Reb Polner and has him arrested and brought to trial for allegedly killing the child in order to use her blood for Passover matzoh. As Goldsmith correctly comments, the remainder of this first half of Singer's novella is largely drawn from a chapter in Rosenberg named "The Wondrous Tale of the Healer's Daughter": "Each story involves the Blood Libel, a missing female witness, the golem's mission to find her and bring her back by the time of the trial, and his dramatic return just in time to save the innocent accused and the whole Jewish community" ("Singer," 41).

In a striking departure from the Rosenberg golem tales, however, Singer invents a holy man to serve as the messenger with instructions for Rabbi Leib (Loew) to create a golem to save the Jewish community. Described as "a little man . . . like a beggar" (19) whom Rabbi Leib realized "might be one of the thirty-six hidden saints through whose merit the world existed" (20), that is, one of the *lamed vov,* the holy man instructs Rabbi Leib to create the golem from clay, engrave God's name on his forehead, and name him Joseph.

Then he admonishes the rabbi: "But take care that he should not fall into the follies of flesh and blood" (23). Indeed, it is just such follies that Singer has already introduced, and they will become a dominant element in this tale, not unlike Singer's other work, again reflecting his boyhood experiences in Warsaw. Singer's description of the creation of the golem must delight his young readers: the shaping of the clay figure is carried out in the synagogue attic by Rabbi Leib alone and is described in sensuous detail. No mystical rituals, no circling of the inert body, no helpers. Then consternation ensues: how will clothing be found for the giant? Rabbi Leib's beadle, Todrus, is commanded to dress the golem and he cleverly purchases, in a local hat maker's shop, clothing from a play about David and Goliath, the latter having had costumes fit for a giant. Implicitly, Singer's golem takes on the heroic stature of this biblical figure.

When the golem is dressed, Rabbi Leib completes the carving of God's name on his forehead, the golem comes to life, and, in yet another departure from most versions, the golem can speak. Rabbi Leib instructs Joseph to find the missing Hanka: "You are part of the earth, and the earth knows many things—how to grow grass, flowers, wheat, rye, fruit" (36). Goldsmith suggests that Singer's emphasis on the tellurian nature of the golem represents another intertextual borrowing, this one from Gershom Scholem's essay "The Idea of the Golem" ("Singer," 43). The delightful illustrations for Singer's book, done by Uri Schulevitz, depict the golem as huge but neatly dressed and possessing regular human features, very unlike the stiff creature with the sculpted hair in Wegener's film. The remainder of this part of the tale involves the golem's search for Hanka and his arrival at the court with Hanka in time to save Reb Polner from the trumped-up accusations of the count.

The second half of Singer's *The Golem* concerns itself with Rabbi Leib's visit to Emperor Rudolf II and with a romance plot between the golem and Miriam, Rabbi Leib's orphan servant girl, another occasion of fleshly temptations. Goldsmith is blunt about his disdain for Singer's innovations here, after the unity and coherence of the first half: "From this point on, Singer's novella falls apart . . . the tone is fractured as the seriousness of the Blood Accusation turns into the comedy of a Walt Disney production. The golem even does a poor imitation of King Kong. Some of the comic episodes have their prototype in the stories of Rosenberg and Bloch, but Singer's structural flaw [the lack of unity after the blood libel plot is resolved] greatly weakens the aesthetic effect" ("Singer," 45).

This part of the novella opens with a command from Rudolf II that Rabbi Leib "bring the giant to his palace immediately after the eight days of Passover" (47). As we saw in chapter 1, a visit by Rabbi Loew to Rudolf II is a historical fact; the visit occurred in 1592, although the contents of their conversation were never revealed. In Singer's tale, the palace guards are so terrified of the rabbi's "monstrous companion" (51) that they flee. Showing more presence of mind, the emperor inquires: "Who is this colossus—your Messiah?" to which Rabbi Leib replies, "Your Majesty . . . he is not our Messiah but a golem made out of clay" (51). But the emperor recognizes the fear instilled in his subjects by the golem and asks Rabbi Leib to destroy the golem as soon as possible. It is interesting to speculate whether Singer might have seen Duvivier's film in which the golem has incited such fear in the emperor that his soldiers come to the Jewish ghetto in order to ferret him out and destroy him; the golem also comes to Rudolf's palace and wreaks havoc there. Duvivier's film was released in 1936, a year after Singer immigrated to America. In 1937 Duvivier came to the United States to work on a film; he returned in 1940 and remained in America until the end of World War II. Thus, it is certainly conceivable that Singer saw his *Le Golem* in New York City and that it influenced Singer's own version of the Jewish folktale.

Although Rabbi Leib has promised quick destruction of the golem to both the emperor and his own congregation, the rabbi's wife, Genendel (another Singer innovation; usually Rabbi Loew's wife's real name, Perl/Pearl, is used in the tales), has other ideas. According to legend (but a legend invented by Singer), a stash of gold, created by "a very rich Jewish man in the city of Prague" (55) through alchemy, is hidden under a rock in the back yard of the rabbi's home and Genendel wants to use the golem to remove the rock and retrieve the gold. When Rabbi Leib commands the golem to undertake this task, the golem refuses, and the rabbi realizes "Such are the rules of all magic that the slightest misuse spoils its power. . . . It was clear to the rabbi that he had lost authority over the golem for good" (58). Thus a woman is subtly blamed for what follows: the golem turns destructive. The theme of the "golem running amok" appears in both the Rosenberg and Bloch versions of the story as well as some earlier versions; it is also seen in Wegener's and Duvivier's films and in David Wisniewski's gorgeously illustrated children's book, *Golem*. But Singer is at pains to reassure his readers that the golem is not dangerous: "He acted like an overgrown child, eager to serve people. Funny stories were told about him" (59). Included here is the story of the golem carrying water buckets until he floods the rabbi's home, of his prodigious appetite (a feature of Cynthia Ozick's golem, as we shall see), and of his playing games with children.

Then comes the somewhat ominous pronouncement: "To his disappointment Rabbi Leib began to realize that the golem was becoming more human from day to day" (65). Ominous because traditionally the golem is mute, does not have a soul, and cannot be counted as part of a *minyan*, and hence his creation by a human being is not an affront to God. But Singer's golem suddenly informs Rabbi Leib that "Golem want Bar Mitzvah" (66) and that "Golem no want be golem" (67) as he feels alone in the world. Shocked, Rabbi Leib endeavors to erase the letters from the golem's forehead in order to disable him, but the golem runs into the street, causing mayhem. An order is issued by the police to seize Joseph, but he eludes capture by running into a *cheder*, a Jewish day school, which causes him to want to learn the alphabet.

By twilight he returns to Rabbi Leib's home, and here Singer becomes even more inventive in his departures from the original tale. The golem begins a flirtation with the orphan Miriam and declares "Miriam golem bride" as he kisses her.[7] Rabbi Leib decides this is the ideal opportunity: he enlists Miriam to erase the Holy Name from Joseph's forehead when he bends down to kiss her, but she is unable to carry this out because of her affection for Joseph. From here, the action moves quickly: Joseph ascends the Tower of Five (provoking Arnold Goldsmith's King Kong analogy); he is notified that he will be drafted into the Bohemian army in eight days; and Rabbi Leib renews his entreaties to Miriam to erase the Holy Name. Miriam plies the golem with wine, and Joseph, "breathing heavily and grunting from pleasure," cries out, "Golem love wine" (82). With these words, he falls into a stupor on the floor, Rabbi Leib erases the Holy Name, and the golem becomes lifeless; he is carried, as is the case in most golem tales, to the attic of the synagogue. Thus the tale comes full circle: the golem is ultimately entrapped by alcohol as was Count Bratislawski at the outset. He has fallen into the "follies of flesh and blood," the very thing against which Rabbi Leib was warned by the holy man who gave him instructions for creating the golem.

Singer brings his tale to a close on a somewhat mystical note: Miriam, who clearly felt affection toward Joseph, disappears and her whereabouts are unknown. Some suspect suicide but "Others believed that the golem was waiting for her in the darkness and took her with him to a place where loving spirits meet. Who knows? Perhaps love has even more power than a Holy Name. Love once engraved in the heart can never be erased. It lives forever" (84). This ending causes Goldsmith to recoil at the "romantic didacticism not found in [Singer's] best adult fiction . . . the sugary closure is an unsatisfactory ending to one of the greatest legends in Jewish culture" ("Singer," 49). However, Goldsmith does not draw a clear conclusion as to what the changes made by Singer mean.

Other critics have been less harsh. Alida Allison remarks that "questions about human nature and *golem* nature become more complex" (122) in the second half of the novella. She continues: "The ending, typically Singer, mixes love and sadness, the perverse and the marvelous." The final lines of the story are, Allison declares, "about as fine an ending for any story as one can find. Love is more mysterious and holy than even the Name of God, even if—or perhaps especially if—it is between a monster and an orphan" (124). Continuing her praise, Allison pronounces: "*The Golem* is one of Singer's best books—for all ages . . . it is the golem's fight to be someone, his fight to survive even though he feels like—and in fact is—a lonely outcast, that resonates with adolescents . . . that resonates with us all" (125). Perhaps the radical difference in opinions here is owing to context: Goldsmith is comparing Singer's golem tale to the long tradition of golem tales and finding it lacking whereas Allison is treating the story in the context of children's literature. In this latter context, Singer's tale received praise from other reviewers such as Barbara Novak in the *New York Times:* "Mr. Singer ends quite properly on this note of love—perhaps the last thing left to draw upon," as well as a reviewer in the *Times Educational Supplement.*[8]

How does Singer's version of the golem tale fit into his overall oeuvre, and what did he hope his readers would take away from his intertextual appropriation? As we have already seen, Singer was steeped in Jewish tradition and mysticism and drew constantly from his experiences as a boy in Jewish communities for his material. His golem tale is certainly no exception: the golem is an ancient Jewish legend and Singer's portrayal of the Prague Jewish community is full of details of Jewish life, worship, habits, and belief. In addition, Singer uses folklore here to depict the conflict between spirituality and piety, on the one hand, and the temptations of the flesh. As one critic has commented: "In general terms, Bashevis is intent on using folklore for its power to depict the moral universe" (Gottesman, 168). This view is shared by Michael Kotzin, who demonstrates persuasively that Singer invests his many children's tales with explicit advocacy for adhering to the Ten Commandments and embodying virtues such as diligence, hard work, kindness to others, honesty, and sincerity (8). Gottesman has further commented: "Bashevis's use of Jewish folklore has become one of the identifying features of his fiction. Demons and devils are integral components of Bashevis's novels and short stories, and in his own words, '[using them] helps me to express myself' because they represent 'the ways of the world.' They are symbolic, bearing a considerable interpretative burden, and cannot be dismissed as simply gratuitous display of Jewish superstition or belief, whether the interpretation of the work in which they appear leans toward parable, politics, psychology, or anything else" (163). Thus, unlike the raw exploitative use of the golem tale for entertainment and financial gain we have seen with Meyrink and Wegener, Isaac Bashevis Singer adopts the golem legend in a respectful (and somewhat playful) manner to carry a moral message to child and adolescent readers. He does so squarely within the Jewish tradition of the tale, though he does ring his own changes on plot and characters. Singer considered his childhood home on Krochmalna Street to be his "literary goldmine" from which all his writing sprang; the encounters with the life of the flesh on this street became a key theme in his golem tale as is the contrast between his eminently practical mother and his mystical father. These changes to the traditional golem narrative are consonant with the themes in his overall opus, a body of work that earned him the recognition of the Nobel Prize. Singer's nostalgia for the destroyed Jewish communities of his youth and his desire to use literature as both a tribute and an instantiation of memory of those Jewish traditions and people make his golem a particularly human and poignant figure.

Isaac Bashevis Singer and Elie Wiesel

Isaac Bashevis Singer and Elie Wiesel published their versions of the golem legend within a year of one another. Though these two writers may seem at first glance very different—one devoting his work to depictions of pre-1939 Jewish life in Poland and the other to the dark and demonic scenes of Auschwitz and after—the two men shared much in common. Both were born in eastern Europe before the Holocaust, both were raised in Hasidic communities, and both spoke Yiddish as their mother tongue. The worlds in which they spent their childhoods vanished before their eyes when they were yet young men. Both immigrated to the United States and worked at the *Jewish Daily Forward*. Both experienced a period of despair after their immigration: Singer had a seven-year writer's block and Wiesel was hit by a taxi cab, requiring a year of hospitalizations and rehabilitation. Singer wrote all his work in Yiddish; Wiesel's original version of his most famous book, *Night,* was written in Yiddish, and he now writes in French. Thus both men required translators for their work to appear in English. Both won a Nobel Prize. Both enjoyed visiting Miami. Both wrote versions of the golem legend, and in both cases these texts have been marketed for children and largely ignored by critics. While Singer's golem is an earthy and very human creature and the text full of Singeresque invention, Wiesel's golem hews more closely to earlier versions and is a more transcendent, philosophical creature.

ELIE WIESEL, *THE GOLEM* (1983)

> After Auschwitz, everything brings us back to Auschwitz.
>
> Elie Wiesel, "Why I Write"

Elie Wiesel is arguably the world's most famous Holocaust survivor: the contours of his life are known to many through his autobiographical texts. Wiesel was born on September 30, 1928, in Sighet, Romania (then Transylvania). He was the only son of four children, with two older sisters, Hilda and Bea, and a younger sister, Tzipora. His parents were shopkeepers. Wiesel describes his childhood home as "a little city . . . a typical *shtetl,* rambunctious and vibrant with beauty and faith, with its yeshivas and its workshops. . . . Immersed in Jewish life, following the rhythms of the Hebrew calendar, the city rested on the Sabbath, fasted on the Day of Atonement, danced on the eve of Simhat Torah" (*Kingdom*, 125).

In his first book, *Night,* which describes the horrors of his deportation and imprisonment in Auschwitz and other camps, Wiesel opens by recounting his growing desire, at age twelve, to study Kabbalah. Rebuffed by his father as too young to undertake such a study, Wiesel turned to Moshe the Beadle who initiated him by reading the Zohar with him. In spring 1944, the Jews of Sighet were rounded up and deported. Wiesel was parted from his mother and Tzipora on the selection platform in Auschwitz and never saw them again. He fought for survival with his father and, when the Russians approached the death camp, he and his father were evacuated to Buchenwald. There, his father died in late January 1945, just months before the camp was liberated in April.

As a displaced person after the war, Wiesel was sent to France, where he studied at the Sorbonne, learned the language, and kept his vow to let a decade elapse before he wrote about the Holocaust. In 1954, when the decade had almost passed, he met the French novelist François Mauriac, who urged him to write about his experiences in Auschwitz. Two years later, Wiesel's Yiddish account of the Holocaust was published in Buenos Aires, and in 1958, a much revised and abridged version appeared in French as *La Nuit.* Two dozen books later, in 1986, Wiesel was awarded the Nobel Peace Prize.

In 1978 Wiesel endeavored to share with his readers his motivations for writing. "Why I Write" is an essay commissioned especially for a volume of scholarly essays on Wiesel, edited by Alvin Rosenfeld and Irving Greenberg. Wiesel reveals in this essay how profoundly he is haunted by his Holocaust experience and, particularly, how everything he writes is an effort to honor the six million Jews who died: "The only role I sought was that of witness. I believed that, having survived by chance, I was duty bound to give meaning to my survival, to justify each moment of my life" (201). Espousing the *mysterium tremendum* school of Holocaust writing, Wiesel warns his readers that they will never understand: "Even if you read all the books ever written, even if you listen to all the testimonies ever given, you will remain on this side of the wall, you will view the agony and death of a people from afar, through the screen of a memory that is not your own" (203–4).

Wiesel confesses that sometimes he forces himself "to turn away from [the dead] and study other periods, explore other destinies and teach other tales: the Bible and the Talmud, Hasidism and its fervor, the *Shtetl* and its songs, Jerusalem and its echoes" (204). But, he acknowledges, "I have not forgotten the dead. . . . They appear in Hasidic and Talmudic legends in which victims forever need defending against forces that would crush them" (204). It is in this spirit, I believe, that, five years after writing this essay, Wiesel composed his golem tale, a tale about a defender of the Jewish community to be sure. Appropriately, Wiesel chooses as his first-person narrator for the story one who is intimately familiar with the dead, Reuven the gravedigger, a character new to the golem legend. Reuven is the "son of Yaakov, who claimed to have witnessed the numerous miracles that legend attributes to the Golem, the most fascinating creature in Jewish lore and fantasy" (12). In biblical style, Wiesel recounts the generations of storytellers who have conveyed Reuven's story since the time of the Maharal. Then Reuven begins to speak: "I truly liked him [the golem], and I was not the only one. We loved him. To us he was a savior. . . . [He had] a single, sacred purpose: to protect the life, the security and the future of the community. . . . He was a saint" (12).

What a stark contrast to Isaac Bashevis Singer's golem! Singer's tale, narrated in the third person, presents us with an increasingly human, that is, flawed, golem, one who indulges in "sins of the flesh" and who is specifically disassociated from any role as savior. Singer's Rabbi Leib tells the community leaders: "According to our Holy Books, this is not the way our salvation will come. Our Messiah will be a holy man of flesh and blood, not a gigantic clay figure" (54). Sharply different is the sacral tone surrounding Wiesel's golem. Already on page three of his text, Wiesel puts into his narrator's mouth an anachronistic allusion to the Holocaust: "I, Reuven, son of Yaakov, declare under oath that 'Yossel the mute' or the 'Golem made of clay,' . . . deserves to be remembered by our people, our persecuted and assassinated and yet immortal people. We owe it to him to evoke his fate with love and gratitude" (13). Reuven seems almost like a figure in a Marc Chagall painting, floating above the story, able to see past and future, and narrating the story from what seems at times to be a twentieth-century vantage point. He tells the reader: "I have lived through too many ordeals not to be able to predict the future" (13), and his role preparing the dead for burial gives him access to the history revealed on the faces of the deceased: "I sometimes read not the past but what the past breeds" (17). Reuven further sanctifies the golem by issuing this gentle complaint: "Ah, if only the Golem were still among us . . . I would sleep more peacefully. Why did the Maharal take him from us? . . . Today, as yesterday, someone must stand between that hatred and us. If only the 'Golem made of clay' could come back to life. None other could prevent the spilling of blood; none other could disarm the murderers and conquer evil" (17–18).

Thus, we see that Wiesel's tone is remarkably different in these opening pages from that of Singer. Though both writers set their stories in sixteenth-century Prague, their golems are quite dissimilar and are used by their respective authors for markedly different purposes: Singer to warn against the temptations that beset human beings, and Wiesel to at once praise and mourn a heroic figure who served as a savior of the Jewish people. From this introduction, which serves almost as an invocation, Wiesel sets Reuven to the task of telling his story.

One constant in many golem tales is the role of the blood libel, the accusation of ritual murder, in fomenting antisemitic hatred in sixteenth-century Prague. Mention of the blood libel appears at the beginning of both Singer's and Wiesel's retellings of the golem legend. While, as we have seen, this is not historically accurate and was a feature of the tale added in the early twentieth century in response to events at that time, it provides a plot and, for Wiesel, an implicit parallel to the Holocaust. Wiesel recounts the confiscation of all Hebrew books from the Prague Jewish Quarter so that they could be examined in Vienna for evidence of such a practice. Nothing was found, and eventually the sacred books were returned to the Jewish community.[9] But, as Reuven tells us, "there are those who continue to secretly spread such lies with only one purpose: to stir up hatred, to provoke violence and the shedding of Jewish blood" (21). So, as in the opening pages of Singer's golem story, Wiesel creates an accusation that leads to an arrest. But here it is an honest merchant, Shmuel, and his family who are arrested on charges of killing a Christian baby; neither alcohol nor gambling is the precipitating factor as in Singer.

The Maharal, realizing the danger to the Jewish community, awakens "Yossel the mute" and chastises him for letting "an enemy pass, carrying the body of a Christian child in his pack" (29). Thus, unlike most golem tales, the man of clay has already been created and activated here. (It is not until a flashback at the midpoint of the story that that creation is described.) Rabbi Loew instructs Yossel to begin a search of the cemeteries for an empty grave from which the baby's body had been stolen.[10] Yossel discovers the grave and saves the day. Reuven exults: "Let me tell you, we do need the Golem" (31). After this opening event, Reuven the narrator addresses the reader: "What did he look like? You would like a portrait. In your own mind he looks like a monster" (31). The portrait Reuven provides is a generous one: the golem is depicted as powerful but decidedly not scary or monstrous. He is tall, but not a giant, "riveted to the ground, but floating in the air . . . he radiated a force which overwhelmed you, moved you, flooded you with emotion . . . he could penetrate the very recesses of your memory" (32). There is the suggestion that the golem and the Maharal are doppelgängers, a theme we have seen in other golem tales: "his shadow . . . followed the Maharal's as if refusing to let go; sometimes in the street at night or in the enchanted forest, the two shadows would unite for a second" (34). Reuven sums up this description of the golem by pronouncing: "In spite of what you think, he was not less human than we, but more human" (34). Again, this is a departure from the usual. Wiesel is creating a heroic savior figure rather than the typical golem whose inability to speak is a symbol for his less than human status: he cannot be counted in a *minyan,* he does chores mindlessly until disaster occurs (e.g., carrying the water buckets), or, like Singer's golem, he succumbs to very human temptations.

From this point in his story, Wiesel has Reuven cast a backward glance to devote a chapter to the life and work of Rabbi Yehuda Lowe (one of the many alternate spellings of Rabbi Loew's name). Wiesel demonstrates here his deep familiarity with and respect for both the facts and the legends surrounding Rabbi Loew. But he concludes the chapter on what some might sense is an autobiographical note. Just as Wiesel's own Holocaust experiences caused him to question God, "the Maharal, attuned to the suffering of his congregation, refused to submit to cruelty. Impotent before the immensity of evil, he chose to question the world above" (44). And what he does, as in other golem tales, is to direct a dream question to God: "And the answer came hidden in the first ten letters of the alphabet of the sacred tongue. For everything is in the word" (44). So again we see the affirmation of the word, the book, the imagination as redemption.

Here Wiesel encounters some difficulty with Reuven as a credible narrator: after all, he did not witness the creation of the golem that he is about to recount. So the following chapter is told largely in the third person and includes not only an account of the creation of the golem but also a brief history of earlier attempts by Jewish mystics to infuse life into a clay figure. The actual creation of the golem follows traditional lines: it occurs on the banks of the Vltava River, Rabbi Lowe is accompanied by two helpers, the ritual includes incantations and circling the lifeless clay figure seven times: "'I name you Yoseph,' said the Maharal. 'Your mission on earth will be to protect the people of Israel from their enemies'" (53).

In the following chapter, our appealing and very child-friendly narrator, Reuven, reappears. Occasionally Wiesel cannot resist the intrusion of an authorial voice that is clearly not that of a ten-year-old, the age of fictional Reuven for many of the events he narrates. For example, this passage: "In truth, all the stories of the 'Golem made of clay' end well. They often begin in the same way: A Jew unjustly accused of imaginary crimes. They end in the same manner: the Golem intervening to put things in their proper place" (65). And, indeed, that is an apt description of the last forty pages of Wiesel's golem story. He borrows liberally from other versions—including, for example, the story of the viciously antisemitic priest, Thadeusz (often spelled Thaddeus), the two Gentile apprentice bakers called the "redbeards," and several other stories found in Rosenberg and elsewhere. In places the text almost reads as if Wiesel got bored with the trope of the golem, as he piles quick anecdotes from earlier golem tales one upon the other, effacing the role of the narrator Reuven.

Wiesel must at last draw his story to a close. We are told that "the Golem, over the years, was less and less busy" (89) and looked at the Maharal "with sadness and shrugged his shoulders as if to indicate frustration" (90). The Maharal took up the habit of visiting him every Friday afternoon for an hour. But we are told nothing of why the golem's role and outlook have changed or what he and Rabbi Lowe discuss. Quite the contrary, Wiesel inserts eighteen questions into this two-page chapter, leaving the reader baffled about the plot and the relationship between the two characters. Suddenly, Reuven's voice reemerges: "I would have liked to hear the Golem's opinion" (91) he says, but his voice is now an intrusion and is unconvincing. The final chapter gives us the familiar story of decommissioning the golem: he is directed to sleep in the attic of the Old-New Synagogue where Rabbi Lowe and his assistants perform in reverse the ritual that created him, and they hide his lifeless clay body under "old ritual vestments" (95). Strangely, we are given no reason for the decision of the Maharal to bring the golem's life to a close. The golem does not "run amok" here as in some versions, nor are we told that attitudes toward the Jewish community have improved, thus making the golem's work unnecessary. However, unlike other golem tales, we are given a precise date on which the reverse ritual occurs: "Ten years after he was created, the Golem returned to dust. . . . It was the 33rd day of Omer, in the year 5350 (or 1590 c.e.)" (92). Like Singer's conclusion, Wiesel's final lines are ambivalent, leaving hope that the golem may yet be among us. We are told that Rabbi Lowe forbade access to the *shul* attic where the golem's remains lay hidden, and Reuven tells us: "But a wandering beggar whom I met recently gave me, under the seal of secrecy, his own explanation: the Maharal had forbidden access to the attic because, in truth, the Golem had remained alive. And he is waiting to be called. As for me, I wish I knew" (96–97).

One cannot close a description of Elie Wiesel's golem tale without mentioning the illustrations in the volume by Mark Podwal. They are a marvel. Including the cover art, Podwal created over forty drawings for the text. Appearing as very finely rendered pen and ink drawings, almost all of them incorporate the Hebrew alphabet, sometimes to form words but, just as frequently, the letters come spilling out on the landscape, forming figures and plumes; they are inscribed on buildings or buzz around a re-creation of a kabbalistic drawing. The drawings realistically depict Prague, the Old-New Synagogue, the Jewish Town Hall with its Hebrew clock, the Charles Bridge, and other landmarks. They are also, at times, fanciful: Prague buildings grow out of the top of a book, the Old-New Synagogue is poised on top of a Torah. Many of the drawings include Jewish symbols and artifacts—the yad, the hamsa hand, the menorah. Such an emphasis on letters, words, the tools of story, underscores the importance of the imagination and its creations in the legend of the golem and in Judaism.

Reviewers and critics had a mixed response to Wiesel's *The Golem*. The *New York Times* reviewer Kenneth Briggs observed that "In the hands of Elie Wiesel, a master storyteller, the tale of Rabbi Loew and his golem takes on a decidedly modern meaning." Briggs praises the text's contemporary nuances: "Clearly, this is a golem suited to the needs of post-Holocaust Judaism, adapted to meet the Jewish longing for a protector. He is a solemn, lonely figure with the ability of devoting his life to others. The tale is told with Mr. Wiesel's taut passion and urgency. In keeping with the story's blend of joy and horror, Mr. Wiesel's rendering is both enchanting and chilling. It is a typical fairy tale dancing over the dangerous abyss." Indeed, as explicated above, this is a tale that reveals the impact of the Holocaust on Wiesel and his resulting commitment to the memory of the six million.

Arnold Goldsmith, who, as we have seen, rendered a somewhat negative opinion of Singer's golem, also finds Wiesel's golem tale "ultimately disappointing" ("Wiesel," 15). In a closely argued essay, Goldsmith traces the arc of Wiesel's narrative, clarifying the etiology of each golem anecdote reused by Wiesel. He carefully catalogues the themes that Wiesel raises and then drops, such as the doppelgänger theme, fairy-tale echoes, moral conflicts: "Wiesel does nothing with this intriguing symbolism and mentions it only to titillate his reader . . . one has to wonder why he deceives the reader with such false starts" (18–19). Noting Wiesel's tendency to summarize very briefly anecdotes fully developed in earlier golem tales—such as those by Rosenberg and Bloch—Goldsmith opines that "The result of such flat condensation is a lessening of pleasure" (21). Goldsmith closes his essay with a very sharp critique: Wiesel's *The Golem* "is neither compelling literary analysis nor exciting narrative. . . . For a writer who in the past has haunted his audience with important moral issues that demand attention, Wiesel is too relaxed, even intellectually lazy, uncertain what to do with what his narrator calls, 'the most fascinating creature in Jewish lore and fantasy'" (26). Goldsmith does, however, single out Mark Podwal's drawings for extraordinary praise. He says they succeed better than any earlier efforts—such as those by Hugo Steiner-Prag or Beverly Brodsky McDermott—in depicting the Maharal, the golem, and the sixteenth-century city of Prague: "These drawings do more than all the words of the text in expressing the mysterious awe of a legend that refuses to die" (25–26). It is perhaps the ways in which Wiesel's golem tale disappoints that explain the almost complete absence of reference to this text in the myriad books analyzing Wiesel's considerable corpus. This title is also missing from chronologies that list key events in Wiesel's life as well as his publications. Nor does Wiesel himself mention *The Golem* in the dozens of interviews he has granted to scholars; these interviews often focus on human rights, political issues, and philosophical controversies rather than on his own writing. Thus, finding his own commentary on *The Golem* has been virtually impossible.

But, without a doubt, Wiesel is keenly aware of the debate surrounding T. W. Adorno's pronouncement about poetry after Auschwitz. He responded in this way to an interviewer's question: "What do you think of Adorno's terrible comment, 'After Auschwitz there can be no poetry'?":

> I understand it. How can we continue to sing, after Auschwitz? How can we put words together, when the murderers used the same words, perhaps in the same way, to cause such ruin, catastrophe, and agony? . . . In Auschwitz we had the wrenching poetry of the dying, and prayers were said for the dead. I therefore prefer to interpret Adorno's remark, like similar statements by other people, as a question. It is better if we end the phrase with a question mark: Can poetry still be written after Auschwitz? (Wiesel and De Saint-Cheron, 190)

This comment from Wiesel, published in 1990, is milder than his pronouncement in a lecture in 1977 that "A novel about Treblinka is either not a novel or not about Treblinka" (Wiesel et al., *Dimensions,* 7), which seemed to foreclose the possibility of imaginative literature about the Shoah. Given this skepticism about the feasibility and/or use of fiction and poetry about the Holocaust, perhaps Wiesel sees the appropriation of a Jewish legend to tell a veiled tale, about the need of the contemporary Jewish people for a savior, as a vehicle to have it both ways. In the sense in which Geoffrey Hartman sees the Jewish imagination as "text dependent," reliant on "older authorities," and inherently intertextual (209), Wiesel may see the reincarnation of the golem legend as not only a permissible tool but also a spiritual one. To quote Hartman again:

> There is no imagination without distrust of the imagination. This interdependence is especially obvious when a powerful religion attempts to subsume imaginative activity. *The relations between religion and fantasy must be intimate,* even complicit, since religion is orbic as well as orphic, wishing to embrace the totality of human life. (201, italics mine)

By infusing the fantasy of the golem with a new, post-Holocaust meaning, Wiesel is arguably not starting *de nouveau* with an imaginative, fictional tale but instead calling upon the resonances of Judaism and Jewish stories. He does so to convey the history of oppression and persecution suffered by the Jewish people, including what he sometimes calls the *hurban* (whirlwind, total destruction),[11] to cry out for a bulwark against such persecution in the post-Holocaust period and to affirm the value of story in our lives.

Wiesel envisions the Messiah as human and so his analogy of the golem to a savior makes perfect sense. An interviewer made the following comment to him: "we might say that the Messiah whom we await is a man, but the man most completely in the Lord's image. What must save man is the human in him—which is to say, his divine component—and not God's intervention." Wiesel replied: "Yes, it is man who must save man. That is the price of freedom God has given us. This freedom itself, of course, comes from God, but it is up to man to lay claim to it" (Wiesel and De Saint-Cheron, 60). By writing the tale of the golem with post-Holocaust nuances, Wiesel is "laying claim" to this notion of a Messiah, to the use of our freedom for peaceful purposes, to the crucial importance of eradicating genocide from our world.[12] And, in a sly way, he is using imaginative literature to validate all these ideas.

As mentioned above, the penultimate chapter of Wiesel's *The Golem* contains eighteen questions, leaving many matters of plot unresolved. Eighteen is a significant number for Wiesel: his number in Auschwitz was 7713, which, when added up, equals eighteen, and in *Gematria* eighteen is the number of *Hai*, life.[13] It is so like Elie Wiesel, the skeptic, the philosopher, the mystic, to end with questions, not answers—but, in so doing, to affirm life symbolically, and implicitly, to affirm the value of literature to help humanity understand that life.

FRANCES SHERWOOD, *THE BOOK OF SPLENDOR* (2002)

Perhaps the best introduction to this novel is that provided by the author herself in her acknowledgments at the conclusion of the book:

> *The Book of Splendor* is a historical fantasy using fictional and non-fictional characters. Most of the events are constructed by the author, some are historically documented, and in a few incidences, the official account has been altered. The book is set in 1601 in Prague, the capital at that time of the Habsburg Empire. The daily life as described in the book—food, furniture, occupations, clothing, court and city political atmosphere and attitudes—is authentic. Rudolph II was Holy Roman Emperor from 1576 to 1612. His strange behavior, family history, passion for collecting, and interest in the elixir of eternal life are part of the record and legend. (347)

Specifically, Sherwood's tale of Prague, Rabbi Loew, and the golem is drawn largely from the existing corpus of golem legends. Her book is almost an early twenty-first-century Yudl Rosenberg–type retelling, except that she does not claim to have found a three-hundred-year-old manuscript as Rosenberg claimed. And the format of her book, unlike that of Rosenberg, is a contemporary novel, largely realistic except, of course, for the golem character.

In a Reading Group Guide included in the book, Sherwood offers further comments on her novel, published in 2002. She calls *The Book of Splendor* "a love story. It is my unabashed love affair with the great city of Prague" (351). She reveals that she has a personal connection to Prague: "My grandmother's relatives lived there until they were killed in Auschwitz. I am attached" (351). Like Wiesel, then, she is using the golem to respond to the Shoah, however implicitly or symbolically. Sherwood describes her three trips to Prague, beginning in 1995, during which she undertook research for the novel, and the extensive reading she did "about the history of opium, tulips, coffee, food, clothing, bathrooms, architecture, fairy tales, art, money, exploration, popular culture" (351–52). It is all these details in the novel, based on this extensive research, that give it a realistic resonance with a bit of magic thrown in.

FRANCES SHERWOOD'S LIFE AND WORK

Frances Sherwood's life story is at once captivating, hardscrabble, and heartbreaking. Her "Autobiographical Essay," contributed to *Contemporary Authors,* is twelve pages long and remarkably candid. Her mother, Barbara, was descended from Scottish immigrants and raised as a Mormon; her father, William, was Jewish; his great-grandparents came to the United States from Prague and the Ukraine. The family lived in Brazil until Frances was five. Her mother attempted suicide after they had relocated to Ossining, New York, and the family then moved to Pacific Grove, California. Sherwood recounts a childhood of money problems, emotional tension, and intense reading as a kind of escape. Describing her parents as "bohemians" and "dilettantes" in the 1950s, Sherwood was raised as an atheist ("Autobiographical Essay," 323). Sherwood's father killed himself in June 1957, just prior to his appearance before the House Un-American Activities Committee. It was also the summer before Sherwood's senior year of high school.

Sherwood's mother, who was not college educated, was left with four children to support: Frances (age seventeen) and her three younger brothers (ages fourteen, ten, and one). The next year was very difficult; her mother increasingly turned to alcohol to cope and Frances received no guidance regarding college applications. Rejected by the University of Chicago, the only place she applied, Sherwood instead leaped into a marriage that turned disastrous. She and her husband "lived on the land" in California until he left her; with a baby daughter, Sherwood attended a start-up college in Monterey. When he returned briefly, he murdered their daughter, was jailed, and was diagnosed as schizophrenic; he subsequently murdered two other people. Sherwood left to attend Howard University, where she received a scholarship and worked as a nanny to support herself, met and married a man from Trinidad, and began to think of herself as a writer. She also experienced discrimination as part of a mixed-race family in the hospital where her twin sons were born in 1962 and in securing housing.

Sherwood's life now became compartmentalized into continuing her education, earning a living, and caring for her young family, to which a daughter was added in 1968. Moving to Brooklyn when her husband got a job there, Sherwood completed her B.A. at Brooklyn College and did graduate work at New York University. She was reading avidly—Henry James, Franz Kafka, Ralph Ellison, Langston Hughes, Lorraine Hansberry. The late 1960s found Sherwood and her family at Berkeley for her husband's graduate education, a time in which she attended a consciousness-raising group, read Grace Paley and Tillie Olsen, began writing daily on an Olivetti typewriter, was hospitalized for depression, and took a job as a typist at the Naval Yard. Then another cross-country move to Washington, D.C., again to facilitate her husband's career. With three children in grammar school, Sherwood, now thirty-five, enrolled in the Johns Hopkins Writing Seminars M.A. program, where she studied with John Barth. Acknowledging that "Johns Hopkins was a major turning point in my life" ("Autobiographical Essay," 329), she went on to a Stegner Fellowship at Stanford that gave her precious time to write. In the next decade, Sherwood worked as a teacher at both the high school and college levels on the East Coast, continued writing, and began to publish short stories. It was not until 1986, when she was forty-six, that she finally landed a position that gave her generous time to write. Her sons had graduated from college, her daughter was in college, and she and her second husband had divorced. She accepted a position as an assistant professor at Indiana University at South Bend: "I felt I had earned the right to work at what I loved" ("Autobiographical Essay," 330). Like so many women, Sherwood delayed her writing career in favor of family responsibilities and earning money; yet these years gave her emotional and experiential memories that she deploys in her fiction.

In quick succession, then, several books appeared to critical acclaim: *Everything You've Heard Is True* (1989), a collection of short stories; *Vindication* (1993), an imagined life of Mary Wollstonecraft; *Green* (1995), a *bildungsroman* about Zoe McLaren in 1950s California, complete with beatniks, bomb scares, sex, and drugs; *The Book of Splendor* (2002); and *Night of Sorrows* (2006), the story of the conflict between Hernán Cortés and the Aztecs in 1519, with Aztec princess Malintzin serving as Cortés's translator-slave-mistress firmly at the center of the story. Sherwood has received many honors for her work: two stories have won O'Henry Awards (1989, 1992), she has won an NEA fellowship (1990), was a finalist for the National Book Critics Circle Award for *Vindication,* and has been nominated for a Nebula Award.

THE BOOK OF SPLENDOR

I have provided a rather full account of Sherwood's life as it is often echoed in her fiction, despite the fact that three of her four novels take place in other centuries and other lands. In the few interviews of Frances Sherwood that are available, she has made two pronouncements about what she considers the purpose of fiction. In 1995 Sherwood stated: "In the end, you see yourself, and I think that's worthwhile. That's what novels are about: the value of the individual, of the individual life lived. And I mean any individual life" (Prenatt, 25). As we will see shortly, Sherwood particularly identifies with Rochel, one of three central characters in *The Book of Splendor,* as she did with Mary Wollstonecraft in her first novel, *Vindication:* "We both had very difficult childhoods, with a lot of trauma. I think that we're both very smart. It's hard enough being a 20th-century woman, growing up in the fifties and being constantly underestimated and made light of—you can imagine what that might have been like in the 18th century. I think that was her experience. That has been my experience" (Prenatt, 22). In 1993 Sherwood told another interviewer: "The emotional life is full of peril. That's what novels are about" (Olshan, 22). Given Sherwood's life experiences—the loss of family in the Holocaust, her mother's suicide attempt and her father's successful suicide, the murder of her first child, two failed marriages, a series of dull jobs in her twenties, thirties, and early forties, her sense of being an outsider—one can understand and sympathize with her notions of womanhood and the life of emotions and how these contribute to her sense of the use and value of fiction.

The Book of Splendor is narrated in the third person, focalized through the minds of various characters, and is divided into five parts, a useful structure for the purpose of recapitulating the key action. Sherwood wastes no time introducing her golem to the plot. She opens the book by intoning some pieties about golem-making:

> Creating a golem requires patience, brilliance, study, prayer, and fasting. The creator must be worthy in character, close to God, free of sin. Traditionally, only rabbis can make such a being, and not any rabbi, but a tzaddik, one of the righteous. Understandably, it is an undertaking filled with presumption and fraught with the possibility

of error. Insight into the magical possibilities of the Hebrew alphabet is imperative, as is the ability to use the exalted language of God's various names. (9)

Here the narrator calls our attention to the act of creation, implicitly drawing a parallel with writing and her own creation of a literary golem. Such a parallel is emphasized further by the mention of the Hebrew alphabet and its magical properties in the Kabbalah.

In chapter 1 the reader is catapulted into the midst of a Jewish wedding between the eighteen-year-old orphan seamstress, Rochel, and Zev, a thirty-three-year-old shoemaker. Both of these characters are Sherwood's invention, not part of the traditional golem legend. Two things of significance occur during the ceremony: according to custom, the bride circles her groom seven times, a ritual that parallels the ritual to bring a golem into life; when the groom tries to put the ring on Rochel's finger, it clatters to the floor, causing a whistling wind to rush through the synagogue, a bad omen. Images of life and death alternate in this chapter, life represented by the wedding and its celebrations and death by Zev's one-room home cum shop located across from the cemetery. Described as "damp and acrid with soot," cold, tanned hides hanging with an "odor . . . of carnage," the bed "like a coffin," the little room causes Rochel to tell herself with a shudder, "I have entered the forest of the dead" (13). Meditations on life and death are central to the novel that follows. Plodding Zev represents an emotional dead end for Rochel, while the golem will come to represent passion.

And the very next chapter recounts Rudolf II's lame attempt to commit suicide, followed by his expression of intense interest in securing eternal life.[14] This suicide attempt occurs on December 31, 1600, the very same day on which Rochel and Zev are being married across the Vltava River in Judenstadt, the Jewish ghetto of Prague, indeed at the very same hour, eight o'clock in the evening, at which the bride is losing her virginity. Sherwood uses this chapter to introduce an extensive cast of characters, including Johannes Kepler and Tycho Brahe, famous astronomers who were actually members of Rudolf's court, Dr. Kirakos (the court physician, later revealed to be an Ottoman spy), and Vaclav, Rudolf's faithful servant (later revealed to be his illegitimate son).

Chapter 3 takes place in three temporal valences: in 1600, as Rochel lies awake in her wedding bed, meditating on the past; in 1595, when Rochel was thirteen, had begun menstruating, and was listening to her grandmother's stories; and in 1582, the time frame of her grandmother's stories themselves, when Rochel's mother and grandmother fled a pogrom in the Ukraine and came to Prague, where Rochel was born. "I am telling you [these stories] so you know what has gone before you and can happen again, anywhere, anytime," Rochel's grandmother intones (33), revealing the necessity of story as history, as warning, as a source of individual identity.

Part 1 concludes with two more chapters that continue to provide the backstory. Rudolf II's desire for eternal life grows apace, and his physician recommends he bring the British magus, John Dee, and his assistant, Edward Kelly, to the court to find the magic potion. A word or two here about Rudolf II will help set the stage. Historians depict him as a smart, quixotic, unapproachable, dilatory, and increasingly strange (some say mad) ruler as he aged. He was obsessed with collections—art works (much of it erotica), clocks, coins, gems, books, medallions, plants, and animals, including a pet lion. He was also obsessed—as we have seen in Wegener's film—with the occult in an age when the efforts, through alchemy, to turn dross into gold and to create a homunculus were already at the forefront of what was then considered science. Rudolf ruled as Holy Roman Emperor from 1575 (when he was twenty-four years old) to 1611, following his father, Maximilian II, who had revoked all expulsion orders against the Jews of Prague in 1567; in 1577 Rudolf confirmed Jewish privileges in the empire and subsequently invited Mordecai Maisel, the richest man in the Judenstadt, to be his "Hofjude"; in fact, Maisel was the emperor's financier and primary source of funds. This friendly (and, one might argue, exploitative) posture toward the Jews of Prague is important in the novel, a time historians often refer to as "the golden age" of the Jewish community. Rudolf II died in 1612.

If chapter 4 in Sherwood's novel concentrates on Rudolf's obsession with a formula for eternal life, then chapter 5, the concluding chapter of part 1, balances that emphasis with a focus on death. It recounts the day, shortly before Passover, when Rochel finds a dead, uncircumcised male baby in the cranny of the wall surrounding the Judenstadt (51–52). Thus Sherwood inserts the myth of the blood libel at the beginning of her novel, an anachronistic device introduced to the golem legend by Yudl Rosenberg, as we saw in chapter 1. Clearly this is also an echo of Sherwood's own lost child, and this is not the only dead baby in the novel. In discussing with Charlotte Templin her second novel, *Green*, Sherwood commented: "The end of *Green*—the child's death—is true. My first child died. That was my impetus for writing the book. I came down from those California hills to tell others my story. The lesson of death is demonstrated throughout the book. That is to say, you cannot flee civilization without great risks. I ran the risk and paid. I continue to pay" (Templin, 119). In her third novel, *The Book of Splendor*, Sherwood continues this death-obsessed theme, writing it into plot and character. Sherwood also includes the antisemitic figure,

Father Thaddeus, and the story of the children of the two Berls, switched at birth, which results in a brother and sister almost unwittingly marrying each other (chapters 15 and 16, respectively, in Rosenberg). Sherwood delineates many aspects of antisemitism in sixteenth-century Prague here and throughout the novel.

The opening chapters of part 2 continue to build both context and characterization. The reader learns more about Vaclav, Rudolf's servant—his childhood friendship with Rochel, his ascension to first valet of the emperor, his marriage, and the death of his first child. We are also introduced to Rabbi Loew's household and to his daughters, Leah, Miriam, and Zelda. It is Leah who tells Rochel that she is the child who resulted from her mother's rape by a Cossack in Ukraine. Sherwood deservedly prides herself on the research she does to bring the environment in her historical fiction to life in an accurate and compelling way, and in these pages she depicts foodways, the Jewish tradition of cutting a bride's hair, the fondness for puppets in Prague, Czech legends and superstitions, the buildings in the Judenstadt, and the clothing of Rudolf II. Such details build credibility and humanity into the novel.

Slowly, Sherwood introduces the plot that will require Rabbi Loew to create the golem: Father Thaddeus, still angry about his defeat in a debate with Rabbi Loew two years earlier[15] and fearful of the privileges granted to the Jewish community by Rudolf, plans a pogrom just before Passover. Rabbi Loew goes to request Rudolf's intercession: he encounters Rudolf in his carriage, returning from Carnival in Venice. The Maharal blocks the way of the carriage and when the citizens of Prague begin to stone the rabbi, the stones turn to roses.[16] Getting no satisfaction from the emperor, Rabbi Loew turns to divine intervention in the form of a golem.

Sherwood's account of the creation of the golem is, for the most part, traditional. "Made of mud" (99) from the Vltava River, he is described as a giant, a mere robot, unable to speak, having no "neshama, no soul": "He was, in all aspects, a golem" (99). Like his predecessors, he is named a variant of Joseph, in this case "Yossel." And, like other predecessors, he has the Hebrew letters EMETH inscribed in his forehead. These spell "Truth," but if the first letter is removed, the word spells "Death," and in some golem variants Rabbi Loew uses this method to decommission the golem when he spins out of control. Again, in Sherwood's tale as in most versions, Rabbi Loew shapes the golem on the banks of the river and walks seven times around the inert figure one way and then the opposite way, reciting "combinations of the twenty-two letters of the Hebrew alphabet" (100).

But, like Isaac Bashevis Singer and Elie Wiesel, Sherwood has introduced some elements of her own: we are told that the golem has no tongue, the cause of his muteness. Rabbi Loew effects the creation solo, without the helpers who usually accompany him to the banks of the river. Rabbi Loew "bunched together blankets, improvised a sort of cloak and breeches for him" (101). Ominously, the reader learns that the golem is tainted at his inception, while the rabbi's back is turned: "something untoward, disturbing, malevolent crept up to the inert figure. A cloud passed over the newly risen sun. . . . Was it a dybbuk, a witch, a restless gilgul, the Evil Eye itself? Whatever, it planted its gruesome kiss on the newly made man's lips" (101). This scene is more reminiscent of fairy tales—the curse being placed on Sleeping Beauty at her christening, for example—than golem legends, but the impact of the kiss will be felt almost immediately in the story. Also noteworthy is Sherwood's metafictional touch in this creation passage. She tells us that to prepare for the creation of a golem, the rabbi "prayed and fasted for seven days, recited parts of the Torah to evoke its secret code, and studied *The Book of Splendor* to discover the profound meaning hidden within its seemingly accessible exemplar" (99).

The Book of Splendor is, of course, Sherwood's own title, but here it refers to the *Zohar,* for which *The Book of Splendor* is an alternative title. Gershom Scholem defines the Zohar as "the most important literary work of the Kabbalah . . . a source of doctrine and revelation equal in authority to the Bible and the Talmud, and of the same canonical rank" (*Zohar,* vii). Most likely written by a Spanish mystic, Rabbi Moses de Leon, in the late thirteenth century, the Zohar reached the zenith of its influence between 1500 and 1800 (*Zohar,* vii–xvi passim).[17] Containing "1,400 pages that deal with every conceivable subject" (Dan, xii), the Zohar nonetheless is not the text usually associated with providing the recipe for creating a golem. That honor belongs, as described in chapter 1, to the *Sefer Yetzirah,* the Book of Creation, which is of earlier (though undetermined) origin (Dan, 17–18), though even that attribution may be incorrect (Dan, 106). Note that Sherwood's Rabbi Loew also chants Psalm 139, which is the psalm in which the notion of a golem, unformed clay, is mentioned.

So why does Sherwood use *The Book of Splendor* as her self-reflexive title? One might speculate that it is simply an error—other errors occur in the book, including the comment by one character that the Altneu (the Old-New) Synagogue was built by Mayor Mordecai Maisel (49) when, in fact, Maisel was a contemporary of Rabbi Loew and the Altneu Synagogue was built three hundred years earlier in the late 1200s. (Maisel built the High Synagogue across the street, and there is also a Maisel Synagogue in Prague that was built as a private house of prayer for Maisel and his family.) One might also speculate that *The Book of Splendor* indeed makes a splendid title. As Richard Eder comments in his *New York Times* review:

"*The Book of Splendor* is not just a title, but truth in advertising." I believe Sherwood chose the title because her novel deals with some of the key themes of the Zohar: appearance versus reality, creation, life, death, love (both erotic and divine), the outsider status of those in exile, and the possibility of redemption.

To return to our story: it is not long before the golem and Rochel begin to flirt. Usually the golem is said to be without much intelligence or emotion, but "unbeknownst to the rabbi, the artificial man could actually feel and think. . . . And emotions? Manifold" (102). Indeed, Sherwood's golem becomes a lusty guy. (This will also be the case when we turn to Cynthia Ozick's female golem in *The Puttermesser Papers*.) Before Rabbi Loew can get him home from the scene of his creation, the golem has exchanged glances with Rochel, who is not wearing a headscarf this early morning. She notices his dimples and he feels "something pierce his groin, and an exquisitely sharp pain spread down his thighs" (105). Such a focus on the erotic, it is implied, is the result of that kiss from the unknown evil source at the golem's creation. Though the golem cannot speak, he can understand and write in German, Hebrew, and Czech (Sherwood's innovation). This is much more than Rochel can do: she is illiterate and longs to be able to read, yet another indication of the importance of words and story. Rochel will not truly be herself until she can read, and indeed write, which she accomplishes by book's end.

Meanwhile, back at the castle, the alchemists John Dee and Edward Kelly have arrived from England, underwritten with funds from Mordecai Maisel. Confronted with Rudolf II's clock collection, they are told by the emperor: "I am most particularly interested in inventions to do with the abolition of time" (112). So the novel begins to take on parallel stories of creation, twin strands of Rabbi Loew creating the golem and Dee and Kelly searching for the elixir of life demanded by Rudolf. Inevitably these strands will collide. Rochel encounters the golem at Rabbi Loew's home, where he functions as a servant; the golem spies on her when she immerses herself, naked, in the mikvah, the ritual bath. They encounter each other again when Zev is hired to make a set of leather clothes for the golem, who must be measured (he is seven feet tall).[18] In alternating chapters, the reader learns of the despair of Dee and Kelly at the viability of actually inventing the elixir of life. Hence, they turn to an elaborate plot involving butterflies to fool the emperor and stave off their execution, the punishment promised by Rudolf for failure to create the elixir he desires.

The relationship between Rochel and the golem continues apace. In one illuminating passage, she is alone with Yossel and very voluble. She reflects: "She wondered at the number of things she had to say . . . as if she were a kind of living book and should she roll up her sleeves and lift her skirts, she would discover letters printed all over her" (189). So both the golem and Rochel are conceived as inscribed with letters, as texts. And shortly thereafter she does have her skirts lifted by the golem, who rescues her from a fall into the river and carefully removes her wet clothing to revive her. He begins to caress and kiss her and she urges him on: "Do not stop, do not ever stop" (192). The bad omen of her wedding ring is fulfilled, again a fairy-tale trope.[19]

Part 4 opens with a meeting between the emperor and his retinue and a delegation from Judenstadt, including Rabbi Loew, the golem, Zev, and Rochel. We know from historical records that such a meeting between Rabbi Loew and the emperor indeed did take place, but the subject matter discussed was never revealed. Here, Sherwood imagines that Rudolf continues to single-mindedly pursue the elusive trophy of eternal life. He offers Rabbi Loew a bargain: "This is what I propose: I send the troops to protect Judenstadt, you make me immortal. A simple exchange. . . . You found the spell in your Kabbalah for making life, now find the spell for making me immortal" (207). If the rabbi fails to produce such a spell, the emperor will wipe out the Jewish community of Prague, which piles another threat upon that of the pogrom planned by the priest Thaddeus.

From here, the novel involves a number of subplots too numerous to re-capitulate. Suffice it to say that a pogrom is launched, that Rochel becomes pregnant by Zev, consummates her passion for the golem in the woods, and then suffers a miscarriage. Rabbi Loew ponders how he will respond to the emperor's demand. Recognizing that "language created the world" (229), he turns to the Torah, rather than the Book of Splendor, for inspiration. He decides to give each member of the community a part of the secret: "a noun or verb, article, adjective . . . a grammar of hope . . . and with the words, the rabbi prayed, may there come a miracle for the People of the Book" (231). This is actually a clever form of protection for the Jewish community, as the emperor will need every person to stay alive in order to reveal his or her word. Rabbi Loew meets again with the emperor, aiming to puzzle and delay him. "In the *Zohar, The Book of Splendor*," Rabbi Loew tells Rudolf, "we read that he who gets up early can see something 'like letters march-ing in the sky, some rising, some descending. These brilliant characters are the letters with which God has formed heaven and earth.' Of course, God is infinite and the universe is a concept that the ordinary man has trouble grasping, but you, the emperor . . . I am sure you comprehend" (263).

By invoking her own title here, Sherwood implies that her novel, too, carries secrets of creation and self-creation. Rochel, by novel's end, has en-dured exile, persecution, and near death, renewed her commitment to Zev, and learned to read and write, fulfilling one of her strongest wishes: "In her old age . . . every weekday night, sitting by the fire, wrapped warmly in her coverlet embroidered with blue and white threads, she wrote in a steady and fine hand, tales, some fanciful, others all too true. On Shabbat, she would read them aloud to Zev and privileged guests" (345). Sherwood and Rochel become doubles at this moment: Rochel could well be the "author" of the tale we have just read and Sherwood often comments on the fact that she became a writer only at middle age. One of the gestures of intertextuality is metafiction, and surely this novel offers us a central character who has re-created herself with words. Sherwood comments: "Rochel, the orphaned seamstress, is both my new baby child and my ancestral mother. Is there a greater love? . . . Rochel is pure invention, but good with the needle like my mother, and like my grandfather, she comes from a small village near Kiev. She is in some ways a Cinderella figure, but she goes through the oven, emerges like the phoenix from the ashes. She stands in homage."[20] And this is Rochel's larger significance: "oven" here is clearly a reference to the Holocaust, and Rochel thus represents the survival of the Jewish people and the critical importance of the imagination for telling the story, for self-creation, for survival.

The intertextual changes, then, that Sherwood rings on her golem tale include the erotic golem in a traditional setting, perhaps the first to successfully seduce a woman, and a golem who is increasingly human and complex. "I have embellished freely on the golem legend, made him good-looking, smart, personable, why not?" (351), Sherwood tells us in her afterword. (Yossel does run amok at the close of his story and is decommissioned in the usual way by Rabbi Loew.) A greater accomplishment, though, is Sherwood's introduction to the golem legend of a highly sympathetic and autobiographical woman character in Rochel, a character that allows her to explore the peril of emotional life and the crucial role that literacy can play for an individual and a community.

Reviews for the book were uniformly enthusiastic, but the novel has received precious little critical attention. Richard Eder in the *New York Times* praises the book for rising above the genre of historical fiction: "Instead of history's retrospective certainty—this is how it was—Ms. Sherwood projects her readers, as if by time machine, back into a place where everything is to be discovered." The *Booklist* reviewer applauds "this ambitious novel [which] blends mysticism, vast political upheaval, and a sexy sweeping love story that reads like 'Beauty and the Beast,'" and also comments on the title: "*The Book of Splendor* is another name for the *Zohar*, a book in the Kabbalah, Judaism's mystical tradition, that explores creation and death, physical and divine love, exile, redemption, and the conviction that nothing is as it appears. Sherwood deftly borrows all of these themes" (Engberg, 1588). The reviewer for *Publishers Weekly* focuses on the golem, "that legendary monster/watchman/savior supposedly created by Rabbi Judah Loew in Prague in 1601 [who] has never lost its ability to inspire the creative imagination" (Zaleski), which brings us full circle to that word again: *imagination.*

In closing, then, we have reviewed in this chapter three post-Holocaust texts which, while appropriating the customary tropes of the golem legend, have simultaneously referenced the temptations and failings of human nature, the crucial importance of literacy, and the treasure of Jewish tradition. By imagining the golem as awakening to eroticism or as a redeemer figure, Singer, Wiesel, and Sherwood demonstrate how intertextuality is at the heart of Judaism, of storytelling, and of postmodern perceptions of the Shoah. Perhaps in using intertextuality as a memory for literature, these three writers re-create a piece of the profound memory loss that was the Holocaust.

"I am a golem, but on weekends I do Domino's."

• •

Above: A photograph of the neighborhood in the Josefov immediately surrounding the Altneu Synagogue, taken c. 1900 by Jindrich Eckert. Reproduced in *The Lost Jewish Town of Prague* by Hana Volavková and Pavel Belina.

Left: A photograph of the Altneu Synagogue in Prague, where Rabbi Loew presided. Note the rungs climbing up the side; according to legend, the golem is buried in the attic of this building. Photograph taken in May 2007 by Elizabeth Baer.

Rabbi Loew's chair, located near the bima in the Altneu Synagogue. Legend has it that no rabbi has used the chair since Rabbi Loew's death. Photograph taken in May 2007 by Elizabeth Baer.

Rabbi Loew's gravestone, located in the famed Old Jewish Cemetery. Photograph taken in May 2007 by Elizabeth Baer.

A Hugo Steiner-Prag illustration from the 1916 edition of Gustav Meyrink's *Der Golem*. Note the influence of German Expressionism on Steiner-Prag's style, the foreboding atmosphere of the Josefov, and the Orientalist depiction of the golem.

From the concluding scene of Paul Wegener's *Der Golem: Wie er in die Welt kam* (1920). The golem is played by Wegener himself; note his clothing and stiff pageboy hair. The gates to the Josefov are shown in the background.

Mark Podwal's drawings for Elie Wiesel's *The Golem* depict actual scenes from Prague, often with exploding alphabets of Hebrew characters, thus invoking the role of words in creating the golem. In this illustration, "The Dream of Rabbi Loew," the letters emanate from the Jewish Town Hall, built in the late 1500s and still located near the Altneu Synagogue. Note that the figures on the lower clock are Hebrew and therefore the clock actually runs "counterclockwise," as Hebrew is read from right to left. The golem appears to emerge from the stream of letters.

Cover image of the October 1974 Marvel Comics issue #176. The golem is depicted here onboard a ship, defending his accomplices against "the devil hordes of the Kaballa." Courtesy of Marvel Entertainment.

Illustration from James Sturm's graphic novel *The Golem's Mighty Swing*, p. 71. Henry Bell, the only African American member of the Jewish team, the Stars of David, plays under the name of Hershl Bloom. Here he is masquerading as the golem, a publicity stunt forced on the team. Note that his costume is exactly like that worn by Paul Wegener in his film *Der Golem: Wie er in die Welt kam*. The publicity agency that proposed the stunt "procured the actual costume worn in the film. All the way from Germany" (29). Courtesy of the Center for Cartoon Studies.

4

The Comics Connection

The Maharal's creature of clay does not act as a mere servant to perform menial tasks at the bidding of his master. Like the superheroes of comic-book culture, the Golem rescues the community from powerful enemies who would do it harm.

Hillel Kieval, *Languages*

You couldn't have torn him away from any movie or TV show or cartoon where there were monsters or spaceships or mutants or doomsday devices or destinies or magic or evil villains.

Junot Diaz, *The Brief Wondrous Life of Oscar Wao*

Their names tell the story. Like their comic creations, America's early and subsequently famous cartoonists had a double identity. Max Ginsberg, credited with creating comic books as we know them today, became Maxwell "Charlie" Gaines; Robert Kahn became Bob Kane; Abraham Jaffee became Al Jaffee; Jacob Kurtzberg became Jack Kirby; Eli Katz became Gil Kane; and Stanley Martin Lieber became Stan Lee. Sometimes they took a new name under pressure, sometimes it was assigned by a sibling, sometimes it was a private gesture: in all cases, it was a quiet recognition of the antisemitism in hiring practices in America in the early to mid-twentieth century and of the fact that a WASPy name could open the door to assimilation and wages.

But the Jewish identity of the founders and giants of America's comics industry can be traced in their creative expression, if not in their monikers. And this Jewish identity, subtextual at best in the early days, became increasingly visible as the generations of comics readers and writers came and went. According to Arie Kaplan,

> the presence of Jews in comic books during this Golden Age [1938–52] was like a drama in two acts. In act one, Jews seeking to escape poverty invented a new medium that melded art and storytelling and projected subconsciously Jewish power fantasies onto their stereotypical gentile superhero creations. And with the advent of World War II, the Jewish metaphors inherent in Nazi-clobbering characters such as Captain America became more pronounced. During the Golden Age's shorter second act, EC's brief but memorable seven-year reign as Entertaining Comics was marked by an overriding concern about morality, sometimes emanating from a Jewish sensibility. (80–81)

In the 1960s and 1970s, the years that followed the Golden Age, Jewish comics professionals began to include Jewish characters in supporting roles while, in these same years, the underground comics displayed Jewish characters in central roles (Kaplan, xv). And that brings us to today, when both graphic novels and comic books feature stories of Jewish life in their pages.

Some historians suggest that it all began with Superman, who first appeared in print nationally in March 1938. He emerged from the imaginations of two Jewish teenagers from Cleveland, and, eerily, was found in their self-published magazine for the first time in the same month that Hitler came to power: January 1933. Jerry Siegel wrote the storyline and Joe Shuster produced the illustrations. Some biographical details of these two teenagers perhaps contributed to the development of their superhero: Siegel's father was murdered in the family dry goods store, he loved movies about muscular heroes, and he is reported to have put his clothes on over his pajamas to avoid being late to school; Shuster was a body builder (Buhle, 54–55).

We can trace their intertextual borrowings in creating Superman—among them, Edgar Rice Burroughs's Tarzan, Lester Dent's fictional hero Doc Savage, and even Nietzsche's notion of an *Übermensch,* from which Siegel and Shuster are said to have derived the name "Superman" (Kaplan, 11–13). But despite these various sources, Kaplan makes a convincing argument for Superman being "the supreme metaphor of the Jewish experience" (14). The evidence he marshals is persuasive: Superman is a refugee, an immigrant from another planet, Krypton, of which he is the last survivor. His parents send him to Earth in a tiny spaceship: Kaplan draws parallels with both the biblical story of Moses and the *Kindertransports*, trains that carried children from Nazi Germany and occupied countries to the safety of Britain during 1938–39. And his real name is Kal-El, which Kaplan notes is Hebrew for "All that God is" (15). And, of course, his name as a mild-mannered reporter is Clark Kent, a WASP name if ever there was one, and probably a nod by Siegel and Shuster to Clark Gable.

If Siegel and Shuster were influenced by earlier characters, such as Tarzan and Doc Savage, in creating their superhero, we can be sure that the golem was also a mighty intertextual force. Will Eisner has remarked: "The Golem was very much the precursor of the super-hero in that in every society there's a need for mythological characters, wish fulfillment. And the wish fulfillment in the Jewish case of the hero would be someone who could protect us. This kind of storytelling seems to dominate in Jewish culture."[1] Superman is, indeed, a modern-day golem. He defends the innocent and the unfairly persecuted, he has superhuman size and strength, and he believes in the possibility of *tikkun olam*, repair of the world.

The Golem Awakens at Marvel Comics

The golem himself had a brief moment in the sun at Marvel, which published three comics featuring "The Golem, the Thing That Walks Like a Man" (as the title went) in June, October, and December 1974, with a semi-sequel the following year. The initial issue #174, written by Len Wein of *X-Men* fame and illustrated by John Buscema, begins with an inset box of history: "In centuries agone, they had called him a myth, a creature formed of stone and clay and the blood of a people's oppression—a moving monolith who rose before the yoke of tyranny—shattered it in his monumental fists—then vanished into the sands of time—there to be almost forgotten—until today! Now, once more, he rises—summoned from his eons-long sleep to protect those he loves, now, for the first time in untold decades" (1). The reader is immediately thrust into those "sands of time" with drawings of a vast Middle Eastern desert, upon which are camped an archaeologist, Professor Abraham Adamson (both significant names, suggesting a founder), his assistants Wayne and his fiancée, Rebecca, Adamson's niece, and her brother Jason. They are digging in the sand to recover the lost golem; finding his assistants discouraged, Abraham tells them the story of Rabbi Loew, who "constructed a creature in humanoid form—breathed life into its rock-like body thru supernatural means—then set the creature against those responsible for our ancestors' plight" (2). In a departure from the traditional story, Rabbi Loew is shown chiseling the golem from rock;

the golem emerges as a huge purple bald figure with glowing yellow eyes. Rabbi Loew looks remarkably like Professor Adamson, a visual suggestion of a doppelgänger, a hint of things to come in the storyline.

Just as they recover the golem from the sands with a huge winch, intruders arrive in the camp, dressed in soldiers' garb with Arab headdress. The reader is told they were fighting "a war of territory, of ideologies" (7), clearly a reference to the Israeli-Palestinian conflict. A dispute breaks out, and Professor Adamson is shot in the ensuing scuffle. His assistants are kidnaped and he is left to die; consulting several ancient scrolls, he endeavors to reanimate the golem, intoning "the mystic alphabets of the 221 gates" (16) but succeeds only when his tear drops on the golem's foot (a comics innovation for the ritual to bring the golem to life). "Aware of the gentle old man [Professor Adamson] who perished that the golem once more might live" (17), the golem pursues his foes in an effort to free Wayne, Rebecca, and Jason. Overtaking them, he swiftly disposes of Colonel Omar and his men and releases the captives. The strip ends as Rebecca recognizes her Uncle Abraham's gleam in the golem's eye.

In the next issue that follows the golem's adventures, the October 1974 issue #176 written by Mike Friedrich with art by Tony De Zuniga, the first four pages recapitulate the story of both Rabbi Loew and Professor Adamson's rediscovery and reawakening of the golem. Many of the illustrations in these four pages are the same or almost exact copies of the June 1974 issue. Then the story continues: the three assistants determine to bring the golem, now reverted to lifeless stone, to the American university where Professor Adamson worked, which had been his intention. But as they endeavor to load the statue, wrapped in fabric, onto the boat, they are again foiled, this time by men in uniforms with different (but still Muslim) head garb. Again, the golem stirs and the leader of the foes exclaims, "Great Allah! The creature lives!" (10). After the golem dispatches this group of enemies, the boat gets underway. In the next frame, the reader sees "a place that exudes pure evil, the home of Kaballa, called the unclean" (11). "I have waited for decades for the golem to reappear—and now that he has I am ready for him! Shortly, his power shall be my power—and all shall fall before me," shouts the curiously named (given the Jewish influence) evil spirit. He is dressed in red and pink spandex with a "K" on his chest and an Egyptian-style headdress from which red horns protrude. Kaballa releases his "air demons" to fly toward the ship and attack the golem, but, of course, the golem knocks 'em all out and, after a lightning bolt hits the ship, takes the three assistants on his back and swims to the shore of a desert island, bringing the second golem episode to a close.

Another feature of great interest in this October 1974 issue is the "Letters to the Golem" column, ostensibly sent in by readers of the June issue. The first one, signed by a Don Vaughan of Florida, proffers his congratulations on the new series and then a correction to the story. "According to Jewish legend" (19), Don claims, the word "emeth" must be inscribed on the golem's forehead, and he goes on to explain how this, as well as an amulet in some versions, would work. Don closes his letter by inquiring, "Did anyone on the staff see the movie 'Der Golem,' produced by Paul Wegener, who also starred as the leading character, before you produced this story?" (19). The editors respond, saying the "inspiration for this series was drawn from the original legend, not from any filmic incarnation of the Golem" (19), but they acknowledge that Len Wein, the scripter, is a "monster movie buff of the first magnitude" (19). They further explain they discarded the amulet idea as it had been used often in other Marvel comics, and "since we wanted to bestow a human intelligence on our Golem, we chose to have Professor Adamson give up his life to instill a life force in old Stone-face. And, too, there was all that symbolism inherent in the Professor's tear falling on the Golem's foot. . . !" (32).

Two other letters respond to the new series, both positively, though both have quibbles about fidelity to the legend. Tim Fish of Paint Lick, Kentucky, and Gordon Abney of Berea, Kentucky, coauthored a complaint about the transfer of the life force from Professor Adamson to the golem as an overused device, but they conclude their letter with kudos for the creators, Wein and Buscema, and this plaudit: "A Jewish hero: who says this isn't the Marvel Age of Firsts? Until Doc Doom rusts over . . . MAKE OURS MARVEL!!" (32). The editors reply that "neither Len nor John was able to remain on the book" (32); pulling the famous Len Wein is perhaps an early forecast that the golem series would last for only one more issue. The last letter in the column addresses point blank the Arab-Israeli war: "What I object to is your taking the political argument between the Arabs and the Israelis and turning it into a question of good and evil. The reason I object to this is that it is the same argument that Hitler used to exterminate the Jews" (32). To this salvo, the editors write a long and thoughtful response, one that rebuts the charge of propaganda and that is personal and revealing: "Regarding the Arab-Israeli conflict . . . there are almost as many differing viewpoints on the question as there are people and that's true in the Marvel Bullpen, too. We have at least one Catholic who's entirely pro-Israel . . . one Jew who wants both sides to blow themselves up and let the rest of the world alone . . . and several people of varying faiths who support the Arab position. There is no one Bullpen position on the issue. We're a true collection of individualists up here" (32, ellipsis in the original). That the editors felt compelled to include such a candid and defensive response to Bohdan Chomiak of Edmonton, Alberta, Canada (assuming these letters are from actual fans), is revealing of the in-between status of Jews in comics in the 1970s—a status that would change radically with the arrival of the graphic novels by Will Eisner, *A Contract with God* (1978), and Art Spiegelman, *Maus* (1986, 1991).

The third and final installment of this golem series appeared in the December 1974 issue #177, created by the same team as issue #176. The story opens with a full-page drawing of the golem who now sports "half-league boots," a loincloth with the Star of David on the belt buckle, wristlets, and a helmet that could be right out of the NFL. Careful scrutiny of the golem's forehead reveals the inscription "emeth." Perhaps Don Vaughan's letter in response to issue #176 was taken to heart. Before the golem stands a man garbed in a red cape and headdress, specifically *not* identified as Rabbi Loew. He barely reaches the golem's thigh and holds an ancient scroll and a magician's globe. The room in which they stand is a cavernous stone room, tricked out as an alchemy laboratory, somewhat reminiscent of Paul Wegener's depiction of Rabbi Loew and his magician's lair. By way of explanation, an inset box tells us: "Since the golem's initial creation by Rabbi Loew in the 15th century, the golem has reappeared many times. His shape may have been different, dependent upon the human hands which fashioned his pre-life clay bulk, but it has always been a life-essence which has given the golem mobility and a semblance of life!" (1). The next page in the issue presents in five frames a story attributed to "Gersham [*sic*]" Scholem's *On the Kabbalah and Its Symbolism* (1965). It is the story of the man who, in endeavoring to erase the "e" in "emeth" to decommission the golem, causes the golem to collapse on top of him and the man (here dressed in the red cape of page one) dies. Then the story picks up where it left off in issue #176, with the wizard Kaballa plotting once again to capture the golem's power. This time, Kaballa is depicted in his underground lair in front of a huge oven filled with fire, an unmistakable emblem of the death camps in the Holocaust. He releases his demons of fire to Florida, where the golem has arrived at the university and is being studied for authenticity by a skeptical Professor Yeates and his assistant, symbolically named Saudia Yamal. She declares the golem to be authentic: "The creature can be . . . is . . . alive" (7). But Professor Yeates dismisses her report in a condescending and sexist manner and seeks to prove the golem is a hoax by turning his torch on the stone golem. As the golem comes to life, the first demons suddenly arrive and a multipage battle ensues from which the fire demons eventually flee back to Kaballa. Recognizing that the golem's power "comes from his emotional affinity with people," Kaballa declares his intention in the final two frames to kill the three people—Wayne, Rebecca, and Jason—who are closest to the golem. The storyline comes to a startling halt with these words: "Notice: see the dramatic announcement on our letters page concerning the shattering fate of the golem" (23).

There, the reader finds a "Special Bullpen Note":

File it under "G."
"G" for "Good idea that didn't work out."
"G" for GOLEM.
"G" for "Good-bye." (32)

"This issue," the note continues, "marks the last appearance in STRANGE TALES of our kosher hunk of clay. After three tries and despite awesome creative efforts . . . our golem strip just hasn't become what we hoped it would" (32). The editors explain: "Deadline hassles" caused a missed issue, resulting in lost continuity; they were unable to decide upon a "direction" for the strip; and thus "we decided to call things to a halt. We goofed" (32). Throwing a sop to the fans, the editors briefly introduce the golem's replacement, Adam Warlock, with this apology: "Okay. So he's not Jewish" (32). And thus, in medias res, the golem lapses back into obscurity.

Marvel subsequently published a series of comics pairing the Fantastic Four character, The Thing, with other Marvel characters and the September 1975 issue #11 was the golem's turn: Marvel Two-in-One "The Thing and the Golem." The Thing is golem-like himself: a man who turned into a hulk of red rocks. This episode does not really add much to the story already told by Marvel of the golem's revival. The Thing and his girlfriend travel by train to Florida and arrive just as Kaballa determines to try once again to capture the golem's powers. This time, Kaballa raises a wall of water that separates the golem from Jason, Wayne, and Rebecca, the source of his strength. Kaballa gains control of the golem's body (through some kind of remote control) and the golem runs amok, much as in the old legends. And, of course, he does battle with The Thing in no fewer than eighteen frames of "POW!" "WHACK!" and "KER-ACKK!" When the trio of assistants approach, the golem regains self-control and reverts to a statue. The episode ends with a hope that the statue will help people understand a little better what a monster is and isn't. In this episode, as in the others recounted above, the golem finds himself in the position of fighting two kinds of evil: the supernatural figure of evil, Kaballa, and the human evil of the Arab armies in the desert or of the man turned into The Thing.

I would be remiss if I did not mention the paratextual material in these Marvel comics, that is, the advertisements that, for example, comprise eleven of the thirty-two pages in comic book #177. In addition, four pages are dedicated to another strip, "The Girl behind the Glass," one to "Letters to the Golem," and two pages of Marvel Bullpen Bulletins, leaving only fourteen pages for the golem story. Three of the four sides of the front and back covers are also advertisements. These ads are fascinating for their intertextual relationship with the storyline of the golem. For example, a half-page ad features a seven-foot Frankenstein "in authentic colors on durable polyethelene [sic]" to be had for only $1.00 (9). A full-page ad offers the reader "All New! The Terrible Truth! Photo news features Hitler: The Horror and the Holocaust," a 100-photograph magazine of the history of the Third Reich, again "only $1.00" (19). Predictably, many ads promise "amazing results" for various bodybuilding methods; others offer self-improvement courses in electronics, motorcycle mechanics, drafting, accounting, and other career fields; and another frequent category is the "sales club" where readers receive "famous name prizes or cash" for selling quotas of sports equipment or greeting cards. The vast majority of these ads are clearly targeted at boys, indicating that the publishers assume that is their primary readership. But squeezed in between small box ads urging "Be Taller (stand 2–6 inches taller in a few weeks)" and "Do Houdini Magic" is the exception: "Have your Poems set to music," probably not aimed at boys enamored of the superhero stories.

DC Comics also ran a golem series, called "The Monolith," which appeared after the demise of the Marvel 1970s golem series. The DC series was written by Jimmy Palmiotti and Justin Gray, with art by Phil Winslade, and, according to Danny Fingeroth, "it was a novel twist on the golem story, set in Brooklyn of the 1930's and today" (*Disguised*, 136). "The Monolith" ran from April 2004 to March 2005 in a dozen issues. It features a golem, the Monolith, created during the Depression in Brooklyn by Alice, a downtrodden factory worker who is a Jewish immigrant from Prague; Rabbi Rava; a Chinese carpenter named Han; and a bootlegger named Peter, whose blood is used to create the golem (and hence the golem is in some sense his doppelgänger, a theme we have seen previously in the legend as well as in the Marvel golem series). "The Monolith" is set in the early twenty-first century with a main character named Alice Cohen, the granddaughter of the factory worker, who inherits a house from her grandmother and discovers therein the golem. The series addresses contemporary issues: drug addiction, prostitution, HIV, sex slavery rings, racism, child pornography, and the "underclasses" of American society. The initial issue was very favorably reviewed by Ryan Paul in the online journal *Pop Matters*: "Palmiotti and Gray have set out to explore the issue of power and disenfranchisement within the alienated and excluded communities of American society, and their metaphor, the Monolith, is a truly apt, and truly frightening, proposition."[2]

The Monolith is drawn as a muscle-bound Hulk-like[3] figure who towers over the other characters, bald, with lines that appear to be incised on his forehead and chin. He sports a bare chest, blue jeans, and a heavy black leather belt, and his feet are wrapped in white binding, mummy fashion. The golem can speak, albeit in short declarative sentences, is associated in various ways with literacy and storytelling, and is in love with Alice. He is squarely in the tradition of Gotham City superheroes and of the golem as a protector and rescuer. Though there are Jewish characters and themes, the golem's sense of responsibility is to the wider world of oppressed people in New York, a city often depicted as dark, menacing, snowy, and decrepit. The series ends, rather curiously, on Christmas Day with the golem, Alice, and her friend Tilt exchanging gifts around a Christmas tree. A brief reference is made to not having "the time or money to follow the tradition of twelve gifts" (Palmiotti and Gray, "The Monolith," #12) as Alice hands the golem a set of Russian nesting dolls and the golem claims, "My name was Peter." This brings the series to a close in a somewhat lackluster fashion.

From Comics to Graphic Novels

If Jews were instrumental in the founding and flourishing of the comic book industry, so were they equally central to launching the graphic novel. But there is a step between these two genres, the "underground comix," which flourished in the 1960s and 1970s. This is the "catch-all term for the alternative comics from this era, which contained subject matter that would never have found its way into mainstream comics . . . sexually charged, drug-fueled, or politically radical (sometimes all three)" (Kaplan, 137). One of the leading pioneers of the underground comix was R. Crumb who, according to legend, peddled his *Zap Comix* (1968) from a baby carriage (Fingeroth, *Graphic Novels,* 16) in San Francisco with his Jewish wife, Aline-Kominsky-Crumb, also a famous cartoonist. These comix appeared in underground newspapers and were sold in head shops and thus evaded the Comics Code Authority, put in place in 1954 after a House UnAmerican Activities Committee investigation into the "harmful influence" of comics on American kids. Two writers who got their start in underground comix, Art Spiegelman and Harvey Pekar, both Jewish and both children of Polish Jewish immigrants, were among those who created the genre of graphic novels.

Will Eisner's *Contract with God* (1978) is usually credited with being the first graphic novel and Eisner with bringing the term into common usage. The text comprises four stories: three set in a block of tenements on

Dropsie Avenue in the Bronx in the 1930s and a fourth about a young boy who travels from the tenements to a resort in the Catskills for a summer; all four chapters depict aspects of Jewish immigrant experience. The title story recounts the life of Frimme Hersh, born in a shtetl in Russia during the pogroms of the early twentieth century. "Above all, Frimmehleh was helpful and kind" (15). His community, recognizing his intelligence and promise, pooled their money to send him to America, where he endeavors to uphold the contract he has made with God: to do good deeds (18). Initially Frimme succeeds: "[H]e became a respected member of the synagogue, trusted with money and social matters" (20). But when his adopted daughter dies suddenly, Frimme cries out that God has violated their contract and, no longer believing he is obligated, he tosses the stone on which the contract was recorded out the window.

Illegally using synagogue funds, he acquires tenement buildings, abuses the tenants, and becomes a wealthy man; he takes up with "a mistress, a 'shikseh' from Scranton, Pa" (38). Eventually Frimme repents, tells the elders of the synagogue what he has done, offers funding, and asks them to draw up a new contract with God. They hesitate about the appropriateness of such a task but eventually deliver what Frimme deems a "bona-fide without question" (50). As he plans to "do charitable work again" (51), Frimme is struck down with a heart attack and dies. In the epilogue a new, Hasidic immigrant boy serves as the "hero of the day" in a fire at 55 Dropsie Avenue and then, somewhat ominously, takes up and signs Frimme's stone contract with God.

The artistic style of *A Contract with God* is rather free form: some pages have the traditional boxes and word balloons of the comics while other pages are full-size pen and ink drawings with wording in a different font, placed appropriately, and no frames or balloons. While *A Contract with God* contains no golem, it does share themes with the post-Holocaust golem appropriations in comics, graphic novels, and fiction: antisemitism; the challenging lives of Jewish immigrants in America; a depiction of New York City as a dark and existential place; and the issues of identity, trauma, and survival. In a 2004 preface written to a new edition of *A Contract with God*, Will Eisner writes autobiographically about his inspiration for the book:

> Born and brought up in New York City and having survived and thrived there, I carry with me a cargo of memories, some painful and some pleasant, which have remained locked in the hold of my mind. I have an ancient mariner's need to share my accumulation of experience and observations. Call me, if you will, a graphic witness

reporting on life, death, heartbreak and the never-ending struggle to prevail . . . or at least to survive. (ix)

Eisner also speaks movingly of the death of his beloved daughter from leukemia, which is part of the plot of Frimme Hersh's story; for Eisner, "The creation of this story was an exercise in personal agony" (xii). Thus, the notion of survival takes on a personal resonance as well as a post-Holocaust reference to the survival of the Jewish people and alludes to the role of story in this survival. *A Contract with God* has been in print for over thirty years now and has been published in eleven languages. Its influence on the field of graphic fiction is inestimable and certainly can be traced in the work of James Sturm.

JAMES STURM, *THE GOLEM'S MIGHTY SWING* (2001)

James Sturm found his calling at a young age. Born in Manhattan in 1965, he amassed a collection of Peanuts comic books early and by first grade was hooked when he saw an interview with Stan Lee on television. The next day he bought an issue of Marvel Comics *The Fantastic Four* and the rest, as they say, is history. Though he vowed to leave this "childish" pursuit behind when he headed off to college at the University of Wisconsin, Madison, as the legend goes he was captivated again two years later when a friend presented him with a box of underground comix. This led to his own comic strip, "Down and Out Dawg," which was published by the *Daily Cardinal*, the campus newspaper. When he graduated in 1987, Sturm self-published a collection of these strips and then headed back to New York City to attend the School of Visual Arts. He landed an internship at *Raw* magazine, where he encountered Art Spiegelman. With MFA in hand, he relocated to Seattle and co-founded an alternative weekly, *The Stranger*.

At this point, his career in the comics really took off. He began a comic book series, *The Cereal Killings*, "a high concept dissection of the American love for consumption," which was later nominated for an Eisner Award, the top prize in the field.[4] Invited to teach at the Savannah College of Art and Design, Sturm lived in Georgia from 1997 to 2001. During this time he continued work on what was to become a trilogy: *The Revival* (1996), an account of the evangelical movement, set in Kentucky in the early nineteenth century; *Hundreds of Feet below Daylight* (1998), which focuses on the exploitation of Chinese mineworkers; and *The Golem's Mighty Swing* (2001). These three historical graphic novels have been collected in an anthology titled *James Sturm's America: God, Gold, and Golems* (2007). Sturm now lives in Vermont, where he co-founded the Center for Cartoon Studies, a two-year program.[5] *Unstable Molecules* (2004), a four-issue series and trade paperback published by Marvel Comics, is an homage to the Fantastic Four, his childhood superheroes.[6] His most recent publication is *Market Day* (2010).

It was *The Golem's Mighty Swing* that catapulted Sturm into national recognition. Time.com named it the best graphic novel of 2001, and it has been translated into five languages. Reviewers from an intriguing range of journals and magazines representing baseball, Judaism, the comics industry, and the general public uniformly praised it. The *American Book Review* called it "an astounding feat of storytelling . . . and an amazing piece of art" (Humphrey). The *Elysian Fields Quarterly: The Baseball Review* exclaimed: "At the heart of baseball is the goal of getting home. Jewish history reflects this goal as well. *The Golem's Mighty Swing* examines what it means to belong both to your new country and to your old traditions. It is a classic baseball story about what it means to be an American." *Flakmagazine,* a journal devoted to comics, raved: "Sturm's dialogue, detail and sense of human interaction are superb. *The Golem's Mighty Swing* has a pacing and sense of drama often lacking in comic books . . . Sturm's clean, engaging drawings bring you into his world. You stay willingly" (Norton).

On the surface, the plot of *The Golem's Mighty Swing* seems as straightforward and clean as the drawings that accompany the narrative. A minor league Jewish baseball team, the Stars of David, barnstorms in the 1920s Midwest, playing games in small towns and traveling by night on their dilapidated team bus. When said bus breaks down and there is no money to fix it, the team captain and narrator of the story, Noah Strauss, reluctantly agrees to the proposition of a promoter: turn one of the players into a golem to bring in the crowds and the money. Mayhem, rhubarbs (baseball slang for fights on the field), and antisemitism ensue. The novel ends inconclusively, with a chapter that feels like an epilogue set ten years later. Perhaps a sequel is envisioned?

But closer scrutiny of this seemingly simple surface reveals the terrific contribution to golem literature (as well as baseball and Jewish American literature) made by Sturm. In Sturm's creation of a golem, we have no Rabbi Loew, no mysticism, no flourishing of the Hebrew alphabet, no secret ritual performed seven times. Instead, we have the African American member of the team, Henry Bell, masquerading as "Hershl Bloom (member of the lost tribe)" (13) who, by virtue of his bulky stature, is designated for transformation into the golem. Henry played in the Negro Leagues for twenty years before joining the Stars of David, and he has no problem with the promotional stunt, a commonplace, he tells his teammates, in the Negro Leagues.

But then a little magic does happen: Sturm creates an intertextual reference to Paul Wegener's film *Der Golem* (1920). The promoter, Victor Paige, has recently seen *Der Golem* on the screen in New York and claims he has obtained the original costume. So when the reader first sees Henry Bell aka Hershl Bloom dressed as the golem, he looks like an exact replica of Paul Wegener's golem: the stiff pageboy hair, the larger than life size, the jacket with the symbolically incorrect five-pointed star implanted firmly on the chest, the broad leather belt, the enigmatic scowl (71). The golem comes up to bat: he grounds out into a double play. But then he comes to the mound to pitch: three up, three down. A full third of the pages of this graphic novel are devoted to frames of baseball games. Perhaps it is the slow nature of the game itself, perhaps it is Sturm's talent as a cartoonist, but he captures beautifully the tension, the bodily movements, and the rhythm of the game.

When the golem succeeds in getting the Putnam All-Americans' best player out on a foul ball caught by Moishe "Mo" Strauss, Noah's younger brother, the crowd turns nasty. They pull Mo into the stands, steal his glove, and begin chanting: "Jews go home" (79). Told by the umpire that they must play or forfeit the game, the Stars of David take the field again. The golem sends a pitch careening toward home plate and it smacks the batter in the head. Now the crowd really erupts, streaming onto the field; the Putnam All-Americans take up their bats and head toward the Jewish team. Noah commands his teammates to head for the dugout and the golem stations himself at the entrance to protect the players. The narrator asks: "How is it possible for a single man with a bat to hold back an angry mob?" The answer: "They are fearful of the Golem. The Golem and his mighty swing" (84).

Now the trick is for the team to escape the field and get to the bus safely. Noah bends his head in prayer: "Please, dear God, let us leave this town alive" (85). Looking around he sees his brother Mo singing the Sh'ma: "For thousands of years Jews have tried to die with the Sh'ma on their lips" (86). This explanation of the Sh'ma appears at the top of a full-page illustration of the heavens opening up with a huge downpour over the Putnam stadium. A cop ducks into the dugout with the ominous pronouncement that the game must continue when the rain clears: "Up to me I'd let the crowd have atcha" (87). But in what is clearly a torrential rainstorm sent from God, the crowd eventually leaves, the river begins to flood, and, after a few hours, the Stars of David slink toward their bus and escape. "We survived our game in Putnam. / Survival. Perhaps that is a victory unto itself. / I don't blame Paige for what happened. He told me he intended to create a golem and I agreed to help him. /It is no surprise that things got out of hand. / That is the nature of a golem" (90).

If parallels between a traveling baseball team, subject to antisemitism in myriad ways, and the trope of the Wandering Jew were not already obvious to the reader, this final page with its emphasis on survival makes a reference to the Holocaust unmistakable. Home plate, too, is a potent metaphor for the desire of Jews to find a home, acceptance, and an identity in America. It is not by accident that their opponents are the "All-Americans." Noah tells us on page one that his life on the road is a difficult one but that he is not complaining: "Had I stayed in New York I'd be a pushcart peddler or worse (like my father, a sweatshop tailor)" (1). He continues on the following page: "My father would be gravely disappointed knowing we are playing on the Sabbath. He will always be a greenhorn. His imagination lives in the old country. Mine lives in America and baseball is America" (2). Baseball is his escape from the fate of his father, an immigrant who has not achieved assimilation. He pursues the American dream of an American imagination.

But the America in which the Stars of David play is still profoundly antisemitic. Sturm finds many devices with which to startle the reader into recognition of this fact. At the book's opening, the kids of Forest Grove await the arrival of the team with the query "Jews here yet?" (2). They are craning their necks over the fence to catch a glimpse of this exotic breed. To emphasize the point, Sturm includes a frame on the following page in which the presence in the ballpark of a stocky, cranky middle-aged woman wearing a crucifix around her neck surprises the home team. "I'm not here for the baseball," she explains, "but to see the *JEWS* . . . thank you very much" (3, italics in original). "Hey, Sheeny!" yells another member of the crowd (4). Jewish team members are seated in the back room of the local restaurant after the game; Henry has joined the local African American community for dinner so it is clear the discrimination is antisemitism (21). As Mo goes for an evening walk, kids gather: "Hey Dino! It's one of those Jew ballplayers. / I want to see his horns, Dino, grab his hat" (24). The kids pelt Mo with rocks. When the team moves on to Putnam, Mr. Putnam himself, a crass capitalist and the owner of Putnam Paper Mill, the Putnam Stadium, the baseball team itself, and the local newspaper, the *Putnam Post Bugle*, calls his team together to prep them. The smokestack of his paper mill is prominently featured in two frames as he begins to talk: the similarity to the chimney of a crematorium is obvious. "The Jews are crafty players. Patient," Putnam tells the players. "They've been waiting for their Messiah a thousand years . . . / Do not try to outsmart a Jew. You must overpower him . . . / I want you men sharp tomorrow! I want you ready for these Hebes!" (44). At the bar the night before the game, a circumcision joke is told by one of the All-American team members: "Let's see them Jews handle McFadden's fastball. He'll cut them down to size—give 'em another circumcision. Cut 'em good" (49).

The *Putnam Post Bugle* serves its purpose in playing on prejudices to draw people to the game. An image of the newspaper shows this story carried in the Friday issue: "Exclusive: When the Golem Comes to Town, Hide Your Women." Careful reading of the fine print reveals that it is Victor Paige, the promoter, who has written the story, intended to arouse curiosity and play on fears (50). What this calls to mind are the stereotypes of Jewish men as licentious rapists, prevalent in such Nazi films as *Jud Süss*. Most blatant in terms of both antisemitism and the metaphorical resonance of the novel is the editorial that appears in Putnam's newspaper on Saturday, the day of the game: "What Is at Stake," cries the headline. "The excitement of Saturday's game should not disguise a simple fact: The Golem is not Putnam's most dangerous adversary. / There is a greater threat that Putnam All-Americans must vanquish, the threat posed by the Jews. / These dirty, long nosed, thick lipped sheenies; they stand not for America, not for baseball, but only themselves. / They will suck the money from this town and then they will leave. / A victory must be had. The playing field is our nation. The soul of our country is what is at stake" (51). This is antisemitic rhetoric at its height: Hitler constantly accused the Jews of being "parasites" and "work-shy," reasons they should be exterminated like vermin. Such images are rampant in Goebbels's propaganda films such as *Der ewige Jude* (The Eternal Jew). The morning of the game, Buttercup Lev, their best pitcher, goes missing. He has been grabbed in a bar the night before, driven into the country, and beaten badly. He is unable to pitch for the team in the big game.

Sturm braids together the theme of antisemitism with a depiction of American racism: the existence of the Negro Leagues; the illustration of the "colored section" of the bleachers (13) and reserved seating for whites; the comment from the promoter, Victor Paige, that Henry Bell "will embrace this new role [as the golem]. Negroes, after all, are born performers" (30). When Lev turns up with broken ribs and a head wound on the morning of the game, Henry recalls the racism his team, the Black Barons, encountered playing in the American South: "My second year we lost three players before we broke training camp. / Outside of Macon, Jimmy Day was hung and set on fire. / Pepper Daniels was stabbed in the throat for smiling at a white woman. / Horace Walker just disappeared. Had he left of his own mind he would have taken his guitar" (57). This period—the novel takes place in 1922—was a time when lynchings in the United States were shockingly frequent. This was the year, in fact, that the Dyer Anti-Lynching Bill was considered by Congress. The early 1920s were also a time when the Ku Klux Klan was resurgent. The reference to "smiling at a white woman" is undoubtedly a reference to Emmett Till, a young African American boy who went to visit relatives in Mississippi from his home in Chicago in 1955. He was murdered in retaliation for a supposed smile or remark to a white woman in a store. Finally, Sturm also works in a reference to racist attitudes toward American Indians with the mention of the "Sioux City Reds, an all Indian [baseball] team" (47).

If many Jewish cartoonists had to hide their identities by assuming WASPy names in the early days of the comics industry, Henry Bell aka Hershl Bloom wears two masks or disguises. First, he becomes "Jewish" to play with the Stars of David, and then he becomes a Wegeneresque golem to pander to the fears and stereotypes of the populace of small-town America. By encompassing various forms of ethnic prejudice in the novel, Sturm makes clear the profound meaning of Paul Lawrence Dunbar's famous line: "We wear the mask that grins and lies."[7] Interestingly, Henry's disguises are also reminiscent of Nazi propaganda films, but in reverse. In *Der ewige Jude*, male Jews are accused of hiding their identities by changing caftans for Western dress, shaving, and cutting their hair. The scene in the film provides "before" and "after" shots in order to warn the "Aryan" audience of this hidden "menace" in their midst. In *The Golem's Mighty Swing*, the reverse process occurs: Henry becomes "Jewish." It is likely that Henry is modeled on Satchel Paige, a famous Negro Leagues player on a team called the House of David and about whom Sturm subsequently wrote a book.[8] When Henry recounts the deaths of his former teammates during spring training, the lesson seems to be that antisemitism is less deadly than racism and that this trumped-up golem—a fake, really—cannot save the Stars of David, the traditional role of a golem. But Henry does ward off the angry crowd by protecting the Stars' dugout and the team does safely exit Putnam. As one reviewer has noted, baseball "provides a theater of difference, in which racial, regional and class antagonisms are heightened but also ritualized and mythologized. These differences become intriguing to the same extent they are threatening" (Hatfield).

Differences and threats in *The Golem's Mighty Swing* are traced by Roxanne Harde through a different lens; her essay "considers the multivalency of Jewish American masculinities through an analysis of Sturm's narrative and visual art. *The Golem's Mighty Swing* denies stereotype to combine aspects of national, religious, and ethnic ideologies into shifting and multiple depictions of Jewish American male identity in the early twentieth century" (64). Though Harde gets some of her facts about the history of the golem legend wrong, her analysis of the "Jewish threat to American capitalism"

(77) and the way in which the novel finally privileges baseball itself as an arena of performance provides useful insights into James Sturm's marvelous book.

America is the land to which Noah, the narrator, aspires to belong, but it is not a utopia: Noah's tale is a caveat for ethnic Americans. Myths can cut both ways: the golem can be a savior or can turn destructive; the American myth, as represented here by baseball, can also be a two-edged sword. By telling his story, Noah creates himself; he imagines and performs himself as a Jew, as an American, and as an aspiring Jewish American. The African American Henry Bell becomes a kind of text, a palimpsest on which are inscribed various identities: first becoming a faux Jew and then a faux golem. His presence on the team illuminates the fluidity of immigrant assimilation as well as the prejudice that serves as an obstacle. Sturm's appropriation of the golem legend is thus uniquely American; Henry Bell's protection of the team at a crucial moment both reaffirms the legend of the traditional golem as protector of his community and reshapes that legend into a contemporary message: the need for the downtrodden in American society to "step up to the plate" for one another.

PETE HAMILL, *SNOW IN AUGUST* (1997)

The golem is a triumphant symbol of the human imagination.

Pete Hamill, afterword to *Snow in August*

Though *The Golem's Mighty Swing* and *Snow in August* are written in very different formats, both novels are a heady mixture of baseball, golems, Jews, and comics. What makes *Snow in August* unique is that it is the only post-Holocaust golem novel written by a non-Jew included in this study. Pete Hamill's parents both immigrated to the United States in the early twentieth century from Belfast, Northern Ireland. Hamill is no stranger to the immigrant experience, to discrimination based on ethnicity, or to religious conflict, all features of most of the golem fiction being treated here. In an essay in which he memorializes John F. Kennedy and his contributions to the status of Irish Americans, Hamill delineates the kinds of prejudice the Irish experienced as immigrants: "the bigotry that went all the way back to the Great Famine; the slurs and the sneers; *Help Wanted No Irish Need Apply;* the insulting acceptance of the stereotype of the drunken and impotent stage Irishman; the doors closed in law firms, and men's clubs, and brokerage houses because of religion and origin" ("Once We Were Kings," 527). In short, Hamill names the environment of prejudice and exclusion suffered by both Irish and Jews: he often refers to the notion that the Irish are the "lost tribe of Israel." *Snow in August* is emphatically a post-Holocaust novel, including as it does several Holocaust survivors and a character who died fighting the Nazis.

Pete Hamill was born in 1935 and grew up in a series of tenements in Brooklyn, New York. Raised as a Catholic, he was the oldest of seven children, and his first job, at age eleven, was as a carrier for the newspaper, the *Brooklyn Eagle*. Like many of his peers, Hamill left school at the age of sixteen to take a job as a sheet-metal worker at the Brooklyn Navy Yard; he subsequently enlisted in the Navy. He earned a high school degree and sporadically attended college after his stint in the navy was complete. Hamill is an inveterate New Yorker, and New York has been his subject during his years as a newspaper reporter, in his fiction, and in his nonfiction. He served as the editor-in-chief of both the *New York Post* and the *New York Daily News*.

But Hamill is also cosmopolitan. He served as a foreign correspondent for the wars in Vietnam, Nicaragua, Lebanon, and Northern Ireland, and has lived in Mexico City, Dublin, Barcelona, San Juan, and Rome.[9] *Snow in August* (1997) is Hamill's eighth novel; it endured on the *New York Times* best-seller list for four months. Hamill has published twenty-three books all told, which include eleven novels, two short story collections, a memoir, *A Drinking Life* (1994), and six volumes of nonfiction, including a book on Diego Rivera and one on Frank Sinatra.

Snow in August opens, appropriately, in a blizzard. Michael, the eleven-year-old through whom the novel is focalized (a child's perspective like Wiesel's golem story), wakes up in his bedroom in Brooklyn in 1946 and notes the radiant light. He struggles into his clothes in the chill morning and heads off into the storm to serve as an altar boy at the early mass. As he pushes his way through waist-deep snow and is literally tossed around by the roaring wind, he hears a voice:

> "Hallo, hallo," the bearded man called, his voice seeming to cross a distance much wider than the street. "Hallo." As if coming from another country.
>
> Michael stood there. The man was beckoning to him.
>
> "Hallo, please," the man shouted. "Please to come over . . ."
>
> The voice sounded very old, muffled by the falling snow. A voice as plain and direct as a spell. Michael still didn't move. This was the *synagogue*, the mysterious building in which the Jews worshipped their God. (15, italics in original)

Eventually Michael overcomes his fear and goes to the aid of the rabbi, who simply wants Michael to turn on the lights on this cold, dark Sabbath morning. Michael becomes his *Shabbos goy*. The rabbi initiates him into Yiddish and Judaism, and he initiates the rabbi into English and American baseball, specifically the Brooklyn Dodgers.

Michael imagines the rabbi's voice that first Saturday as "plain and direct as a spell," and the reader already knows that Michael is susceptible to spells: the spells of *Captain Marvel* comics, of films like *The Four Feathers* and *Gunga Din,* and of books—Jack London, Edgar Allen Poe, Robert Louis Stevenson, Charles Dickens.

The opening chapter of the novel reveals the importance of fantasies of power to Michael and the ability of comics, especially, to deliver that fantasy. Michael's father was killed in the Battle of the Bulge; his mother is often sad. Michael feels keenly the powerlessness of his age and status. He clearly identifies with Captain Marvel: "On that night in the mysterious cave, the wizard named Shazam told Billy Batson he had been chosen to fight the forces of evil because he was pure of heart. And no matter how monstrous their weapons, all he needed to fight them was to shout the magic word. *Shazam*!" (3). Michael thinks the magic of the word *Shazam* "might be true" (3). He further identifies with Billy Batson because both were newspaperboys.[10] He valorizes his trip through the blizzard by imagining literary heroes and their adventures: "a phrase that he had memorized from Jack London rose in his mind—*sole speck of life journeying across the ghastly wastes of a dead world*—and he tingled with excitement" (10). Thus, at the outset of the novel, Hamill privileges words and story as a way to frame, explain, and embolden one's life. Just as words of the Kabbalah create the golem, so "*Shazam*!" creates Captain Marvel, and so the words of his beloved books and comics create Michael.

Read simultaneously with Hamill's memoir *A Drinking Life, Snow in August* is revealed as a highly autobiographical novel. "I'm one of those countless writers who must begin with the rough material of my own life," Hamill has declared (*Snow,* 363). Snow and comics played key roles for the young Pete as they do for Michael. One of Hamill's earliest memories is how the "winter snow garnished the limbs of the elm tree" outside their kitchen window (*Life,* 3); this tree will come to stand for the happiness and innocence of his early childhood. Though his father, Billy Hamill, was not killed in World War II, he is a largely absent father—working blue-collar jobs, spending long hours in neighborhood bars. Billy uses a wooden leg to replace the one he lost due to careless medical practice after he broke the leg in a soccer game. Pete never manages to attract the affection or approval he so craves from his alcoholic father.

He recalls taking "a great mound of pure fresh-fallen snow in my mittens" and beginning to eat it: "the snow was just so clean and white I wanted it inside me" (*Life*, 6). His kindergarten peers ridicule him but his teacher assures him it's all right. Hamill tells of long walks in the snow that occurred periodically in his life and often brought epiphanies. He closes the memoir with a final snow scene: he has walked to Brooklyn's Prospect Park, "which was whitening under the heavy snowfall" of a January day. He has himself given up drinking and been sober for five years. He imagines the important people in his life walking across the snowy meadow as across life's stage. He experiences a sense of peace. "And I loved my life, with all its hurts and injuries and failures . . . I reached down and took a great mound of fresh snow in my hands and began to eat. I was home. I was free. I'd leave the rest to Providence and Paddy McGinty's goat"[11] are the closing lines of the book (*Life*, 265).

Just as snow serves as an important touchstone for memory, epiphanies, and the cherished and lost sweetness of childhood in Hamill's work, comics are also a central symbol of his childhood. Hamill recounts his growing consciousness during the fall of 1941, when he entered first grade: that he was Irish, that bigotry existed in the world, and that his father was crippled, all of this explained kindly and directly by his mother. And then a new friend entered his life: "Best of all, Ronnie Zellins introduced me to comic books. He had a collection but he couldn't read them yet. . . . I . . . explain[ed] to him what was in the balloons and how the words helped make the pictures more exciting" (*Life*, 14).

Given coins by his father's friends at the neighborhood bar, Hamill began his own collection of comics: "*Superman, Captain Marvel* and *Batman*, the *Human Torch* and the *Sub-Mariner*" (*Life*, 18). In a lyrical passage, Hamill makes clear the profound impact these comics had on him:

Until I learned the names of Simon and Kirby, around 1943, I didn't know that men actually sat down to write and draw comics. That knowledge would change my life. But when we lived on Thirteenth Street, the *content* of the comics was driving deep into me. They filled me with the secret and lurid narratives, a notion of the hero, a sense of the existence of evil. They showed me the uses of the mask, insisting that heroism was possible only when you fashioned an elaborate disguise. Most important was the lesson of the magic potion. The comics taught me, and millions of other kids, that even the weakest human being could take a drink and be magically transformed into someone smarter, bigger, braver. All you needed was the right drink. (*Life*, 19)

After a street fight with a classmate in which Hamill is humiliated, the comics become imbricated in the narrative of his life: "I could not emerge from my room in a mask and cape to avenge myself . . . I could not, like Billy Batson, the orphaned newsboy, say the word *Shazam*! and be transformed into Captain Marvel" (*Life*, 22). The magic of the comics changed from being a possibility to a fantasy. But Hamill has another epiphany: "Maybe words, like potions were also capable of magic" (*Life*, 24). It will be with words that magic will be wrought in Hamill's life.

With the threat of the Nazis omnipresent in his life by this time, Hamill's sense of the dangers of the world extended beyond the conflicts in the comics and on the streets of his neighborhood to those of the world. Pearl Harbor was bombed during his first grade year; the fathers of other kids were joining the military. And he becomes aware of the Holocaust. Ten years old when the war ended, he "played a game called concentration camp, made up of jailers and the pursued, sprinkling our talk with German words learned from comic books and movies: *Achtung!* and *Schweinhund!*" (*Life*, 57). This game was suddenly halted when Hamill sees a newsreel from Buchenwald in his local RKO theater:

> Grizzled American soldiers were at the edge of the camp, some of them weeping. And just past them, beyond the barbed wire, were men and women and children in striped pajamas, unable to move, full of fear, staring with eyes that couldn't be seen. Some were lying on tiers of bunks, too close to death to ask for help, their long skeletal hands limply hanging to the floor. Their arms were tattooed with numbers. Their heads were shaven. . . . This was what Hitler had left behind after killing himself in the bunker: these silvery gray images of European horror. (*Life*, 57)

Hamill's efforts to get an adequate explanation from his parents to his question of how this happened were futile; in school, there was only silence. In his own life in Brooklyn, his contact with Jews was minimal at best. Educated in parochial school from first grade, he did not have Jewish classmates. He does meet a Jewish boy at a summer camp he attends one year; he learns the meaning of the word "antisemitism" at age thirteen in school (*Life*, 108); he serves, like Michael, as a *Shabbos goy* (*Snow*, 367); he mentions living next to a synagogue on Ninth Street in Brooklyn after his release from the navy (*Life*, 186). Though such personal knowledge of Jews and Judaism was limited, Hamill recalls being haunted by the images of the Holocaust. When food scarcity meant eating kelp after the war, Hamill would try to console himself by reciting silently: "*You have it good, you have a bed, you have food to heat up at night . . . you are not being buried by a tractor, fatherless, motherless, brotherless, sisterless, you are not a Jew"* (*Life,* 66, italics in original).

Just as ethnic and neighborhood boundaries prevent Pete Hamill from having Jewish friends and classmates, so Michael, wrapped in his Italian and Irish Catholic environs, is similarly bereft. Reading an encyclopedia entry to learn more about Judaism, "Michael suddenly realized that he knew almost no Jews" (*Snow,* 47). Hamill uses this ignorance of Judaism and Jewish legends advantageously. As Michael's relationship with Rabbi Judah Hirsch grows apace, Rabbi Hirsch gradually begins to tell him stories of his home in Prague, where he was born in 1908. He reveals that he was named after Rabbi Judah Loew (*Snow,* 106) and, with a book full of Prague illustrations, he literally transports the boy to Prague, a "magical city of goblins and ghosts and doppelgängers" (*Snow,* 103). Hamill's descriptions bristle with details: Hradcany Castle, the Vltava River, the Charles Bridge, "the royal gardens where the Hapsburgs grew their tulips in vast dazzling rows . . . the orange tile roofs and cobblestoned streets and weeping willows of the Mala Strana" (*Snow,* 93), Mucha and Kafka, the astronomical clock and Wenceslas Square. Gradually Rabbi Hirsch leads Michael back, back to sixteenth-century Prague, the time of Rudolf II and Rabbi Loew and the Josefov. He tells Michael of the alchemists in the royal court, and Michael envisions a man "in a dark robe covered with silver stars, a man who looked like what the wizard Shazam might have looked like" (*Snow,* 103). So Michael's longing for magic and miracles and power in his own life begins to merge with the stories of Rabbi Hirsch. Hamill is carefully setting the scene for the arrival of the golem.

By using a child narrator, Hamill creates the perfect condition for raising antisemitic stereotypes and puncturing them. This and the careful lessons in Jewish beliefs and legends distinguish this golem novel from those by Jewish American writers who often assume more knowledge on the part of their readers. Michael's friendship with the rabbi and his personal experience of being inside the synagogue, of which he was initially fearful, go a long way to contradict the lies and myths told by his friends. These include the usual: "After all, didn't everybody on Ellison Avenue say that the Jews killed Jesus" (16) and "he'd heard all the stories about Jews being greedy" (37). His friend Sonny urges him to find the treasure hidden in the synagogue: "All the Jews, they give money and jewels and rubies and gold and shit like that to the rabbis. But these rabbis, they don't put it in banks . . . They hide it . . . so if one morning they gotta run, they pack it all in a bag and get the fuck out of there" (55). But in a vicious attack, a neighborhood bully slams the cash register on a kindly Jewish candy and comics store-owner, who was trying to defend Michael; this has a profound impact on the young boy. The bully screams: "You cocksucker, you Jew cocksucker! You motherfucker!" (34). After the bully departs, Michael calls an ambulance to attend to the severely injured Mister G.[12] and later reflects on how this incident contradicts the stereotypes of Jews as greedy Christ killers.

While Hamill is carefully building and braiding Michael's desire to learn about Judaism ("I want to find out about those secrets" [23]), his exposure to antisemitism, the magical atmosphere of Prague, and Michael's infatuation with comics, he is also building Michael's growing realization of the seduction and searing supremacy of words. Studying his encyclopedia, Michael discovers that Jews "gave the world the Bible and the first alphabet. The goddamned *alphabet!*" (45, italics in original). As he trades languages with Rabbi Hirsch, he reflects further: "Words themselves had a special power and mystery. . . . In Latin or Yiddish, they were like those secret codes used by spies, or members of secret societies, which he sometimes wrote down while listening to *Captain Midnight* on the radio. . . . Words had assumed another importance as well . . . the rabbi treated words as if they were jewels. He caressed them, handled them with his tongue, repeated them with delight" (80–81). Without knowing the phrase, Michael, a bibliophile himself, begins to perceive the Jews as the people of the book. As Rabbi Hirsch gives Michael his virtual tour of Prague, he tells him about the magic there. "Snow fell in August" (104), he says, providing the reader with one of the meanings of the novel's title. And the Jews have "the magic of the Kabbalah," he continues, defining Kabbalah as "the secret wisdom . . . contain[ing] special alphabets and magic words, the most important of which, the most powerful, the most awesome, was the secret name of God" (104–5).

Finally, about a third of the way into the novel, Rabbi Hirsch begins to tell Michael in earnest the legends surrounding Rabbi Loew. Again Hamill demonstrates careful research as he rehearses traditional stories: of the magic palace created so Rabbi Loew could entertain Rudolf II, of the antisemitic Father Thaddeus and the blood libel, of stones turning into roses.[13] At first, Michael sees Rabbi Loew "as if he were at a movie" (116), then Michael "was suddenly huddled in a doorway, as a mob marched on the Jewish Quarter" [of Prague] (118), and then, just as suddenly, Rabbi Loew asks Michael to take a letter to Rudolf, imploring the emperor to protect the Jews: "After all, Michael was a *Shabbos goy.* Nobody could stop him on the streets beyond the ghetto" (119).

So Michael becomes, temporarily, a time traveler—he is enticed, indeed abducted, by the power of books, story, words, such that he has crossed into the centuries' old Jewish legend of the golem. He watches breathlessly as Rabbi Loew creates the golem. Hamill has added his own touches to the creation story, including a large "silver spoon that was mentioned in the Book of Creation" (120) that carries a Hebrew inscription and is given to Rabbi Loew by Rudolf. Using the *shem*, a piece of parchment containing the word for God, the magic word that will invoke the golem, and the ritual of circling the mud form, Rabbi Loew brings the golem to life: "Shazam! 'It's like Captain Marvel,' Michael said" (122). This golem also pisses and farts, inevitable additions of an eleven-year-old boy's scatological universe.

Across the next two hundred pages, events conspire to bring Michael to the point where he, himself, must create a golem. Hamill masterfully realizes the world of postwar Brooklyn, the world of his own childhood, a world where gangs were beginning to appear, where class differences were sharply felt by many families, where Jackie Robinson was breaking color barriers as the first black American to play in the major leagues, for Michael's beloved Brooklyn Dodgers. Michael is faced with a dilemma: he knows the gang member who beat up Mister G., now hospitalized in a coma, but community (especially Irish) codes prevent him from "squealing" to the police. On the other hand, he recognizes, through his talks with Rabbi Hirsch, that to withhold this information is to be a bystander. He struggles with this as with the issue of racism in professional sports.

A series of interlocking events brings things to the breaking point: antisemitic graffiti is sprayed on the walls of the synagogue, including a dozen swastikas, and Michael is attacked, called a "Jew-lover" (233), and severely beaten by the gang members who mistakenly believe he has turned informer: they break his leg and he lands in the hospital for an extended stay. After his release, Rabbi Hirsch comes to visit and tells Michael and his mother the story of his wife's death at the hands of the Nazis. Michael and Rabbi Hirsch go to a Dodgers game to see Jackie Robinson play; this passage is lyrical and full of laughter as Hamill, no doubt, recalls the first baseball game he attended in Ebbets field.[14] Though the rabbi joyously finds that baseball is "his key to understanding America" (226) (much like Sturm's immigrant players), all the conflicts of America are played out in the bleachers: racial, religious, class confrontations. Even the Holocaust is alluded to: black fans of Jackie Robinson lend Michael binoculars with the revelation: "I took them off a dead German" (286).

Then, the ultimate offense: the gang again attacks Michael, still hobbling along on his leg cast, and his mother, molesting her sexually in an assault that stops just short of rape. Shortly thereafter, the gang returns to the synagogue, carving a swastika on the door and leaving Rabbi Hirsch for dead. Michael decides they must be punished here on earth: "Not in Purgatory or Hell. Here. And then he thought about the only way that punishment might be certain" (303). Sneaking into the intensive care ward, Michael elicits from the battered rabbi the secret name of God and sets out for a Quaker cemetery to gather enough pure dirt. Locating in the synagogue a small box from the time of Rabbi Loew, brought by Rabbi Hirsch from Prague, Michael discovers therein the silver spoon and the *shem* and shapes a clay man, writing EMET on his forehead. Michael chants "YHVH" [Yahweh] (330): "Feeling his own body charged with power and mystery. Believe, he thought. . . . Here is the Kabbalah. . . . For the mystery was all about letters . . . for from letters we make words, and words are the names of life" (331). Michael, who has fallen under spells himself, now conceives one: "Michael danced and chanted, repeating the letters in pairs and in triplets . . . tried to will himself into the inert mud. He rose into a frenzy of words and letters, hearing sounds from his mouth that he did not think, moving to music that nobody played . . . soaring and swooping and breaking for third [as Jackie Robinson had done], up, rising up . . . borne by the letters, swept through the golden skies . . . above Brooklyn, above Ireland, above Prague, above the fields of Belgium [where his father died]" (331). Michael falls to his knees "in utter emptiness" (331), and the reader is expended, too, at that point.

The magic works:

> And then two dark hands gripped the sides of the tub and the Golem pulled himself up.
> It was him.
> The Golem.
> Everything was true. (332)

Michael trembles and finds that the golem, eight feet tall and "as dark as Jackie Robinson" (332), is a creature way beyond the figure he had imagined from Rabbi Hirsch's stories of Prague. That imagined golem was a kind of comic book character "made of pen lines and brush marks. Simple, sometimes even humorous, sent on missions of justice by a good rabbi. He did not expect this naked creature" (333). Providing the golem with an old cape he finds in the synagogue, Michael leads him outside and finds, to his astonishment, that it is snowing in August: "In the churning, gyrating, eddying frenzy of the sudden storm, nobody saw the white boy and his giant black companion" (337). (It is intriguing to consider a comparison of this black golem with that of James Sturm.) In a wonderful scene, the pair makes short work of revenge against the gang: "Don't you ever read *Crime Does Not Pay* comics?" Michael asks the gang leader. "This is the part near the end" (347). In a triumphal conclusion, the golem heals Rabbi Hirsch, even repairing his broken teeth; restores the dilapidated sanctuary of the synagogue; revives the congregation including not only Mister G. but millions of Holocaust survivors; and brings back Leah, the rabbi's wife. Rabbi Hirsch confesses to Michael that during the Holocaust he had tried to create a golem and failed: "I was not pure enough . . . I did not believe enough" (352). It has taken a child, already full of marvels and belief and a deep love of the word, to bring the golem back. The novel ends as "birds talked and stones became roses . . . and the rabbi, at last, danced with his wife" (354). Such a conclusion is a wonderful example of Sidra Ezrahi's concept of "alternative history" as a response to the debate over representation of the Holocaust, discussed in the introduction. Hamill creates a liminal space between history and fiction; in a sense, he reinvents Rabbi Hirsch's memory. The juxtaposition of the reality of Rabbi Hirsch's losses and their restoration to him affront the reader with the power of the imagination.[15]

In the afterword of his novel, as well as in an interview with the Jewish journal *Tikkun,* Pete Hamill has been very specific about what he hoped to accomplish with *Snow in August:* "I wanted to acknowledge the great gifts that I, and all Americans, had received from the Jews: tenacity, irony and moral intelligence" (367). Hamill acknowledges "Jewish intellectual brilliance" (367) and the profound influence it had on "American thought and sensibility" (367) in the postwar period. He talks of the darkness of McCarthyism. And he recounts "two momentous events [that] forced us to think in new ways" (368): the Holocaust and Jackie Robinson playing in the major leagues, both of which Hamill puts in the novel. Hamill was first exposed to the Holocaust through newsreels from Buchenwald: "I was horrified and had nightmares for months. . . . Those gray images of skeletal figures, of bony bodies stacked upon each other like offal, of eyes staring from gaunt faces like silent accusations: they drove themselves deep into my mind and my *imagination.* At school that fall, I asked the first moral questions of my life: How could this happen? . . . There were no adequate answers. There are none now" (*Snow,* 368, italics mine). Jackie Robinson also taught Hamill something about evil, in a world where racism was just not discussed, and how to confront it: "Robinson is crucial to this novel" (369). It was a trip to Prague, and specifically to the Jewish Cemetery there, when he learned about the golem legend, that coalesced the novel for Hamill: "God, I wish I'd had a golem when I was eleven" (371).

Hamill repeatedly uses the word "imagination" to delineate the heft and message of *Snow in August.*

> Here is that novel, set in a time before television, when our imaginations were stirred by talk at kitchen tables, by books, by songs, by an occasional movie, and by the radio. . . . It was a time when boys could

believe in magic words [and] . . . the extraordinary transformations of
Irish legends and myths. . . . They could believe in the secret language
of the Kaballah. Again, this is a novel, not a tract. But it has a very
simple theme: first we imagine, then we live . . . imagine your entire
lives, not simply your youth. (*Snow*, 371)

Snow in August gives the reader a portrait of a young boy who struggles
viscerally with several manifestations of evil in the mid-twentieth century:
the Holocaust and ongoing antisemitism, racism, gang warfare, the death of
his father, fear, jealousy, and class animosities. Entwined with these struggles are his joys: learning, comic books, stickball games with friends, the
pleasure of Yiddish and his relationship with Rabbi Hirsch, baseball, and
belief in the marvelous. *Snow in August* is a *bildungsroman* with a touch of
magical realism. It is just this magic, engendered by the imagination, that
Hamill wishes to privilege, and not "just" imagination but *moral* imagination:

The Golem is a triumphant symbol of the human imagination. On
its simplest level, his tale is a parable about the power of moral intelligence. The imagination allows us to confront all horror and evil. In
the end, the imagination opens out, like a great symphony, to encom-
pass all the living and the dead, to say to the forces of evil, as the Jews
continue to say, a half century after the Holocaust: You cannot win.
You can kill us. You can insult us. You can marginalize us. But we
shall triumph. And we shall dance. (*Snow*, 372)

Michael Chabon, *The Amazing Adventures of Kavalier and Clay* (2001)

All novels are sequels; influence is bliss.

Michael Chabon, *Maps and Legends*

In my largely non-Jewish circle of friends, I often draw a blank look when I
tell them I am writing a book about the golem, a Jewish legend. But if they
have heard of the golem, it is almost always in connection with Michael
Chabon's Pulitzer Prize–winning novel, a towering intertextual appropriation of the golem legend and the comics genre. In the epigraph to this section, Chabon protests Harold Bloom's notion of "the anxiety of influence,"
instead finding his bliss in influence, in the intertextual gesture of revising
and reimagining. Critics often speak of Chabon's tendency to write "genre

fiction," that is, that he experiments with a traditional genre in each new book (much as the Coen brothers do in each new film). The book that followed *The Amazing Adventures of Kavalier and Clay* provides a good example: *The Final Solution* (2004) is subtitled *A Story of Detection;* it features a very elderly retired detective who is drawn back into his profession by the inexplicable appearance in London in 1944 of a small Jewish boy and his talking parrot. Though he is never named, the detective is Sherlock Holmes and he indeed provides "a final solution" to the murder in the story as well as the origin of the boy, a Kindertransport child. Thus, the clever title both initially misleads and, in the end, provides a satisfying double entendre.

Like the afterword of Pete Hamill's novel, which acts as a coda to his deployment of the golem in his autobiographical *bildungsroman*, Chabon's essay "Golems I Have Known, or, Why My Elder Son's Middle Name Is Napoleon: A Trickster's Memoir" (*Maps*, 193–222) comments on *The Amazing Adventures of Kavalier and Clay*. Chabon opens the essay by declaring: "I saw my first golem in 1968, in Flushing, New York, shortly before my fifth birthday" (*Maps*, 193). With this arresting sentence, Chabon launches into an autobiographical account of how his interest in golems arose. It is a raucous, funny, and convincing account—until the reader hits the subsection toward the end of the essay titled "Postscript, August 2007" where Chabon confesses:

> The preceding is the text of a talk that I delivered publicly several times over the course of 2003–04. Its subject is the interrelationship between truth and lies, memory and invention, history and story, memoir and fiction, the sources of narrative and the storytelling impulse; the inevitable fate of liars to be swallowed up or crushed by their lies; and *the risks inherent both in discounting the power of outright fiction to reveal the truths of a life, and in taking at face value the fictions that writers of memoir present as fact."* (217, italics mine)

He goes on to reveal that much of what he has just confided in his audience has been "pure invention" (218). Yet, he says, this is at the heart of the writer's enterprise: "The writing of fiction is akin to the work of a stage magician, a feat of sustained deception . . . the essential difference between fiction and lies [is] . . . a contract between the writer of fiction and the readers he or she lies to, as there is between a magician and the audience he hoodwinks; they are in it together. They are helping each other to bring a story to apparent life" (218). Thus Chabon dares the reader to interrogate pronouncements that imaginative literature about the Holocaust is "barbaric" or, conversely, that everything Holocaust survivors say in their memoirs must be recognized as unalloyed truth, the facts as opposed to the "fiction" of fiction. The string of opposites in this quotation, "truth and lies" and so forth, are a series of dichotomies that Chabon means to collapse. In so doing, he affirms the usefulness of all story to render human experience and emotion and to make visible the value of story itself.

If Chabon did not see golems in his youth as the essay in *Maps and Legends* coyly asserts, then how did he come to include the legend in *The Amazing Adventures of Kavalier and Clay?* An interviewer put this question to Chabon and writes about his response:

> Chabon says golems were the key. . . . The breakthrough came while Chabon was researching comics and interviewed Will Eisner, the creator of the classic newspaper strip *The Spirit.* Eisner brought up golems without prompting, mentioning how most of the golden-age comic-book creators were Jewish, how Superman is very golemlike, how there is something inherently Jewish about many superheroes. This jelled the story in Chabon's mind, made things start to pop. "That's when I first realized," he says, "I was onto something more than comic books." (Binelli and Duffy, 58)

The portion of Chabon's essay in *Maps and Legends* before the postscript makes clear that he has carefully studied the golem legend, as does the author's note at the end of the novel that documents his reading and research. He provides a perfectly adequate definition of a golem and describes accurately the process of creating one. He mentions Paul Wegener's 1920 film *Der Golem* and Gershom Scholem's famous essay "The Idea of the Golem." These references to real sources, as well as his father's (supposed) "revelation" that the Chabons are "descended from Rabbi Judah ben Loew" (200), build credibility, as does his childish innocence at the time of "seeing" these real golems. A further ploy to captivate and "hoodwink" his audience are the frequent protestations that this is all true, despite its seeming implausibility: "I don't know what exactly is prompting me to come forward now and come out with the truth" (195). He refers to a couple of writers he admired as a kid—both real—C. B. Colby and Philip Jose Farmer; the latter was famous as a sci-fi writer who intertextually riffed on superheroes and wrote an imagined genealogy for Tarzan. This, too, adds to the credibility of the golem sightings he claims. But then, cheek by jowl in the essay, he shares with his audience his totally fictitious adventures with C. B. Colby who, in fact, is "really Joseph Adler," a Holocaust survivor who supposedly lived down the street from the Chabons; this part of the story, seemingly verified by physical proximity to Michael Chabon in his childhood, is "pure invention."[16] The memoir that Chabon claims Adler wrote, *The Book of Hell*, does not exist.

Chabon goes on to talk about his first "sustained work of fiction" titled "The Revenge of Captain Nemo," written at ten years of age in which he "consciously adopted" the literary style of Arthur Conan Doyle (202). (One is tempted to ask: really?) But the key thing is his revelation about the bliss of influence: "the intense pleasure . . . derived from attempting to impersonate Sir Arthur Conan Doyle" (203). Chabon draws a comparison between "the pleasure that a liar takes in his lie as it enters the world wearing the accent and raiment of truth" and "the pleasure that a maker of golems takes as the force of his words, the rhythm and accuracy of his alphabetical spells, blow life into the cold nostrils, and the great stony hand unclenches and reaches for his own" (203). Chabon describes an imagined room filled with his favorite writers—from Judy Blume to Edgar Allan Poe to H. P. Lovecraft—"*their intersection defined me . . . I derived from them, they explained me*"—and his profound desire to be one of them: "This was the wish . . . I have sought to express in the infinitely malleable clay of language, ever since" (204, italics mine). This is the bliss of influence for Chabon: to see himself as part of an infinite network of writers, to be defined by them and to redefine them in his own writing. Chabon makes palpable the parallel between golem-making and text-making.

The Amazing Adventures of Kavalier and Clay is itself a golem: outsized (636 pages), unwieldy, transformative, magical, composed from the alphabet swirling around its author. And both of the main characters have golem references in their names: Josef Kavalier (Joseph is the first name usually assigned to Prague's golem) and Samuel Klayman (the surname being an obvious reference to the golem). Samuel Klayman changes his name to Sam Clay early in the novel, a clear reference to the many Jewish men in the comics industry who also changed their names (see the opening of this chapter for several examples). *Kavalier and Clay* shares with *Snow in August* a setting: largely New York during and after World War II; a consciousness of the Holocaust (like Rabbi Hirsch in *Snow*, Joe Kavalier is an immigrant to America as a result of the Holocaust); and a valorization of the comics as both framework and subject matter. Only the emphasis on baseball, prevalent in *Snow*, is missing here.

Joe and Sam are doppelgängers, both creative artists for whom comics are cosmic. By the end of the novel, they are both, in essence, married to the same woman and father to the same son. Chabon has created a variation on the familiar golem theme of the affirmation of the imagination in post-Holocaust texts. The golem is both a real character in this novel and a comic book character; he represents comics, an often denigrated form of art; he represents the passion of Joe and Sam (and, likely, Chabon himself) to foster greater appreciation for the art of the comic; he represents also how the comics industry has morphed and how the comic has, indeed, become a genre that is more widely accepted, analyzed, and valued. Incorporated into the novel is a great deal of the history of the comics industry and some inside jokes (e.g., a detective who appears near the end of the book is named Detective Lieber: Lieber was Stan Lee's name before he neutralized it to Lee).

A huge theme in this sprawling novel is that of escape.[17] Josef Kavalier, growing up in prewar Prague, apprentices himself to Bernard Kornblum to learn magic, and specifically to learn how to escape, Houdini-like, from handcuffs, locked cabinets, underwater confinement, and so forth. When the Nazis occupy Prague, Josef needs to engineer another kind of escape: one from the city itself. His family pools all their resources to buy him a train ticket and legal documents for travel to another country; in a typical Nazi move, the regulations are changed at the last minute, and Josef is denied permission to leave. Utterly dejected, he returns not to his family (Josef is unable to tell them about the failure, given their sacrifice) but to his teacher, Kornblum. In a remarkably convoluted and comics-inflected series of plot twists, Josef escapes Prague by riding out secretly in the coffin of Prague's golem, who is being sent for safekeeping to Vilna. From this first "death," Josef rises from the coffin, golem-like, and sets out on his own, traveling across eastern Europe, Asia, and the Pacific Ocean. Josef eventually arrives at the home of his cousin, Sam Clay, in Brooklyn, where they literally share a bed. Sharing a bed, the second time figuratively, will be one of the final gestures of the novel for this pair. Again golem-like, Josef undergoes a metamorphosis, dubbing himself with the American nickname Joe, learning the language, and apprenticing himself once again, this time as an illustrator for the burgeoning comic book industry. It is 1939.

Joe has dark premonitions about the future in Prague and his one goal in life is to bring his family—his father, mother, grandfather, and younger brother Tommy—to join him in America. That will require money. Joe and Sam decide to capitalize on the superhero craze in comics that followed the appearance of Superman in 1938 by creating a superhero of their own. Joe initially proposes a golem—after all, the golem has functioned as a superhero in the Jewish ghetto in Prague in latter-day incarnations of the legend. But this idea is nixed by Sheldon P. Anapol, the owner of Empire Novelty, which is soon to be Empire Comics. Even Sammy understands the obvious objection to the golem: "but, Joe . . . the Golem is . . . well . . . Jewish," Sam says (86, ellipsis in the original). So instead, the cousins create a Superman-like character whom they call, appropriately, the Escapist; the character becomes enormously popular and they do make money. (More than a slight parallel exists between Joe and Sam and the actual creators of Superman, Joe Shuster and Jerry Siegel, two Jewish kids from Cleveland. Later in the novel, the fact that Joe and Sam were swindled out of their fair share of profits for the Escapist by the Empire Comics corporation is emphasized; this is a clear echo of the way in which Shuster and Siegel were treated by Detective Comics, commonly known as DC.)[18] The Escapist heads the League of the Golden Key, dedicated to fighting oppression everywhere: "Such men roamed the world acting, always anonymously, to procure the freedom of others, whether physical or metaphysical, emotional or economic" (133). The League's primary foe is the Iron Chain, an underground organization whose goals "were opposite and sinister" (133) and found purchase in Germany in 1939. The Escapist is part Joe—a literal escapist and an idealist—and part Sam—American and walking with a limp as does their comic character Tom Mayflower until he morphs into the Escapist (Sam had polio as a child and has the same symbolic limp). As the Escapist series develops, Joe and Sam increasingly imagine the Escapist as the archenemy of Nazis, seeing their comics as a potent weapon on the side of the Allies in World War II. But despite Joe's best efforts, he loses his family: his father dies of illness; his mother and grandfather die in a camp (probably Terezin); and his brother dies when the ship on which he is sailing to America, sponsored by Joe, sinks after a U-Boat attack.

After his brother's death, Joe enlists in the navy and is stationed, much to his disappointment, about as far from the Nazis as possible: in the Antarctic.[19] Existing underground to escape the cold, Joe ultimately pulls off yet another daring escape, wounded, piloting a homemade airplane, to be rescued and ultimately to return to New York City at the close of World War II. There Joe holes up in the Empire State Building much of this time, writing a 2,200+-page comic manuscript on the golem—all illustrations, no text. He has thus returned to his original idea for a superhero. Sam, despite his growing recognition that he is gay, has been living with his wife, Rosa, and Tommy, who is Joe's biological son.[20] In this postwar period, Joe and Sam spend ten years separated. Through various disappointments and financial downturns (and hundreds of pages of plot twists), they finally reunite. As the novel ends, Sam accepts his homosexuality (not an easy feat in the 1950s) and Joe buys Empire Comics, now a failing enterprise in the aftermath of the Golden Age of the comics, with the hope of producing the golem series. They have managed a double escape: Joe from the solitary, hidden existence he was living to be reunited with Rosa, his "true love," and Sam from the "closet," with a train ticket in his pocket to Los Angeles and a hoped-for career in the movies.

The theme of escape is, of course, tied to the genre of comics, which is often sneeringly labeled by cultural elitists as "escape literature" (if the term "literature" is even used). Just as affirming the value of the genre of comics is one of the thrusts of *Kavalier and Clay*, so the reader is urged to discard old notions of high and low culture, of dichotomies between good literature and escape literature, to see that a book can be both. And, in the same vein, Chabon is urging readers and critics to accept the critical importance of the imagination and imaginative literature (in all its genres) in the post-Holocaust era. Some critics have simplistically reduced Chabon's valorization of comics to a formulaic acceptance of comics as pure escapism: "Chabon's novel explores a major moral and aesthetic issue . . . the fact that fantasy itself, no matter how disruptive . . . can give pleasure to an artist and an audience, and *that pleasure may be a distraction from the past* . . . his novel guardedly presents the idea that that distraction may be itself a valid response" (Behlman, 62, italics mine). This is a reductionist view of Chabon's novel: "pleasure" is never the goal of Kavalier and Clay's creation of the Escapist nor is distraction or pure "escape." The point of the Escapist series in the novel is rather to serve as a vehicle to arouse American awareness of the menace of Hitler in the pre-1941 period. Chabon's larger point is that denigrated genres, such as comics, have the often unrecognized capability to provide readers the frisson of pleasure which, in turn, induces awareness; that they can represent the "real" and that imaginative literature is a valid response to trauma. Marc Singer takes Behlman to task: "while Lee Behlman claims that Chabon's superhero comics are 'a form of fantasy that resolutely avoids the real' (57), Joe actually confronts the real by representing his political, familial, sexual, and artistic desires through hypostasis" (286). Chabon is actually endeavoring to accomplish something much more complicated than escape qua escape: to acknowledge the deeply conflicted debate about Holocaust representation and to weigh in against dichotomies and hierarchies (a structure particularly anathema to those who write on the Holocaust, which resulted from a society's embrace of spurious racial hierarchies). "*Kavalier and Clay* is a work of historical fiction that asks how one responds to or registers history—especially traumatic history—in a popular medium . . . Chabon suggests that trauma breaks the boundaries of form, mutating the very shape of representation" (Chute, 280, 286).

Chabon acknowledges that "I was a big comics reader when I was a kid, from about six to fifteen. I collected them, I read them, I even created my own characters in comics" (Weich). He also recalls tying a towel into a cape as he and a friend walked to the swimming pool when he was about ten, and "becoming" two superheroes, Dark Lord and Aztec (Binelli and Duffy).

He acknowledges that initially the seeming disparity of the elements in the novel was "scary," but:

> When I started writing about the golem, I trusted that it belonged in the book just as I trusted that escape artistry belonged. . . . There was something about the golem which tied in with Superman and the superhero figure, the messianic figure who would redeem the suffering and helplessness of the world. There was a Jewish element to all that, and the creators of all these golden age comic books, many of them were Jewish kids. When I started working the Houdini vein, very quickly I realized that escapism is always a charge leveled against comics: why would one want to waste time reading them? It all belonged together. (Weich)

Chabon signals to the reader in the first paragraph of the novel that his book will focus on the themes of mask/lies, escape, transformation/metamorphosis, comics, and the imagination. He sets up Sam, now a kind of comics patriarch attending the fictional equivalent of the annual comics extravaganza, Comic-Con International, reminiscing about the Golden Age of comics. Sam talks about how Clark Kent in the phone booth and Houdini in a packing crate "were one and the same thing. . . . It was never just a question of escape. It was also a question of *transformation*" (3, italics in original). The narrator interrupts to confide in the reader that, in fact, Sam did not care about Houdini that much, yet "his account of his role—of the role of his own imagination—in the Escapist's birth, like all his best fabulations, rang true" (3). The exploration of imagination and creativity in all their ramifications continues throughout the coming 600+ pages. When the narrator describes the moment of the Escapist's birth as a concept in Sam's head, the emphasis is placed on the liberating role of the imagination in our lives, on emotion, on chance, and on retrospective invention:

> Over the years . . . Sammy would devise and relate all manner of origin stories, fanciful and mundane and often conflicting, but it was out of a conjunction of desire, the buried memory of his father, and the chance illumination of a row-house window, that the Escapist was born. . . . Sammy felt an ache in his chest that turned out to be, as so often occurs when memory and desire conjoin with a transient effect of weather, the pang of creation. . . . It was, in part, a longing—common enough among the inventors of heroes—to be someone else. (112–13)

As he did in his essay in *Map and Legends,* Chabon is fusing here the act of artistic creation with that of golem creation.

Several pages later, the reader is introduced to the history of the Escapist. The opening of chapter 8 is a sleight of hand. Chabon typically changes scenes radically and rapidly from chapter to chapter. For example, in part 1, "The Escape Artist," chapter 1 takes place in Brooklyn in 1939, chapter 2 in Prague in 1938, and chapter 4 in Prague around 1900. Thus the reader initially takes the opening sentence of part 2, "A Couple of Boy Geniuses," chapter 8, as just part of the realistic frame of the novel: "The curtain itself is legendary: its dimensions, its weight, its darker-than-chocolate color, the Continental fineness of its stuff" (123). Gradually, however, we realize that we are inside the comic inside Chabon's novel, in an underground theater, and witnessing the actual birth of the Escapist. Tom Mayflower is having trouble with the equipment of escape artist Misterioso prior to the opening of a show; when it malfunctions, injuring Misterioso, Tom must be sure the "show goes on" so he performs the tricks and thus is born the Escapist. Initiated into the League of the Golden Key by the aging Misterioso, the Escapist vows to carry on its mission. The chapter ends by returning to Joe and Sam, who are walking past the theater where this scene supposedly just occurred, "dreaming their elaborate dream, wishing their wish, teasing their golem into life" (134).

By using only the sheerest of scrims here, Chabon models the collapsing of the dichotomies, eliminating distinctions between high and low culture, valorizing the comics. He performs a similar feat in part 3, "The Funny Book War," when, without warning, the reader is again plunged below ground, this time into Office 99 of the Empire City Public Library where we meet "Miss Judy Dark, Under Assistant Cataloguer of Decommissioned Volumes" (267). Again, it may take readers several paragraphs to realize we are witnessing the creation of another comic character, the Luna Moth (the moth, of course, being the perfect symbol of metamorphosis). Miss Judy Dark grows "an immense pair of swallowtailed moth's wings" (270), having been chosen to be the next Mistress of the Night by the moth goddess Lo. "I really think I'll need some clothes" (272), Judy Dark complains, Cinderella-like; to which the moth goddess replies: "You will find, Judy Dark, that you have only to imagine something to make it so. . . . Take care—there is no force more powerful than that of an unbridled imagination" (272). This declaration, which embraces the creation not only of clothes but also of comic book characters, golems, and Holocaust fiction, serves as a response to the deflation that Joe Kavalier has been feeling. Increasingly desperate to get his family out of Prague, in 1940 he hears a radio announcement that France's Jews are being transported to labor camps in Germany. This does not bode well for his own family in Nazi-occupied Prague, and suddenly all of his efforts to fight the Nazis vicariously through his character, the Escapist, seem in vain: "The Escapist was an impossible champion, ludicrous and above all *imaginary*, fighting a war that could never be won. His cheeks burned with embarrassment. He was wasting his time" (168, italics in original). As Marc Singer has noted, "The displacement of the real war onto its fictional analogue becomes insufficient, unsatisfying, and futile" (285). Despite the $7,000 that Joe has managed to save, visas are impossible to obtain and he is rendered largely impotent to save his family. But despair does not overtake Joe for long. After he and Sammy create storyboards for the Luna Moth, they approach their boss at Empire Comics with a proposal for a new series. Though Mr. Ashkenazy is impressed ("'Look at those . . . those . . .' 'They're called knockers,' said Anapol" [276]), a long negotiation ensues in which Ashkenazy demands that in return for accepting the Luna Moth character and raises for Joe and Sam, they must "lay off the Nazis for awhile" (285). This is the moment of truth for Joe and a lot of money hangs in the balance. But he refuses to eliminate the battle against Hitler from the Escapist series: "I believe in the power of my imagination. I believe . . . in the power of my art" (286).

Chabon talks in the 2007 postscript to his *Maps and Legends* essay on golems about the fact that some readers of *Kavalier and Clay* were convinced that Sam Clay and Joe Kavalier really existed, that *there really had been* a comics character name the Escapist, and "that somewhere out there you would be able to find and purchase old Escapist comic books. . . . These people wrote me letters and emails asking me how they could obtain such things" (221). He also mentions in an interview in *Rolling Stone* that he had offers to make the Escapist into a comic, but he declined due to time constraints (Binelli and Duffy). However, *there is an Escapist comic book series* and Michael Chabon is described therein as the Master of Ceremonies. So Chabon has actually crossed through that scrim to intertextually riff on his own creation in the form of these full-color comic books.

Chabon provides the introduction to volume 1 of *The Amazing Adventures of the Escapist,* as well as the first story, "The Passing of the Key," which is essentially an illustrated version of part 2, chapter 8 (described above) of *Kavalier and Clay,* the "origin story" of the Escapist, a classic opening gambit for a superhero story. This volume also includes a chapter titled "Escapism 101" written by one Malachi B. Cohen (an anagram of Michael Chabon). It presents a six-page history of Empire Comics and the fate of the Escapist from 1940 to the present. This entire volume acts as a kind of gloss on *Kavalier and Clay,* and of course, the reverse is true:

having read the novel brings a delicious frisson to reading the comic. All told, there are ten other stories in volume 1, written and illustrated by a variety of artists. Luna Moth makes her appearance in two stories that hew closely to her story in *Kavalier and Clay*. One reviewer asked, "Where are the Nazis?" implicitly demanding even more parallels between the novel and its offspring, the Escapist comic (Barsanti). In subsequent issues, such stories do appear; for example, "Heil and Fear Well" in volume 2. Other stories continue the themes of the novel: "The Death of the Escapist" in volume 3 is set in an evil dictatorship in Quodesia, an Asian country whose buildings sport huge posters of the Lenin-lookalike leader, who plots to kill the Escapist. Also in this volume is "The Escapist in a Fair to Remember," a story set in the Empire City's World's Fair; a key scene in Sam's journey to accepting his homosexuality occurs in the deserted World's Fair grounds in *Kavalier and Clay*.

And, of course, the entire Escapist series raises issues of fact and fiction, imagination and reality, truth and lies. Chabon opens his introduction by saying, "I still remember the first *Escapist* comic I ever came across" (*Escapist*, 1:4). Since we know that this character never existed in the real 1940s comics, we know our collective legs are being pulled. Ditto the spurious history of Empire Comics he presents under a pseudonym.[21] The back cover of the book represents a side-splitting parody of the kinds of advertisements that were found in 1940s comics. On offer are costumes for the Escapist, Omar, Luna Moth, and other characters from Chabon's novel and a coupon to be mailed in to obtain "free to all purchasers of this book" a midget radio (again, an intertextual reference to the novel, where such radios were one of the novelties offered by Empire Novelties before it became Empire Comics), as well as a "deluded sense of efficacy" and an "absentee father" (a reference to a theme in the novel). A one-inch by one-inch box offers a "Clay Lump: Silty earth of a fine, compact texture and consistency, allowing for formation into any shape or figure. Make your own collectibles, imaginary friends, heroes, idols, or just let dry into a hard rock. Specify grey, red, brown, tan or black. No. 74 Metaphor. . . . . FREE." An obvious nod to the golem, this is the only reference in the entire volume to this key theme of *Kavalier and Clay*. Volumes 2 and 3 carry similar parodies: both the front and back covers of volume 2 simulate "Stars of the Screen" cards, much like baseball cards; one such card depicts Chabon himself, identified as Malachi B. Cohen, who "made one small appearance as 'The Puppet Master' in the classic film 'Like a Moth to the Chains.'" The back cover of volume 3 offers kids the opportunity to "Create Chaos: Get Prizes with Fast Selling Seeds of Destruction." Prizes such as lunch boxes and action figures are pictured; kids only have to sell (the symbolically significant number of) 666 seed packages to qualify. Neither of these volumes features Chabon's writing (unless included under yet another pseudonym), but the storied Will Eisner made a contribution to volume 3, submitted shortly before his death in January 2005. This series was still issuing editions in 2009.[22]

Chabon's most recent novel, *The Yiddish Policemen's Union* (2007), continues his tradition of breaking boundaries among genres. Described as science fiction, mystery, and alternative history, the novel was nominated for two prizes for best crime fiction and won the Nebula Award for best sci-fi novel. Chabon was interviewed by the United States Holocaust Memorial Museum in its "Voices on Antisemitism" podcast series. Once again, he speaks to the role of the imagination in the post-Holocaust period:

> I think more than anything else the question that I've wrestled with in my own writing in terms of the Holocaust is how much of a right do I have to quote unquote "use" the Holocaust for fictional purposes? You know, is it okay for me to write about the Holocaust, having had no direct personal experience of it whatsoever? To what degree am I entitled to portray or represent it in my work?
>
> Ultimately, I'm trying to tell stories, and it's such an unconscious process of having a kind of image occur to me. Having a sort of wish or a desire or a longing or reading this Yiddish phrase book, *Say It in Yiddish: A Phrase Book for Travelers,* a Yiddish phrase book for travelers that was published in the late 1950s. And it was the source of inspiration for me to write *The Yiddish Policemen's Union,* but before that I wrote an essay trying to come to terms with the idea of a phrase book for travelers in Yiddish. Trying to address the question of where would you go with such a book? Where could you take it? To what destination would you travel with a Yiddish phrase book that told you how to do things like order a dental appliance in Yiddish, or something like that?
>
> I think in *The Yiddish Policemen's Union* I tried to use my imagination to undo at least some of the effects of the Holocaust, and to imagine a way out of the catastrophe. And again, I suspect that part of the force that drives that novel is the consciousness that ultimately that's a tragically futile *wish*.[23] (italics mine)

Thus, instead of reviling the idea of post-Holocaust imaginative literature, Chabon honors its potential usefulness for enabling us to recognize the Shoah's grievous losses (Yiddish being one of them), to instantiate memory of the People of the Book, and to endeavor to grasp what it tells us about humanity. By creating, as defined by Sidra Ezrahi, an alternative history, Chabon, like Pete Hamill, has interrogated the issue of representation and induced consciousness of what might have been; such counterhistory may serve as "the future's answer to the past" (Ezrahi, "Auschwitz," 136).

Chabon's focus on the imagination figures significantly in his most recent book, *Manhood for Amateurs: The Pleasures and Regrets of a Husband, Father, and Son.* Here he tells us what fired his own imagination during childhood (see, for example, "A Woman of Valor," an essay on comic book character Big Barda, one of many Amazons whom Chabon loved as a boy). He devotes a chapter to *Planet of the Apes,* a show he loved as a child and now acknowledges was "crap" (80). But it had "crucially, to my theory of what makes great mass art—the powerful quality of being open-ended, vague at the borders. . . . There was room for you and your imagination in the narrative map of the show" (80). In contrast to his own childhood are the childhoods of the twenty-first century, of his own four children, about which Chabon expresses his fears, lacking as these childhoods are in opportunities for nourishing the imagination: "Our children have become cult objects to us, too precious to be risked. . . . What is the impact of the closing down of the Wilderness on the development of children's imaginations? This is what I worry about the most. . . . Art is a form of exploration, of sailing off into the unknown alone, heading for those unmarked places on the map. If children are not permitted—not taught—to be adventurers and explorers as children, what will become of the world of adventure, of stories, of literature itself" (65–66). The very future of literature itself—for Chabon—is staked on the healthy development of the imagination.

I'd like to close this chapter with a rather long excerpt from *The Amazing Adventures of Kavalier and Clay,* as it speaks to the overarching theme of not only this book but of the other books explored in this chapter and indeed in *The Golem Redux* itself:

In literature and folklore, the significance and the fascination of golems—from Rabbi Loew's to Victor von Frankenstein's—lay in their soullessness, in their tireless inhuman strength, in their metaphorical association with overweening human ambition, and in the frightening ease with which they passed beyond the control of their horrified and admiring creators. But it seemed to Joe that none of these—Faustian hubris, least of all—were among the true reasons that impelled men, time after time, to hazard the making of golems. The shaping of a golem, to him, was a gesture of hope, offered against hope, in a time of desperation. It was the expression of a yearning that a few magic words and an artful hand might produce something— one poor, dumb, powerful thing—exempt from the crushing strictures, from the ills, cruelties, and inevitable failures of the greater Creation. It was the voicing of a vain wish, when you got down to it, to escape . . . into the mysterious sprit world that lay beyond. (584)

5

Golems to the Rescue

The golem, you see, has not been forgotten. It is still here.

I. L. Peretz, "The Golem"

As we saw in chapter 4, comic books of the 1930s and 1940s transformed the venerable Jewish tradition of the golem into Superman and other superheroes, and Marvel Comics returned to the trope of the heroic golem in the 1970s; the merging of the golem with comic images led, in turn, to such writers as James Sturm, Pete Hamill, and Michael Chabon. Writers of post-Holocaust fiction in the 1990s and early twenty-first century again appropriated the golem as a rescuer figure but this time without such comic associations. Cynthia Ozick's *The Puttermesser Papers* (1997) is set in New York City, a place that is literally and metaphorically gritty, the latter by virtue of political corruption. For the first time we have a woman character who creates a female golem, and she arrives with mighty ambitions for cleaning up the Big Apple. But her utopian visions go wrong in a most sobering manner; the Holocaust is the shadow of evil lurking behind this novel. With Thane Rosenbaum's *The Golems of Gotham* (2002), we encounter a story in which the Holocaust is central: Rosenbaum gives us no fewer than eight golems, most of them the ghosts of famous Holocaust survivors who took their own lives. Rosenbaum is a member of the Second Generation, the dominant theme of his novel, which explores literature and the imagination as tools for working through the trauma of post-memory. The impact of the Holocaust on one's family is the theme to be found again in a curious episode of *The X-Files* (1997) in which a Holocaust survivor from Prague brings Kabbalah, Jewish mysticism, and the golem tradition from the old country to Brooklyn.

This chapter concludes with a brief analysis of Daniel Handler's novel *Watch Your Mouth* (2000). Handler is also the child of Holocaust survivors; his vision of the world as harboring dark threats is embodied in his best-selling series for children, *A Series of Unfortunate Events* (written under the pseudonym Lemony Snicket); discovery of his bawdy golem novel will come as a surprise to some readers.

Cynthia Ozick, *The Puttermesser Papers* (1997)

"Not even the Maharal could make a woman out of clay," Kornblum said. "For that you need a rib."

Michael Chabon, *The Amazing Adventures of Kavalier and Clay*

The story itself is a golem, and we are right to be suspicious of it.

John Leonard, "Levitation"

With Cynthia Ozick we encounter a fiercely intellectual author who writes about the Holocaust almost as if against her will. Having agreed with Adorno and Wiesel that the notion of "Holocaust literature" verges on the obscene, Ozick nonetheless wrote one of the most compelling and widely read stories about the camps, "The Shawl," and another about the aftermath of the Shoah for survivors, "Rosa," which Joseph Lowin has insightfully called "a midrash on ['The Shawl'] . . . a rewriting" (*Cynthia Ozick,* 109).[1] Ozick, like Michael Chabon, is neither a survivor herself nor a member of the Second Generation. She has wrestled with the issues of agency and the authority to speak about the Holocaust. Unlike Aharon Appelfeld, for example, whose fiction is displaced, set on the edges of the Shoah in time and place, Ozick places "The Shawl" in the immediacy of a death camp, with all the attendant tropes of Nazi boots, barbed wire, and the killing of babies: "a highly focused, close-up rendition of concentration camp reality" (Friedrich, 94). Lillian Kremer has noted that "The Shawl" "marks the sole instance in which Ozick locates her fiction within the lice-infested, disease-ridden, death-dominated concentration camp universe and focuses exclusively on the gender-based Holocaust suffering of women and the murder of their innocent children" (*Women's Holocaust Writing,* 150).[2] Unlike "The Shawl," *The Puttermesser Papers,* Ozick's golem book, is set at a remove: in New York City in the 1970s.

After "The Shawl" was published (initially in *The New Yorker* in 1980), Ozick received a letter from a survivor who essentially told Ozick that she was "falsifying" and "desecrating" the Holocaust by writing about it without having actually experienced it. Ozick responded to the survivor with a passionate defense of her act of imagination:

> Every Jew should feel as if he himself came out of Egypt. . . . The Exodus took place 4000 years ago, and yet the *Haggadah* enjoins me to incorporate it into my own mind and flesh, to so act as if it happened directly and intensely to me, not as mere witness but as participant. Well, if I am enjoined to belong to an event that occurred 4000 years ago, how much more strongly am I obliged to belong to an event that occurred only 40 years ago. (Cohen, *Comic*, 148)

As Sarah Blacher Cohen notes, it is through the use of synecdoche in "The Shawl" that Ozick manages to convey so powerfully the "major torments of the *Shoah* experience" (*Comic*, 150).

In a 1987 roundtable in which Ozick participated (with Raul Hilberg, Aharon Appelfeld, and Saul Friedländer), she stated: "In theory, I'm with Theodor Adorno's famous dictum: After Auschwitz, no more poetry. And yet, my writing has touched on the Holocaust again and again. I cannot *not* write about it. It rises up and claims my furies" (Lang, 284, italics in original). Two years later she told a *New York Times* interviewer that she had put the manuscripts for both Shoah stories away in a drawer after writing them in 1977; quoting Ozick, the interviewer said: "The reason was her great abiding fear of 'making art out of the Holocaust,' of 'mytho-poeticizing, making little stories out of a torrent of truth. I worry very much that this subject is corrupted by fiction and that fiction in general corrupts history'" (Heron). By 1999, in an article in *Commentary*, Ozick had complicated the issue of Holocaust fiction. Titling her article "The Rights of History and the Rights of the Imagination," Ozick struggles with the question of whether there are/should be limits on imaginative fiction about the Holocaust. Ozick begins her closely argued essay by noting the differences between genres: "History is that which is owed to reality. Imagination—fiction—is freer than that; is freed altogether. . . . Imagination owes nothing to what we call reality; it owes nothing to history. The phrase 'historical novel' is mainly an oxymoron. History is rooted in document and archive. History is what we make out of memory. Fiction flees libraries and loves lies." Acknowledging that "impersonation" (i.e., creating a character that the author "enters" and becomes) is a prerogative of fiction, Ozick takes serious issue when "impersonation escapes the bounds of fiction and invades life." This, she says, we call a hoax or fraud, and she cites the by now infamous example of Binjamin Wilkomirski's *Fragments,* a text masquerading as a nonfiction Holocaust memoir that was revealed to have been entirely falsified. "What is permissible to the playfully ingenious author of *Robinson Crusoe*—fiction masking as chronicle—is not permitted to those who touch on the destruction of six million souls, and on the extirpation of their millennial civilization in Europe."

But what of the avowed Holocaust novel, Ozick proceeds to ask. She offers as a response an analysis of two such novels: William Styron's *Sophie's Choice* and Bernhard Schlink's *The Reader.* "What does the autonomy of the imagination owe to demographic datum?" Ozick explores how in each novel the main character defies the reality of demographics: Sophie is a Polish Catholic in Auschwitz of which there were only 75,000 of the 1.5 million murdered at that death camp; Hannah, in *The Reader,* is illiterate, in a nation renowned for its literacy rates, and "Illiteracy is her exculpation" for taking on the role of a Nazi death camp guard. Ozick condemns both novels for the misrepresentation of reality when they purport to be historically, factually based: "When a novel comes to us with the claim that it is directed consciously toward history, that the divide between history and the imagination is being purposefully bridged, that the bridging is the very point, and that the design of the novel is to put human flesh on historical notation, then the argument for fictional autonomy collapses, and the rights of history can begin to urge their own force."

Ozick, though a champion of the imagination, thus does put the brakes on its deployment where the Holocaust is concerned. When speaking to students at Yale University a few years ago, Ozick advised them to read all the nonfiction literature on the Holocaust before turning to "The Shawl" (Hungerford, 155). She feels some guilt that as a high school student during the Holocaust she was oblivious: "Like everyone else, I did not know what was happening; like everyone else, I required a dawning"; but now she has the knowledge and "knowledge makes everybody a witness" (Heron).

Ozick was born in 1928 in New York City to Russian Jewish immigrants. Joseph Lowin notes that Ozick's parents "came from the Litvak (Lithuanian) Jewish tradition . . . of skepticism, rationalism, and antimysticism" and that, though she calls herself "a *mitnagged,* an opponent of mystic religion, [i]n her stories, however, she wallows in mysticism" (*Ozick,* 2). We will certainly see this tendency in *The Puttermesser Papers.* The Ozicks owned a pharmacy where a typical workday lasted fourteen hours; as a young girl, Ozick contributed by delivering prescriptions and working at the counter. One of the stories she consistently tells about her parents is their refusal, in the 1930s, to sell Bayer aspirin in the store, despite the constant request from customers for this name brand (and the subsequent loss of those customers' business). Their reason for this refusal was the German origin of Bayer. Even before the Holocaust reached its height in 1942, Ozick's parents had properly sized up the threat that Hitler posed, and their protest made a significant impact on their daughter. She continues this protest by refusing to buy German products or to accept invitations to speak in Germany, terming this her "private memorial" for the six million (Lang, 282).

Ozick began attending *cheder* at age five and a half; despite the fact that the rabbi dismissed her with the admonition "Take her home; a girl doesn't have to study," her grandmother brought her back, enabling her to learn Yiddish and Hebrew (Lowin, *Ozick*, 3). This was the epiphany that made her a feminist.[3] Ozick experienced persistent antisemitism in elementary school. Her escape was reading, and she determined at an early age to become a writer. Asked about her childhood reading, she mentions Alcott's *Little Women:* "Like every other little girl, I identified with Jo, and knew I was going to be a writer, and longed to do what Jo did, which was to write for money and put down a new carpet" (Frumkes, 18). After attending New York University in Greenwich Village and graduating cum laude, Phi Beta Kappa in 1949 with a degree in English, Ozick earned an M.A. in English from Ohio State University in 1950 where she wrote a thesis titled "Parable in the Later Novels of Henry James." She describes herself as an "autodidact" in the years immediately after graduate school: "I was 22—[I] sat down and read 16 hours a day. I went to the public library and came back with heaps of books. I was filling in the gaps" (Frumkes, 18). The range of her reading is quite astounding: fiction from England, Russia, France, and America, literary criticism, history, philosophy, and Heinrich Graetz's *The History of the Jews* in six volumes. Of this book, Ozick said: "It has an anti-mystical point of view, which happens to be mine also. I feel myself to be a rationalist, except in fiction, where I do like magic and folklore" (Frumkes, 18). This predilection for folklore she explores in full in *The Puttermesser Papers*. In 1952 she married Bernard Hallote, who would be employed as an attorney for New York City as Ruth Puttermesser is. In what was very unusual for a woman in the 1950s, Ozick waited thirteen years before having a child, Rachel, in 1965. In that interval she began to write seriously and also commercially, for Filene's Department Store in Boston. Her first novel, *Trust,* was published in 1966, followed by *The Cannibal Galaxy* in 1983, *The Messiah of Stockholm* in 1987, *The Shawl* in 1989, and *The Puttermesser Papers* in 1997. The latter two volumes had had earlier publications as short stories. Ozick has also published seven volumes of short stories and seven volumes of essays. *Heir to the Glimmering World* appeared in 2004; narrated in the first person by Rose Meadows, the novel tells the story of her entry into the lives of the tumultuous Mitwisser family, refugees from Hitler brought to America in the 1930s by the Quakers after expulsion from academia in Germany. Her most recent novel, *Foreign Bodies* (2010), is yet another intertextual tour de force, this one in conversation with Henry James's magisterial novel *The Ambassadors*. Despite what Ozick considers her late start by publishing her first novel at the age of thirty-seven, she has won many literary awards as well as a Guggenheim Fellowship and the American Academy of Arts and Letters Straus Living Award (which carried an annual stipend of $35,000 for five years).

Given her voracious reading habits, it is not surprising that intertextuality is a frequent gesture in Ozick's work. In addition to the observation mentioned above that "Rosa" serves as an intertext of "The Shawl," scholars have commented on the likelihood that Susan Fromberg Schaeffer's *Anya* served as an intertext for the story.[4] Ozick has acknowledged that it was a line from William Shirer's *The Rise and Fall of the Third Reich* that engendered "The Shawl" (Heron). Her novel *The Messiah of Stockholm* references the Polish writer Bruno Schulz, who was murdered by a Nazi in 1942, and her short story "Envy" references Isaac Bashevis Singer.

It is intertextuality with the centuries-old golem legend that informs *The Puttermesser Papers*. Published as it was in 1997,[5] two decades after the publication of *The Pentagon Papers*, Ozick's title tempts one to make a comparison: the title has the scent of politics and of the archive, of secrecy and revelation. And, indeed, New York City politics do play a large role in the story. The sense of nonfiction and biography is enhanced by the title of part 1: "Puttermesser: Her Work History, Her Ancestry, Her Afterlife." But this is no "historical novel." Ozick makes it clear very early in the text that she is writing a series of interlinked stories with fantasy threaded throughout, and this exonerates her from the strictures that she discussed in the *Commentary* essay. Thus a frisson is established between the title and setting, on the one hand, and the use of the golem legend on the other. How Ozick merges and blurs these two forms is part of the genius of the text. James Gardner has applied the label "postmodernist" to this aspect of Ozick's work: "The conjunction of the miraculous and the everyday, which causes ["Puttermesser and Xanthippe"] to seem so postmodern, recalls both the magic realism of South American writers and that deep vein of fable in Jewish tradition that stretches all the way from the Talmud to Franz Kafka and Bruno Schulz." Richard Bernstein also discerns a "clash" in the novel between a "sharply satirical commentary on contemporary urban life" and a "reworking of an ancient, mystical, redemptive, Jewish legend." This clash results, he says, in a novel that seems to be unsure what it is: "a modern tale of the supernatural or a naturalistic tale of the modern."

Our story opens with an introduction to Ruth Puttermesser, who is a thirty-four-year-old attorney living in the Bronx; she graduated summa cum laude, Phi Beta Kappa from Barnard with a major in history and was the editor-in-chief of the *Yale Law Review.* Puttermesser is Yiddish for "butterknife," and Ozick explained that she called her main character Puttermesser because "like a butterknife, she doesn't have a very sharp cutting edge. She's ineffectual but fanatically intellectual" (Frumkes, 18). The fact that she is so intellectual and that Ozick gave her the age of thirty-four when Ozick herself was thirty-four as she began to write the story and that both are of Russian Jewish descent suggests more than a little "impersonation" between author and character.[6] Despite Puttermesser's illustrious career as a student, her law firm discriminates against her as a woman and as a Jew; she studies Hebrew in her spare time with Uncle Zindel (who has been dead several years, our first clue that this will not be a novel representing reality). Ozick establishes promptly the themes of texts, of the alphabet, and of the Hebrew language that is always essential to creating a golem. We are told that Puttermesser studies Hebrew grammar in bed and it "elates" her: "it seemed to her not so much a language for expression as a code for the world's design, indissoluble, predetermined, translucent" (5). Thus the fecund power of language is emphasized, the act of studying in bed linking Hebrew to sexuality and creativity. This link between language and birth is reiterated when the narrator provides a description of the pedagogical method of Uncle Zindel. He eats an egg while giving Puttermesser a mnemonic device for remembering certain Hebrew letters: "Mrs. *Zayen* pregnant in one direction, Mrs. *Gimel* in the other" (16).[7]

We learn that Puttermesser is a voracious reader; references to texts in her head and texts she wants to read abound; she quotes Anatole France on Dreyfus (7). Puttermesser has a dream of what Eden would be like: an infinite supply of fudge at her left hand, an infinite supply of books at her right, an infinite supply of time to sit under a tree and consume both. She yearns to read an unlimited list of books: "anthropology, zoology, physical chemistry, philosophy . . . about quarks, about primate sign language, theories of the origins of the races, religions of ancient civilizations, what Stonehenge meant" (13–14). And after the nonfiction, she'll start on the fiction: all of Balzac, Dickens, Turgenev, and Dostoevsky; *The Magic Mountain, The Faerie Queen, The Ring and the Book;* biographies of Beatrix Potter, and Walter Scott and Lytton Strachey (14) and more—her appetite for texts is insatiable.

Just as the reader is becoming comfortable with who Puttermesser is and with the third person, omniscient narration, we are suddenly interrupted. "Stop. Stop, stop! Puttermesser's biographer, stop! Though it is true that biographies are invented, not recorded, here you invent too much. A symbol is allowed, but not a whole scene" (16). So another kind of frisson is interjected, a tension among the multiple tellers of the tale. "The scene with Uncle Zindel did not occur," we are told twice (18). This new narrator, speaking in the second person, chides the first narrator to return to the "real" story of Puttermesser at her job at the government office of Receipts and Disbursements and quit with the fantasy of her lessons with Uncle Zindel, who died four years before she was born. "Hey! Puttermesser's biographer! What will you do with her now?" (19), this new voice teases at the end of part 1, calling attention to the "lie" that has been told to the reader, to the blurring of boundaries of nonfiction and fantasy, and thus creating a metafiction.

Twelve years have passed as part 2 of the novel, titled "Puttermesser and Xanthippe," begins with section 1, "Puttermesser's Brief Love Life, Her Troubles, Her Titles." Puttermesser, now forty-six (and, again, the age of Ozick when she wrote this story), is reading in bed. The night prior to the opening scene, she had read aloud to her lover, Morris Rappoport, a passage from Plato's *Theaetetus* on the nature, powers, and properties of man that distinguish him from other beings, a kind of foreshadowing of the golem creation that will occur shortly. Now, in bed, Puttermesser is eager to finish the *Theaetetus*, and Rappoport, a married man from Toronto, decides to walk out on her since she obviously prefers her book to sex with him. Puttermesser equates the loss of Rappoport with the recently discovered bone loss in her jaw (she has periodontal disease) and with the loss of her home in the Bronx to arson. Her periodontal disease is a synecdoche, one critic has claimed, for the imperfectability of humanity; significantly, the mouth is traditionally where a golem holds a piece of paper with the name of G-d inscribed on it.[8] It can also be read as a loss of "roots" in the sense of Zadie Smith's *White Teeth*, a loss of her traditions, her ancestry; the fire represents an additional loss: "her shoes were ash, her piano was ash, her piano teacher's 'Excellent' written in fine large letters at the top of 'Humoresque' . . . had vanished among the cinders" (25), a Holocaust reference. As if to re/create generations, Puttermesser fills her new apartment with plants that she grows herself from seed: "Every window sill . . . was fringed with fronds, foliage, soaring or drooping leaf-tips" (26). Yet her work life is "arid" (26); a new boss, the eponymous Alvin Turtelman, has arrived, with his patience and his "steady ogle" (27). Her office becomes a perfect exemplar of a Kafkaesque bureaucracy. Injecting more intertexts by comparing the environment to a fairy tale and envisioning herself as Alice in Wonderland, Puttermesser is dismayed at the "spoils quota" (28) that is the operating principle of the office; she begins to dream of "an ideal Civil Service" where the motto would be "justice, justice shalt thou pursue" (30).

As section 2, "Puttermesser's Fall, and the History of the Genus Golem," begins, our heroine is called into Turtelman's office and summarily informed that she is being fired. After a mild protest on her part, Turtelman relents, instead relegating her to a windowless cubicle and replacing her with an old classmate, Adam Marmel, and then assigning her to a low rank in the taxation department. In the few pages just preceding the arrival of the golem in Puttermesser's apartment, Ozick includes intertexts of various kinds, a foreshadowing of the role of texts in the generative act of creating the golem. First there is the entire text of a letter Puttermesser writes to the mayor of New York City, one Malachy Mavett,[9] complaining about the shabby treatment she has received from Turtelman. She points out the hypocrisy of the language used by Turtelman, accusing him of making appointments on the basis of "getting the spoils": "Power and connections are never called power and connections. They are called principle. . . . They are called restructuring. They are called exigency. . . . They are called government" (34). Ozick thus points out the proclivity of bureaucrats to lie; lies exist not only as/in fiction but in "reality" as well, a nod to the controversy over Holocaust fiction. The next reference to a text is to a novel titled *Pyke's Pique*, "an obscure book no one had ever heard of, published by a shadowy California press" (35). One of Puttermesser's colleagues, Leon Cracow, has, without an ounce of evidence, decided that the main character of the book is a caricature of him and is suing the author for defamation.[10] Puttermesser eggs him on because she "believed in the uses of fantasy," a sly and comic reference to the pastiche of her own text and the imminent appearance of the fantastic golem. When Cracow asks Puttermesser to accompany him on a date, her mind slides toward the unhappy prospect of remaining single and childless: "Sometimes the thought that she would never give birth tore at her heart. She imagined daughters" (36).

Sunday morning, Puttermesser rises from bed to retrieve Sunday's edition of the *New York Times* and return to read it between the sheets. She is still thinking about daughters and yet another text, Goethe's *Erlkönig*. When she returns to her bed, she is startled to find a naked girl lying there; the link with the line she has quoted from Goethe is unmistakable: " '*In seinem Armen das Kind war tot.*' . . . She looked dead—she was all white, bloodless. . . . A small white square was visible on her tongue" (37). This is, of course, the *shem* that carries the name of God and in many golem stories is the means of activating and deactivating the clay figure. In several riveting paragraphs, Ozick recounts the circling of the bed that Puttermesser does in wonder and confusion, thinking perhaps this is a junkie or prostitute who has somehow slipped into her apartment (this is, of course, the required ritual circling performed to infuse life into the clay figure). Touching the girl, Puttermesser finds a reddish powder—clay—on her hand; she pokes at the figure's face and hand to provide a more perfect shape to the creature. Taking the white square of paper to the window to read the inscription, Puttermesser notes that all of her flowerpots have been upended and emptied of dirt; the piece of paper "was a single primeval Hebrew word, shimmering with its lightning holiness, the Name of Names, that which one dare not take in vain" (40). Puttermesser speaks the name aloud and the creature leaps from the bed and finishes forming, growing fingernails and eyelashes and dark red hair "the color of clay" (40). Puttermesser provides her with clothing. The golem grabs a notebook and pen and begins to scribble: as is the tradition, she is unable to speak. She writes: "My mother" (41), further confusing Puttermesser, who has not quite grasped yet that she has unwittingly created a golem. Puttermesser names her Leah, but the creature insists upon being called Xanthippe, the name of Socrates' wife.

At this point in the novel, Ozick launches into a dense five-page recapitulation of the history of the golem through the vehicle of Puttermesser, who dives into a two-volume study of golems that she has read many times before. For the reader who may be unaware of the tradition, Ozick leaves no room for doubt about her intertextual appropriation. Puttermesser contradicts Xanthippe's claim that she is the first female golem by recounting the story of the medieval Spanish mystic, Ibn Gabirol, who is said to have created a female golem from wood and hinges to work as his servant. "That was not a true golem," Xanthippe saucily replies (43). One of the books Puttermesser consults is clearly Chayim Bloch's *The Golem: Legends of the Ghetto Prague*, easily identifiable as Ozick provides the publication date and place as Austria, 1925 (43). (Since Ozick composed this section of *The Puttermesser Papers*, Bloch's work has been revealed to be derivative of Yudl Rosenberg's *Golem and the Wondrous Deeds of the Maharal of Prague* [1909] and thus has been largely discredited.)[11] The narrator tells us that "Puttermesser's intelligence was brambly with the confusion of too much history. . . . She had pruned out allegory, metaphor; Puttermesser was no mystic, enthusiast, pneumaticist, ecstatic, kabbalist" (44); this comment emphasizes the division between historical and imaginary texts as discussed in Ozick's (later) *Commentary* essay. And in being a "rationalist" (44), the narrator tells us, Puttermesser is like the creator of the most famous golem, Rabbi Judah Loew, who was "a reasonable man of biting understanding, a solid scholar, a pragmatic leader" (44). In recapitulating the process by which Rabbi Loew formed the golem, Ozick relies heavily on Bloch's text, often quoting verbatim. Thus she links the creation of the golem to the blood libel, which we now know was an anachronism. Piling on the intertexts, Ozick goes even further back to the golems of Rabbi Rava and Rabbi Eleazar of Worms, to the mention of *The Book of Creation,* Paracelsus's homunculus, and finally forward to Gershom Scholem's famous essay "The Idea of the Golem" (46–48). The reader comes away suitably impressed with Puttermesser's scholarly knowledge of the golem; Puttermesser, having reviewed this history, accepts herself as a golem-maker because she notes that earlier such creators "were, by and large, scientific realists" (48). So, once again, Ozick reminds us of the divide between history and imagination, rather ironically as she valorizes the former while actually writing in the latter mode.

Section 3, "The Golem Cooks, Cleans, and Shops," follows the traditional tropes of the golem as servant, as Xanthippe performs these tasks for Puttermesser. But Xanthippe is discontented and writes notes to Puttermesser: "I can have uses far beyond the mere domestic" (49), and "I need a wider world. . . . Take me with you to your place of employment" (53). Thus the stage is set for another common trope in golem stories: the golem's transition from servant to crusader against antisemitism, to reformer, to hero. So Puttermesser duly takes Xanthippe to the office, where the golem types a mysterious document intently all day and where, by the end of section 4, "Xanthippe at Work," Puttermesser is summarily fired. Which brings us to section 5, "Why the Golem Was Created: Puttermesser's Purpose."

In her newly found leisure and her bitterness about the culture of political spoils that caused her to be fired, Puttermesser begins to contemplate a better world, a better New York City. Again, the parallel with Rabbi Loew is reified: "Ah, how this idea glowed for Puttermesser! The civic reforms of Prague—the broad, crannied city of Prague. . . . All that manifold urban shimmer choked off by evil corruption, the blood libel, the strong dampened hearts of wicked politicos" (63). Puttermesser conceives a vision of New York as a paradise, "a city washed pure" (64), over against her perception of the decay and decline of the city in the late 1970s. The golem has already conceived a PLAN: to get Puttermesser elected mayor of New York; this is the document she has been typing and Puttermesser sits down to read it. In a flash/flashback of insight, Puttermesser remembers now that *she had created* the golem and how she had gone about that task. Having set down the *New York Times* with its "record of multiple chaos and urban misfortune" (66), she went to work, and now, belatedly, she recognizes that she did so "because of the wilderness inside" the newspaper (66): "Her craving was to cleanse the wilderness; her craving was to excise every black instance of injustice; her craving was to erase outrage" (66–67).

Joseph Lowin has asserted that one of the major themes of *The Puttermesser Papers* is the "repair of the world" (*Ozick*, 122–43), what is sometimes termed *tikkun olam*, a uniquely Jewish notion that embraces the idea of social justice and the role of art in achieving both social change and memorialization. The sense of social responsibility toward others is at the heart of the notion of *tikkun olam*. The term carries the sense of mending, healing, or perfecting the world, and it appears as early as the fourth century C.E. Emil Fackenheim, a leading twentieth-century Jewish philosopher and theologian, proposed the idea of a new *tikkun* for the post-Holocaust period, a *tikkun* that focuses on witness and survival after the profound rupture of the Shoah (Suomala, 120).

In an epiphany, Puttermesser realizes that she is the author of the "PLAN for the Resuscitation, Reformation, Reinvigoration, & Redemption of the City of New York" (67) and that the golem has been her amanuensis. Again a trope common in golem stories, Xanthippe is depicted as Puttermesser's doppelgänger: "I express you. I copy and record you," Xanthippe tells her (67). So we see that the golem has emerged from a text (*New York Times*) and is, in turn, the recorder of Puttermesser's text. Xanthippe is the very embodiment of intertextuality: she is the trope, the text that is re-created with each new golem story. With Xanthippe as her tireless campaign manager (a Xanthippe who now seems suddenly to be growing in stature and who sports the word *emet* spelled out on her forehead in freckles), Puttermesser is, within two pages, elected mayor of New York City, a position that enables her to put into place reforms to "mend the world." "Justice, justice shalt thou pursue" (72) becomes her mantra. Just as Rabbi Loew does with his golem, Joseph, Puttermesser sends Xanthippe out into the urban wilderness to serve as a spy. And then the reforms begin, some so improbable that they are remarkably funny: lost wallets are always returned with cash and cards intact, and gangs magically wash subway cars clean at night and dance in Central Park by day with crowns of clover on their heads. Gardens and books become prominent features of the new city, reminiscent of Puttermesser's vision of paradise. Streets are turned into garden rows, hawkers sell books from wheelbarrows, schoolchildren build bookshelves, and a poet composes a poem for each burial of an unknown body in Potter's Field. Due process and "visionary hearts" replace the rapaciousness and spoils quota as the order of the day in government offices. "The Bureau of Venereal Disease Control has closed down. The ex-pimps are learning computer skills" (78).

But a slight worry begins to creep into Puttermesser's mind: who is the true golem, she or Xanthippe? Puttermesser comes to see "that she is the golem's golem" (79) (a kind of doubling of the doppelgänger effect). And here utopia begins to unravel. Rappoport, her former lover, appears suddenly in Gracie Mansion where Puttermesser and Xanthippe live; staying for dinner, he ends up in bed with Xanthippe, whose sexual appetite grows out of bounds as does her body, so large now she must sew together sheets to create a kind of toga for clothing. Ozick first published "Puttermesser and Xanthippe," which she wrote in the 1970s, in *Salmagundi* in 1982; it is intriguing to recall that 1982 was also the publication date of Isaac Bashevis Singer's *The Golem,* an incarnation of the legendary figure who also grows physically and lustfully. And just as Singer's golem wants the girl Miriam and an independent existence of his own, Xanthippe declares: "I want a life of my own. My blood is hot" (84). Declaring that she has worn Rappoport out, Xanthippe begins to disappear for days at a time, visiting men from Puttermesser's past—Turtelman, former Mayor Mavett, and others. "The golem will no longer obey. She cannot be contained" (86), Puttermesser realizes. Likening herself to Rabbi Loew, Puttermesser wonders how long he waited when his golem began to "run amok." The paradise Puttermesser has created is disrupted and drains away: "O lost New York! . . . Xanthippe ravishes prestigious trustees, committee chairmen, council members. . . . Sex! Sex! The golem wants sex! . . . Mayor Puttermesser is finished. . . . The golem has destroyed her utterly" (86–87). As Anolik notes, "Xanthippe's rampant sexuality [is] the cause of Puttermesser's downfall (reminding the reader that Puttermesser's is not the first Paradise to be lost by female appetite.) . . . The golem ravishes every commissioner of Puttermesser's utopian government; succubus-like, she drains them of their powers" (46–47).

And so, as in many versions of the golem legend, Puttermesser is faced with the problem of how to dispatch Xanthippe. She chides herself: her intertextual knowledge should have served as a warning: "[H]adn't she read in her books, a thousand times, that a golem will at length undo its creator? The turning against the creator is an attribute of the golem, comparable to its speechlessness, its incapacity for procreation, its soullessness. A golem has no soul, therefore cannot die—rather, it is returned to the elements of its making" (88). She sets a trap for Xanthippe by calling upon Rappoport to lie in wait in Xanthippe's commodious bed; in return, she offers Rappoport a government post, thus stooping to political favors, a corruption she had swept clean in her reforms.

The snare works and Puttermesser and Rappoport duly reverse the process of creation to return the golem to the elements. This reversal includes ritually walking around the golem counterclockwise seven times and summoning evil rather than pure thoughts. Puttermesser thinks "of City filth, of mugging, of robbery, arson, assault, even murder. Murder!" (97). These thoughts serve as a chilling foreboding of Puttermesser's own demise. Suddenly, as her life runs out, the golem finds a voice and speaks, pleading for "Life! Life! More!" (98) to which Puttermesser bitterly responds: "Too much paradise is greed. Eden disintegrates from too much Eden. Eden sinks from a surfeit of itself" (99). The urge to create an Eden is unattainable, finally, and Ozick issues a caveat to her readers: ideological efforts such as fascism and communism, purporting to create heaven on earth, are doomed to fail precisely because of their desire for homogeneity and perfection, for more paradise. As the Czech Holocaust survivor Ivan Klima has said: "There is no idea in the world good enough to justify a fanatical attempt to implement it. The only hope for salvation of the world in our time is tolerance" (26–27). Rappoport makes the final deathly stroke by scraping the *aleph* from Xanthippe's forehead, leaving the word *met*, death, inscribed there. Xanthippe's clay remains are consigned to the blood-red geranium flowerbed outside Gracie Mansion.

In the final three chapters of *The Puttermesser Papers*, Ozick retains her emphasis on intertextuality in humorous and innovative ways. Chapter 3, "Puttermesser Paired," invokes the story of the Victorian novelist Mary Ann Evans, aka George Eliot. Puttermesser, unemployed again as her stint as mayor has ended in failure, begins to read the personal ads: "What she was concentrating on was marriage: the marriage of true minds" (111). She also reads a biography of George Eliot and finds in Eliot's long-term partnership with George Lewes, already a married man, the ideal romantic relationship.

Puttermesser meets one Rupert Rabeeno, first at a party and then by happenstance in the Metropolitan Museum of Art where he is making a copy of a painting titled *The Death of Socrates*.[12] Thus Ozick interjects more intertextual references, one to Socrates, whose wife was named Xanthippe, and another one that Ozick interrogates by having her two characters argue. Puttermesser claims that Rupert is making a copy; he insists "It's the act I care about. I don't copy. I reenact" (125–26). This debate becomes even more pointed when Puttermesser learns that Rabeeno has his copies photographed and then sold as postcards in bookstores around New York. What is "real" and what is "imitation" is at issue: what is the text and what is the intertext?

Wanting to see Rabeeno as a "simulacrum of George Lewes" (132), Puttermesser yet worries about the age difference of two decades between them. Nonetheless, they read books together, often books by and about Eliot, and eventually Rabeeno proposes marriage. The pair plan their honeymoon, which, of course, is to be a replica of Eliot's honeymoon—not with the married George Lewes but rather with Johnny Cross, a man two decades her junior, whom Eliot actually did marry after Lewes's death. Cross, asserts Rupert, "was going to be Lewes for [Eliot]. A reasonable facsimile" (144). So now the reader has three layers on this particular palimpsest: Rupert (Ozick's character) imitating Cross who was imitating/replacing Lewes. Ozick has created a clever and very funny parody of the whole notion of intertextuality and simulacrum. Indeed, it is all so dizzying that one begins to question the reality of Rupert himself and all that follows in the story. The reader's nagging doubt is enhanced by this passage from Puttermesser's ponderings on her wedding night: "he seemed new-made—as if she had ejected him from a secret spectral egg lodged in her frontal lobe, or under her tongue where the sour saliva gave birth to desire" (163). Perhaps not a golem—but the production of Puttermesser's imagination nonetheless. And with that, Rupert walks out of the apartment door, disappears into the snowy night, and the reader is left to question: was he real or imaginary? A copyist or a copy? Of Lewes? Of Cross? A character from Puttermesser's imagination or Ozick's?

"Puttermesser and the Moscovite Cousin," the fourth installment in Puttermesser's saga, also raises questions of copies and conceptions. Puttermesser, now "white-haired, in her sixties—retired, *unmarried* [so perhaps Rabeeno was a mirage?], cranky in the way of a woman alone" (170, italics mine), is still living in New York; it is, we are told, the ninth decade of the twentieth century, just before the fall of communism. Historically, this period saw a large Russian Jewish population fleeing antisemitism and immigrating to the United States. Puttermesser agrees to host her father's Russian relative, Lidia, who is thirty-three years old and a lab technician for Soviet sports teams. Lidia and Puttermesser soon find themselves at cross-purposes. Puttermesser, recalling accusations of blood libel in Russia in the early twentieth century, sees herself as "saving" Lidia. Lidia, however, is all about entrepreneurial endeavors, claiming never to have heard of the blood libel. Lidia lands a job as a nanny and housekeeper for a neighbor of Puttermesser's; meanwhile, she leaves a terrible tangle of her own things in Puttermesser's apartment. She acquires an American boyfriend and, through him, fences Russian memorabilia, making a sizable amount of cash. Ozick introduces a very funny intertextual subplot about one Schuyler "Sky" Hartstein (heart of stone), who has founded a periodical titled *Shekhina:* "a mixture of global utopianism and strenuous self-gratulation" [192]).[13] Puttermesser cancels her subscription after a year, but a list of the dozen other journals she reads regularly is included in the story. *Shekhina*, a Hebrew word for "dwelling," also carries implications of the feminine attributes of the divine and has a special place in Kabbalah.[14] So, though Ozick does not introduce a golem in this story, she references the mystical aspects of Judaism and parodies their appropriation by self-serving idealists. In the end, lovely Lidia boards a plane for Sakhalin, ignoring all of Puttermesser's generous and well-meant gestures to obtain legal refugee status for her. Sakhalin, a Russian island in the North Pacific, holds the promise of more entrepreneurial opportunities, as a letter from Lidia's mother to Puttermesser, the final text of the story, makes clear. Paleolithic mammoth tusks have been dug up there and Lidia, though "somewhat doubtful about their authenticity" (209), relocates with her Russian boyfriend to capitalize on them. She leaves behind Pyotr, an innocent from North Dakota who helped her sell her Russian wares and whose child she carries. She has told her mother that Pyotr "sells icons for a living (but they are of course only reproductions)" (210), when, in point of fact, Pyotr has a sporting goods store where Lidia set up shop.

The final chapter in the book, "Puttermesser in Paradise," is a mirror image, an intertext, a midrash on "Puttermesser and Xanthippe." As this chapter opens, we once again find Puttermesser reading in bed in her apartment in New York City. Indeed, the opening sentence of this chapter is the opening sentence of Thomas Mann's *Joseph and His Brothers,* a 1,400-page intertextual novel based on the biblical story of Joseph; Mann wrote it in four parts between the late 1920s and 1943; it was his primary literary task during the Third Reich. Puttermesser, now almost seventy years old, is, we are told, "one moment before her death" (213). Just as Xanthippe began, as all golems do, with letters and words, so Puttermesser contemplates the Hebrew word *pardes,* meaning "orchard . . . garden . . . Paradise" (213) as she is about to expire. She is also thinking of all the puns one could make on writers' names, just as her own name signifies "butterknife": "the poet Wordsworth giving exact value for each syllable. . . . Joyce's Molly rejoicing. Bellow fanning the fires" (214), and many more.

An intruder enters her apartment, carrying not a butterknife but a genuine weapon of a knife. In six excruciatingly detailed and grisly pages, Ozick recounts his demands for jewelry and other items of value that Puttermesser does not have; his use of the knife to murder her; and his subsequent necrophiliac rape. The reader, who has become fond of Puttermesser, recoils. While one critic has taken Ozick to task for this "cruel" treatment of her heroine (Katz), another has noted that her murder is "a sign of judgment on the world at large, New York City in particular," and that Ozick promptly transports Puttermesser to paradise and bestows upon her "the ability to rewrite the script of her life, her last golem/double" (Sivan, 55). As readers, we follow Puttermesser in Ozick's imagined afterlife.

Initially Ozick defines paradise in terms of what it is not: it has "no gate . . . no before or after . . . no up or down . . . no happy or sad . . . no hours, minutes, or seconds" (220). What it does have are neighborhoods with theaters and poetry readings and people Puttermesser knows to be still alive. "Paradise was the place—though it was not exactly a *place*—**where she could walk freely inside her imagination**, and call up anything she desired" (222, boldface mine). So while this is not the Eden that Puttermesser had envisioned with infinite books, chocolate, and time, it is freedom from her reliance on rationality and freedom to call up "the lost, the missing, the wished-for" (222). She summons a first love whom she had lost, a college boy who "as a child of eleven or twelve . . . had fled from Hitler's Germany with his parents" (223). The story of her painful rejection by this young man, Emil, is told in the form of a flashback in which the two argue about the relationship of religion and art, a focus of Ozick as a Jewish American writer. The flashback concludes with mention of Emil's wedding to another woman and then the declaration: "In Paradise [Puttermesser] married him" (232). This second fantasy marriage of the novel results in the birth of a son whose skin is "silken gold" (233).

But the intellectual Ozick is not content to leave it at that; the Ozick who has looked deep into the abyss of the Shoah cannot countenance such a blissful conclusion to this novel about creativity, greed, deceit, *tikkun olam,* and the role of the imagination in our lives. Paradoxically, because the paradise she has created for Puttermesser has no time, "nothing is permanent. . . . Paradise is a dream bearing the inscription on Solomon's seal: *this too will pass.* And that is the secret meaning of Paradise: Solomon's truth. . . . The secret meaning of Paradise is that it too is hell" (234). Thus, Puttermesser loses her husband and son and as she walks through Paradise, she is confronted with "loss and tragedy and heartbreak" (235). She sees Charles Dickens led back to the blacking factory and Henry James about to suffer humiliation from his failed play. Worst of all, "[s]he sees the alphabet fleeing from having been invented" (235). Time flies backward and the means of creativity—letters—endeavor to disappear. Ozick ends the novel with a bitter ditty:

> *Better never to have loved than loved at all.*
> *Better never to have risen than had a fall.*
>   *Oh bitter, bitter, bitter*
>   *butter*
>   *knife.*

In rejecting the idea of Paradise, Ozick is rejecting the possibility of a human creation of utopia. *Mending the world* may be possible on a limited scale, but achieving perfection is a dangerous goal. For Ozick, rejection of a utopian trajectory is also a rejection of the notion that texts about the Holocaust can have a consolatory meaning. Kauvar reads the dissolution of paradise in the novel as instantiating "the Judaic injunction against idolatry and Ozick's injunction against artistic veneration," and she calls "Puttermesser and Xanthippe" Ozick's "Book of Creation" ("Book of Creation," 54). If it is Ozick's *Book of Creation,* it is an ironic one indeed, and in a very different sense in which Frances Sherwood's *The Book of Splendor* is *The Book of Splendor.* Utopias, we know, are impossible in the post-Holocaust era; indeed, some scholars and artists have pointed to the impulse of humanity to create utopias as a self-destructive impulse that potentially leads to genocide.[15]

But such a rejection does not mean that Ozick is rejecting the importance of the imagination. More than a decade before *The Puttermesser Papers,* Ozick published a luminous essay titled "Innovation and Redemption: What Literature Means."[16] She bemoans the trend in contemporary theory that focuses on language as constituting reality. As an example, she cites a writer who said to her at a party: "For me, the Holocaust and a corncob are the same" (244). "I want to stand against this view," declares Ozick (245). She envisions texts as having a kind of corona that is interpretation, "the nimbus of meaning that envelopes the story" (246). Continuing, Ozick affirms the ineluctability of the imagination: "Imagination is more than make-believe. . . . It is also the power to penetrate evil, to take on evil. . . . The imagination seeks out the unsayable and the undoable, and says and does them." Here is a direct contradiction to those who say the imagination has no role in post-Holocaust literature. Ozick further claims: "So a redemptive literature, a literature that interprets and decodes the world, beaten out for the sake of humanity, must wrestle with its own body, with its own flesh and blood, with its own life" (247). This internal struggle has been embodied in Ozick's use of rationality and folklore, the doppelgänger motif, and the dueling narrators in *The Puttermesser Papers.* It is also embodied in her appropriation of golem intertexts, at once critiquing outmoded assumptions and affirming the importance of creating a memory for literature.

As we turn from Cynthia Ozick's *Puttermesser Papers* to Rosenbaum's *Golems of Gotham,* we find provocative similarities: both are set in New York City, both involve the creation of a golem as a helper (which, in fact, was the original purpose of Rabbi Loew's golem), and the golems in both novels work to transform the city into a kind of utopia. And in both novels, as in many of the early golem stories, the golems turn to destructive behavior before they are eliminated.

For me, the post-Holocaust universe is a perpetual way station of interrupted life, and for this reason, the post-Holocaust, by definition, must offer some elements of a ghost story.

Thane Rosenbaum

Thane Rosenbaum, a member of the Second Generation, precedes chapter 1 of *The Golems of Gotham* with a caveat: "A warning to all readers: Please take the labeling of this book as a novel seriously. It is indeed a work of fiction" (xi). Rosenbaum goes on to note that many of the characters in his book are actual Holocaust survivors who committed suicide but nonetheless participate in this story. Primo Levi, Jean Amery, Paul Celan, Piotr Rawicz, Jerzy Kosinski, and Tadeusz Borowski all return to life in New York City as ghostly golems, though Rosenbaum acknowledges that he has manufactured many of the circumstances of both their lives and their deaths. Rosenbaum continues: "The effort here is *to recruit the imagination* into the service of answering the unanswerable, to find the logic in numbers that simply don't add up, to find an acceptable way to respond to so much collective longing, to seek hope and reconciliation in a world that provides so little reason to do so—but yet we must try" (xi, italics mine). Thus, as readers, we receive right at the beginning of this fantastical and humorous story a crucial validation of the key role of the imagination in post-Holocaust literary texts and an explicit rejection of Adorno's prohibition. Rosenbaum *boasts* that he is writing fiction and that such a story has validity and authority. Somewhat later in the novel, Rosenbaum applauds Celan's work by saying: "The philosopher Theodor Adorno had warned that it was barbarous to make poetry after Auschwitz. And yet that's what Paul did . . . it was through verse that he demanded from Germany's mother tongue the acknowledgement of the atrocity" (63).

Rosenbaum was born on January 8, 1960, in New York City; when he was nine years old, he and his parents relocated to Miami Beach. He is the only child of Holocaust survivors: his mother was interned in Majdanek and his father in various camps, including Auschwitz, "but the subject of the Nazi death camps was unmentionable within the household" (Royal, 1). His parents died when he was young (Peacock, 303). He earned his B.A. degree, summa cum laude, in 1981 from the University of Florida and went on to earn an MPA from Columbia University in 1983 and a JD from the University of Miami in 1986. He told an interviewer that he studied law "because he felt that the security of a law degree would help to mitigate his inherited sense of vulnerability" as a member of the Second Generation (Royal, 2). Initially Rosenbaum pursued a career in law, clerking for a district judge in Florida and working for a law firm as an associate from 1987 to 1991. But at some point he realized, "I simply didn't want to be a lawyer anymore and I did want to write fiction" (Royal, 6). The Shoah, particularly its impact on the Second Generation, is the obsessive theme of his first publication, a linked short story collection, *Elijah Visible* (1996), as well as his novels, *Second Hand Smoke* (1999) and *The Golems of Gotham* (2002); Rosenbaum sees these three books as a "post-Holocaust trilogy" (Royal, 5). He won the Edgar Lewis Wallant Prize for the best book of Jewish American fiction for *Elijah Visible,* was a finalist for the National Jewish Book Award for *Second Hand Smoke,* and was listed among the San Francisco Chronicle Top 100 Books of 2002 for *The Golems of Gotham.* He held the position of literary editor of *Tikkun* magazine from 1996 to 2002.

Rosenbaum currently serves as director of the Forum on Law, Culture, and Society at Fordham University, where he is the John Whelan Distinguished Lecturer in Law and teaches classes on human rights and law and literature. These intellectual interests have resulted in two books, *The Myth of Moral Justice: What Our Legal System Fails to Do Right* (2004) and the recent anthology, *Law Lit, from Atticus Finch to "The Practice": A Collection of Great Writing about the Law* (2007). His forthcoming book is titled *Revenge and Its Rewards.*[17] Rosenbaum has one daughter, Basia Tess, to whom he dedicated *The Golems of Gotham,* a book about father-daughter relationships, among other things.

That Thane Rosenbaum is an avid believer in the importance of the imagination in post-Holocaust literature and life is evident in several sources. Rosenbaum's nonfiction study, *The Myth of Moral Justice,* is an extended critique of the American justice system in which Rosenbaum finds that the courtroom process fails the majority of defendants: they feel as if their story has not been told, as if they did not receive an apology, as if morality is entirely absent from the proceedings and their outcome. In short, Rosenbaum finds that the legal system suffers from *a failure of imagination.*[18] In his introduction to the book, Rosenbaum describes himself as "stuck in two seemingly irreconcilable worlds—the storyteller who depends on the imagination, emotion, nuance, and the uncertainty of direction; and the lawyer, whose world is increasingly narrowed, isolated, cut off from human experience and focused far too much on achieving prescribed, predictable results" (2).

Similarly, in reviews Rosenbaum has written for the *New York Times* about recent Holocaust narratives, he praises the willingness of their creators to "imagine a life after the unimaginable" ("Imagining"). This review, which appeared in 1998, applauds the film *The Truce,* based on Primo Levi's memoir *The Reawakening* about Levi's journey home from Auschwitz to Italy and his more gradual return to art and life. While acknowledging the precipice of danger over which such a film dances—dangers of sentimentality, inaccuracy, and lack of nuance—Rosenbaum nonetheless finds that the film brings home to the viewer the complexities of a survivor's experiences in the aftermath of the Shoah. In a similar review, which appeared in the *New York Times* a year later, Rosenbaum responds to a Broadway play titled *The Gathering,* by Arje Shaw. He opens the piece by noting the "one-dimensional cliché, a cartoon of a stock character" that is the common representation of Holocaust survivors in contemporary texts and films: "lifeless . . . unfixably broken, unrelievedly angry and volatile; . . . self-pitying, incapable of experiencing love or generating any emotion other than bitterness, isolation and rage" ("Holocaust Survivor"). By contrast, *The Gathering* presents a survivor who has benefited from the imagination of his creator. Shaw, a child survivor, "offers a more searching and textured vision of the survivor," claims Rosenbaum, and he concludes by suggesting: "But wouldn't it be better if we returned home [from the theater] knowing a little more about the actual lives of those whose experiences have been fictionalized for our entertainment?" In other words, there is value in the imagination stretching audiences beyond the usual clichés employed in portraying survivors.

Like Cynthia Ozick, Rosenbaum has given a great deal of thought to issues of voice and authority in writing about the Holocaust. While Ozick acknowledges that she has no direct link to the Holocaust and yet wrote "The Shawl," a story set in a death camp, Rosenbaum, by contrast, the child of Holocaust survivors, takes a much more tentative approach as a writer: "I generally recoil at the idea of being thought of as a Holocaust writer . . . I don't write about the years 1933–45, nor would I ever. My characters all live in the aftermath of Auschwitz . . . I have no claims to the Holocaust as an event, only its generational consequences . . . I have focused almost entirely . . . on the huge shadow of darkness and forgetfulness that the Holocaust cast on humanity in the post-Holocaust era" (Royal, 3–4).

The Golems of Gotham opens with two arresting chapters, recounted by a sassy, irreverent omniscient narrator who presents us with three shocking images. Set in Miami in 1980, chapter 1 begins by recounting the suicide of Lothar Levin, who is in his synagogue on Shabbat, is called to the Torah, pulls a gun from his *tallis,* and shoots himself in the temple: "A Jewish brain shot out from his head and splattered all over the unscrolled sheepskin as though the synagogue had just hosted its first animal sacrifice" (1). Seated nearby, Lothar's wife, Rose, ingests a cyanide pill and crumples over dead. The narrator adopts a jaunty, casual, and seemingly inappropriate tone in which to describe this event: "A *Shabbos* suicide pact is not exactly what God had in mind for his day of rest. But Lothar and Rose were Holocaust survivors; God would have no say in the matter. He had become irrelevant, a lame duck divinity" (3). The narrator continues expostulating in the language of advertisement: "And what about sin? Well, nobody took that seriously anymore either. Another house specialty of Auschwitz. The Nazis had given new meaning to sin, raising the ante on atrocity, showing the world the deluxe model. Original sin seemed puny, and frankly unoriginal, by comparison. Zyklon B was now the ultimate forbidden fruit. Faster-acting, easier on the stomach. All Eve would have had to do was get Adam to inhale, then say Kaddish" (3). By employing this tongue-in-cheek tone, the narrator achieves two seemingly opposite effects: he desacralizes the notion of the survivor as saint while at the same time pointing to the commodification of the Holocaust in contemporary culture.

Chapter 2 begins nineteen years later in New York City in front of the famed delicatessen Zabar's in what could almost be a scene from a Marc Chagall painting, presenting the reader with a second shocking image. A teenage girl withdraws from a battered violin case "a weird, bruised blue" (11) violin and begins to play piercingly beautiful and technically flawless klezmer music, an astonishing feat as she has had no formal training. A crowd gathers, listening reverently. However, our omniscient narrator cannot resist undercutting the scene again with racy analysis: "But in the post-Holocaust era, klezmer had all too often become no better than kitsch, cosmetic music that filled in that awkward gap between the serving of the fruit cup and the main course at Jewish weddings and bar mitzvahs" (12). The violinist is fourteen-year-old Ariel Levin, the granddaughter of the Holocaust survivors of chapter 1. She lives on Edgar Allan Poe Street on the Upper West Side and, significantly, the song she plays again and again is "Invitation to the Dead." This chapter closes with a third shocking image, contributing to the sense of magical realism: "A baby carriage of sturdy Swedish design, with large rubber wheels and a blue canvas hood, strolled up and down Broadway" in the twilight (18). Curiously, it had neither passenger inside nor parent or nanny propelling it: "Just the stroller itself, freely traversing the avenue, parading along Broadway" (18). Some readers may hear, faintly, that chorus "Who you gonna call? Ghostbusters!" as the novel is off to a spooky start, indeed.

In chapter 3 the narration switches to that of Ariel in first person: "All I wanted was to fix my father, and that's why I did it" (19), she informs us at the outset, not yet revealing what "it" is. She then launches into a description of a favorite book of her childhood about a lighthouse on the Hudson River that, though modest in size, rescues boats in danger. This text becomes a kind of intertext throughout *The Golems of Gotham*, underscoring the importance of story, Ariel's effort to rescue her father, and the role of the golem historically to rescue the Jewish people.[19] Ariel, a perceptive and sensitive ninth grader, tells us that her father is a writer; that he was profoundly saddened when his wife abandoned him twelve years earlier, a loss that echoed the loss of his parents to suicide; that he is suffering from writer's block; and that she has decided to create a golem to help him.[20] She collects mud from the Hudson River on a school field trip to the very lighthouse that is in her childhood book, acknowledging that this was not exactly "like the story I heard in Hebrew school, about the rabbi who went off in the middle of the night to dig up mud from some river in Prague" (24). Filling her backpack with the mud, Ariel inadvertently cuts her hand on broken glass at the river's edge and thus adds a few drops of blood to the mud.

As chapter 4 opens, we encounter a third narrative voice, that of Ariel's father, Oliver. He is holding forth on writer's block and suicide, continuing themes to which the reader has already been introduced. References are made to Hamlet's "to be or not to be" dilemma and to Vincent van Gogh's suicide. Rosenbaum elevates our awareness of this novel as a metafiction by including Oliver's meditations on the role of art: "for the artist, the outtakes of life loaded down with disappointment inevitably get reimagined as art" (29). Echoing Freud's view of the artist as neurotic, Oliver further intones, "The artist has no other alternative. Repression is not an option. Neither is forgetting nor denial. The artist becomes the warden of his own prison, a jailer without mercy" (29). Oliver denigrates his own publications as failing to reach the gold standard: "I *am* a writer but I'm no artist. Far from it. I write gothic mysteries; courtroom legal thrillers" (30). (We learn that Oliver was formerly a practicing attorney, one of several biographical links to Rosenbaum.) He can no longer bring himself to write formula fiction: "But a real artist doesn't care about facts, details, adventure, intrigue, or even plot—just truth. When art is pumping on all emotional cylinders, *when it aspires not to copy but to reinvent,* not to please but to disturb . . . the result can split your veins" (30–31, italics mine). Again, Rosenbaum is here emphasizing the importance of the imagination and the uses of intertextuality—reinventing—in responding to atrocity. As Oliver continues his confession, he acknowledges that his writer's block is due to his "refusal to emotionally confront all that had gone wrong, and all that had walked away" (31). He decides to come clean with the reader; his tone switches to one of irony and popular culture, much like that of the omniscient narrator: "My parents were Holocaust survivors. Need I say more, or should I just go ahead and ruin your day" (31), an echo of Clint Eastwood's famous line "Go ahead, make my day" in the film *Sudden Impact* (1983). In a somewhat cryptic reference to the novel we are reading, Oliver notes: "This book in your hands, the words inverted in your eyes, is a new beginning for me" (31). Passages later in the text will clarify this assertion.

From here on, the chapters alternate between Ariel and Oliver as narrators, with the occasional return of the omniscient narrator. This pattern (or lack thereof) is reminiscent of Rosenbaum's first book, *Elijah Visible*, which has both a fractured chronology and fractured narration. Rosenbaum has commented about the main character who is the son of Holocaust survivors: "I wrote the chapters as a fragmented novel—a metaphor for Adam Posner (who in one guise or another appears in each chapter, a broken man living in a broken world)" (Royal, 6). The fracturing of narration in *The Golems of Gotham* has a similar impact, conveying to the reader the broken perspective of Oliver Levin but also serving as a kind of Brechtian "alienation effect," calling the reader's attention to the metafiction.

The next several chapters form the nexus of the golem story within the novel. Ariel recounts her creation of the golems, a process that represents a clever riff on Rabbi Loew's proven formula. An artist in her own right as a violinist, she hopes to create the golem to rescue her dad from his muffled emotions and writer's block. "I'm not really good with my hands," she begins. "But I did remember that in the story I heard in Hebrew school, Rabbi Loew's creature wasn't pretty. . . . The golem was an early-model Terminator without all the cyborg nuts and bolts" (40). Gathering together the mud she has filched, eight *yahrzeit* candles, and the death camp numbers inscribed on her grandparents' arms (which she has obtained by getting old photos blown up until she can read the numbers on the forearms; the numbers are 20167 and 14822), she withdraws into the attic of the brownstone where she lives with Oliver; the attic resembles Prague's Old-New Synagogue. Mixing some water and matzoh meal with her mud, she plays "Invitation to the Dead" on her violin, chants the numbers from her grandparents, and then "improvises some more" by calling out the names of death camps: "Auschwitz, Birkenau, Majdanek, Treblinka, Bergen-Belsen" (48). She recognizes that she has included some "uncalled-for ingredient[s] in the golem recipe, but I felt like I had to improvise with my own formula" (47). And it works! "I started to feel dizzy. But then I looked at the golem, and he looked dizzy too, as if his head was filling with the same things that were in mine" (48). In fact, what Ariel has succeeded in doing is creating not one but *eight* golems, one for each *yahrzeit* candle. She has summoned the six actual Holocaust survivors mentioned above, as well as her two deceased grandparents. Significantly, these golems have been summoned not only to rescue a people but to rescue art, to enable her father to write again. Such a gesture is yet another indication of Rosenbaum's emphasis on the importance of story and imagination in the post-Holocaust era.

A few days later Oliver is suffering through an excruciating dinner in a restaurant with his agent, whose name is, suggestively, Evelyn Eisenberg (iron mountain). She is impatiently badgering him about his now "obscenely late" book manuscript (52). Oliver is struggling to tell her about his writer's block and his desire to try writing something different: "A literary novel, perhaps. Maybe something with a Jewish theme" (52). It is at this pregnant moment, as Oliver is beginning to confront his blocked emotions that in turn block his creativity, that the golems Ariel has summoned first appear to Oliver.

Out the window, in the bare branches of winter trees, the six famous Holocaust survivors perch: "each blinking at me, dead eyes sending out private messages. . . . They were wearing uniforms . . . like threadbare gray pajamas . . . black stripes on white" (54). Oliver rushes into the restaurant's courtyard to get a better look and, after a schmaltzy moment when he dances with the unwitting Evelyn to "Strangers in the Night" (another humorous passage in which Rosenbaum again undercuts the Gothic ghost tale), Oliver faints and is taken to the hospital. In the following chapter, the omniscient narrator returns to introduce the reader to each of the six survivor-writers, again using notes of levity at places; for example, Jerzy Kosinski is introduced by means of an interview on an American television talk show. As Rosenbaum has warned the reader, some of the "facts" about these survivors' biographies are fictional; in some cases, they represent rumors or exaggerations that have gained currency in the aftermath of their suicides.

When Oliver arrives home on Edgar Allan Poe Street, he discovers that the golems have taken up residence together with his parents; they explain that Ariel's "golem experiment [had] gone haywire" and they were the result (77). A conversation about writing ensues in which Rosenbaum again introduces the theme of the value of story, this time through the voice of Primo Levi: "We lived through the unimaginable, but as writers we spent our lives trying to actually imagine it, to give it an image, to make it more real, as we had remembered it, even though the task itself was impossible, because we could never succeed in describing it" (79). Levi here poses the classic dilemma of Holocaust literature: existing language is simply insufficient to describe an experience that was unimaginable before it happened, and yet, for the sake of memory, one must try and the imagination is the best tool we have. The other survivors weigh in on the importance of story in the aftermath of atrocity, and in the midst of this serious discourse, Jerzy Kosinski makes an explicit reference to Jewish Monica Lewinsky and the sex act she performed for President Clinton—again the intrusion of popular culture and a bit of humor, bringing the reader up short, desacralizing at a moment in the novel that might have morphed into pontificating.

The next several chapters recount the changes that the golems wreak in New York City. These passages are somewhat reminiscent of Ozick's *The Puttermesser Papers* as many of the things the golems change are Holocaust related: all tattoos and body art disappear from people's skin; all showers stop working; the stripes on the Yankee uniforms are eradicated as well as on the zebras in the zoo; all smoking is banned; barbers are forbidden to shave people's heads. In perhaps the funniest move, the narrator declares that "Con Edison switched from gas and went entirely electric" (104). A robust Jewish community reemerges on the Upper West Side, dancing the hora in the streets. "The original golem was a creature of rescue and retribution, but the latest models came outfitted with shrewd minds, big souls, and a flair for restoration" (104).

Chapter 12 is devoted to a lively debate among the golems about what is possible in the post-Holocaust era and why they have returned to life. Primo Levi intones: "We are here to teach how to move on, how not to live in the past" (123); such dwelling in the past has, of course, hampered Oliver in his efforts to write. While Jean Amery protests the impossibility of reconciliation or redemption, Paul Celan, who is given the voice of gravitas by the narrator, pronounces: "We need to show the world how to finally come to terms with the inhumanity of the twentieth century" (124). "Words are important. . . . Poetry can and must change the world" (129). When speaking of his post-Holocaust trilogy, Rosenbaum asserts that "The aesthetics of the trilogy called for a redemptive closure. . . . As the golems teach in *The Golems of Gotham*, it is essential to somehow mediate the moral imperative to remember and never forget with the equally moral duty to reconcile with the past and aspire to a life filled with meaning and possibility" (Royal, 4–5). Like Ozick, Rosenbaum believes in the possibility of a "redemptive" literature, and what better creature to inhabit such a literature that the golem, representing creativity, protection, and rescue.

Rosenbaum's novel stretches on for another two hundred pages, much of it a kind of magical realism journey through a Gotham transformed by the golems. Rosenbaum continues to explore the theme of art after Auschwitz, particularly as it relates to the Second Generation. Elie Wiesel makes a cameo appearance, a flashback to Oliver's wife's departure is inserted, and there are continued notes of humor and references to popular culture. Eventually, the novel as metafiction takes a new turn; Oliver recovers from his block and begins to furiously work on another novel, titled *Salt and Stone,* which the reader suspects is the novel he or she is holding: "The emotions in the book," we are told, "were relentless" (262) as indeed they are in *The Golems of Gotham.* The novel ends with a conflagration and a resolution. The golems go on a rampage, creating mayhem in New York; Oliver tries to take his life after his new novel is rejected ("The literary, postmodern elements are impressive indeed but, Holocaust novels don't sell," says the rejection letter [264]).

But then the golems and Oliver and Ariel sit down to a Passover seder during which the conversation includes a number of questions such as "How is it that mankind continues on when there are so many reasons not to?" which manifest the paradox of post-Holocaust life and literature and the key to Rosenbaum's novel. Elsewhere Rosenbaum has written: "I am a post-Holocaust novelist, which means that *I rely on my imagination—my capacity to reinvent worlds and reveal emotional truths*—in order to speak to the Holocaust and its aftermath" ("Art and Atrocity," 125, italics mine).

Alan Berger, who has written extensively and sensitively on Second Generation literature as well as on Thane Rosenbaum and his reification of golems, describes *The Golems of Gotham* thus: "The novel's thirty-six chapters, a number which itself has mythico-mystical significance—thirty six being twice the numerical equivalent of the Hebrew word *chai* [life]— deal with moral philosophy, the nature of memory, the role of religion in post-Holocaust Jewish identity, Jewish-Christian relations, and the fact that the immensity of the Holocaust precludes the possibility of undoing the trauma, even for the third generation" (2). Though the trauma cannot be undone, Berger praises Rosenbaum for his effort at "working through" by deploying a variety of resources in *The Golems of Gotham:* "On the one hand, they are *specifically Jewish:* biblical and rabbinic thought, mysticism in its kabbalistic and Hasidic expressions, the notion of the Golem, the search for *tikkun.* On the other hand, they are *particularly literary:* magical realism, post-modernism, and the preoccupation with identity" (4). Finally, Berger affirms the intertextual gesture: "Rosenbaum's novel boldly recruits the imagination in seeking moral guidance from the ghosts of Holocaust victims. . . . Rosenbaum's greatest moral and literary leap lies in imagining what the ghosts of the dead would say about Holocaust memory in the new millennium" (2–3).

THE GOLEM ON *THE X-FILES:* EPISODE 4-12, "KADDISH" (1997)

In turning from Rosenbaum to an *X-Files* episode from season 4 titled "Kaddish," we encounter another post-Holocaust text that focuses on the topic of the Second Generation and "working through." In "Kaddish," originally aired February 16, 1997, a young Hasidic man from Brooklyn, brutally murdered by three men in his grocery store, is the spirit in the golem created by his grieving fiancée, Ariel (also an intriguing comparison to Rosenbaum: another Ariel creating a golem; we now have looked in this chapter at three instances of women creating golems—Puttermesser and the two Ariels). Ariel's father is a Holocaust survivor from Prague and was an apprentice jeweler when the Nazis arrived in Prague. He concealed a large ring made in the form of a castle and managed to keep it through the Holocaust and bring it to America when he immigrated. He has revealed the ring to his daughter upon her engagement, promising to present the ring to her on her wedding day.

The funeral of Ariel's fiancé—Isaac Luria—opens the episode: a brooding day with shots of Ariel, who cannot bring herself to throw the requisite handful of dirt upon the coffin of her beloved.[21] When one of the killers is subsequently strangled in the cemetery, the stars of *The X-Files,* heroic FBI agents Fox Mulder and Dana Scully, are baffled: the fingerprints of Isaac are found on the strangled man—how could this be? Isaac is dead—or is he? Suspicion falls upon Ariel's father, Jacob Weiss, as his copy of the *Sefer Yetsirah, The Book of Creation* that supposedly gives the mystical formula for creating a golem, is found in Isaac's coffin.

The suspicion that Isaac's death was a hate crime is bolstered by antisemitic threats received by Jacob Weiss, including a brochure titled "How AIDS Was Created by the Jews." These brochures are traced to a white supremacist who owns a business across from Isaac's grocery. A huge swastika flag hangs in his back room where he pumps out the brochures on a hand-cranked printer. He, too, is strangled while printing a new pamphlet titled "Only through Blood Can the Jewish Scourge Be Killed." Meanwhile, Scully goes to the Jewish Archives to learn more about the creation and power of golems. She is given a lesson about the *Sefer Yetsirah* and the "power of letters to create and kill"; commentary from the scholar of Jewish Studies at the Archives is cinematically juxtaposed with the printing of the antisemitic brochures, calling attention as we have seen so often in variants of the golem tale to the importance of letters, words, and story.

The episode concludes with an eerie scene in the synagogue in which Ariel appears in her wedding dress. The golem—representing Isaac and looking rather Frankensteinish—emerges from the shadows and, after Ariel says her wedding vows, Isaac puts the castle ring on her finger. Immediately the golem's body begins to crack and melt, reverting to a corpse as the life essence seeps away.

This strange episode, though dealing with the "paranormal," the focus of *The X-Files*, has no sequel; it is a single golem episode. It can be read as an account of the impact of the Holocaust survivor father on his daughter. This ring had meant so much to him and he was so deeply pleased by his daughter's engagement to Isaac. At some level, Ariel, who is depicted as much saner and more balanced than her survivor father, needs to complete the wedding ceremony to satisfy him and to put the ring to its proper use. It is a Spiegelman *Maus*-esque story of a Holocaust survivor and the Second Generation. "Love," we are told, "created the golem." That is, Ariel creates a golem and gives him Isaac's fingerprints not only out of her love for him as her fiancé but also out of love for her father. We can see some parallels with the pop culture golem episodes in the Marvel comics: love was also the animating force of Marvel's golem and that golem was a kind of reincarnation of Professor Adamson who had been murdered.

Enacted here is a perfectly realized example of what Marianne Hirsch has called "postmemory." The child of Holocaust survivors herself, Hirsch conceptualized the impact on the Second Generation of growing up with survivors as parents and provided the concept with the name "postmemory." These children do not have the actual memory of the Holocaust but instead a kind of ghostly remnant of that memory:

> Postmemory is a powerful and very particular form of memory precisely because its connection to its object or source is mediated not through recollection but through an imaginative investment and creation. . . . Postmemory characterizes the experience of those who grow up dominated by narratives that preceded their birth, whose own belated stories are evacuated by the stories of the previous generation shaped by traumatic events that can be neither understood nor re-created. (Hirsch, 22)

Though it is Ariel who has lost a fiancé, it is Jacob, her father, who seems to suffer more, to be undone completely by this loss. The perceptive viewer will conclude that it is *all the losses* in his life that he mourns. His daughter's wedding symbolizes for him the return of life, the possibility of future generations. When that possibility is cut off by the murder just a few days before the wedding, his daughter internalizes his enormous grief and creates the golem, using her father's knowledge of Kabbalah. Isaac's spirit inhabits the golem just long enough to complete the ritual, albeit in a creepy, ghostly manner.

After this episode aired, fans (known as X-Philes) of the program shared their responses—both positive and negative—on the Internet newsgroup alt.tv.x-files. Some of these responses were collated and compared by Mikel Koven in an article titled "'Have I Got a Monster for You!': Some Thoughts on the Golem, *The X-Files*, and the Jewish Horror Movie." Much of the back-and-forth among the X-Philes is devoted to pinpointing ways in which the episode breaks golem tradition, for example, the *emet* is inscribed on the golem's hand, not forehead; the golem is created by a woman; mud is used from a cemetery whereas the mud traditionally must be from a pure source; and so forth. Some fans decry these changes as irreverent; others, including Koven, recognize the role of intertextuality and the power of literary adaptations to analyze contemporary times and issues. Koven provides a creditable history of the golem legend as a prelude to his analysis of the "Kaddish" episode. He notes appropriately that the "golem acts as a literal metaphor for the series' ultimate theme 'the truth is out there' . . . [and] the 'Kaddish' episode also presents a metatextual meditation for us on the power of words" (221). Curiously, though, Koven fails to mention anything about Ariel's father, Jacob, a Holocaust survivor; about her status as a member of the Second Generation; or about the symbol of the ring. Instead, he includes a section titled "The Monstrous Feminine" in which he arrives at the conclusion that because Ariel deviates from Hasidic traditions in various ways and creates a golem "to be her phallus" as well as for revenge, she is "doubly guilty of being 'monstrous'" (225). This is an unfortunate conclusion that smacks of "blaming the victim" and ignores a whole layer of meaning in the episode.

DANIEL HANDLER, *WATCH YOUR MOUTH* (2000)

The golem, like so many aspects of Judaism, is inundated with the power of the Word.

Daniel Handler, *Watch Your Mouth*

In this chapter we have looked at a range of golem appropriations: Cynthia Ozick's fiercely intellectual hypertext; Thane Rosenbaum's fiercely emotional adaptation; and an episode from *The X-Files* that invites viewers to consider the many hatreds white supremacists harbor as well as the impact of the Holocaust on the Second Generation. I'd like now to briefly discuss another sort of intertext, this one a hyperbolic satire or even a parody of the golem legend. Daniel Handler, who wrote *Watch Your Mouth*, is none other than Lemony Snicket, author of the wildly popular books for children, *A Series of Unfortunate Events*. Published in thirteen volumes beginning in 1999, this series presents the plight of three orphaned children turned over to a greedy uncle who plots to eliminate them and grab their considerable inheritance; the series was made into a film starring Jim Carrey (2004).

Handler is the child of Holocaust survivors and, prior to his editor's realization that his talents were far better suited for children's books, Handler published two novels for adults, both of which were remaindered. *Watch Your Mouth*, which one critic aptly described as being "Like Kafka on Prozac,"[22] is a bawdy romp set in a steamy summer in Pittsburgh and a winter in California. In part 1, appropriating the tropes of opera, the narrator repeatedly announces "the curtain rises," the chapters are labeled as acts and scenes, and the reader is afforded several "Brief Intermissions." Part 2, printed in red ink, adapts as its structure the twelve-step program to recover from an addiction. This novel is not for the faint of heart—incest is a prominent theme and there are seemingly endless scenes of the main character having sex with his girlfriend, slyly nicknamed Cyn (sin).

Speaking of names, that of the narrator is Joseph, the name given by Rabbi Loew to the golem he creates. And all evidence points to the narrator being such a golem. Indeed, golems abound in this book: Joseph teaches the kids at the Jewish summer camp where he works how to make a golem; the opera *The Golem* is performed in the novel; Mrs. Glass, Cyn's mother, creates a golem in her basement; and the title of the novel, *Watch Your Mouth*, is a reference to the life-giving *shem* placed in the golem's mouth.

Familiar golem themes are here: the doppelgänger motif; the golem running amok (various murders are committed); and many literary allusions (to Tolstoy, Ann Rice, Robert Frost, Euripides, and Shakespeare, to name just a few). Handler metatextually acknowledges the difficulty of following the plot of his novel by having his narrator opine: "It's often hard to describe the plot of a book to others, even when it's still going on" (221); the narrator also reveals the parodic intent: "The golem is a figure in Jewish myth—sort of a Jewish lie, sort of a Jewish truth. It appears to wreak havoc but really, it'll do anything you say. You don't have to tell it twice. If it tries to speak for itself, the Word of God tumbles out and the golem turns back into clay. It's a monster, sort of, but who isn't a monster occasionally, particularly among family?" (222).

While the novel contains no overt references to the Holocaust, Handler has acknowledged in an interview that the Holocaust was an early influence on him and his views of Jewish literature: "I think you learn something from any good book, and I think that one's education comes largely from

literature. But over and over, the message of children's books is, 'If you be-
have well, you'll be rewarded.' Which is not a very Jewish message. It is just
not an interesting message to me, and not a true one." Handler's father fled
Germany as a young boy. "I knew about the Holocaust at an earlier age than
most people learn about it, I think, and so the idea that the world could
suddenly go very wrong—and that it had no bearing on what sort of person
you were—sunk in pretty early. And it's affected my politics and my writing and my life. . . . It was a big lesson for me very young and I think Jewish
literature encompasses impending disaster—even pre-Holocaust—in every
age, there's been one, sadly. And I think my books incorporate that tradition."[23] Thus in Handler's literary vision we see the markers we have traced
in many adaptations of the golem legend: the pastiche of intertextuality,
metafiction, and history.

AFTERWORD

And so the golem lives on and golem literature also lives on. As I completed
work on this book, I read another golem novel, this one for fun: *Vienna
Secrets* by Frank Tallis (2009). Set in that august Austrian city in 1903, the
novel opens with the discovery of a murder: the victim has been beheaded
with a force that seems superhuman. Clumps of mud are found at the murder scene. Sigmund Freud is a character in the novel and is reputed to have
a collection of Judaica that includes several volumes on Kabbalah and a
copy of the Zohar. According to the afterword to the book, the existence of
this collection was confirmed by Chayim Bloch; he visited Freud and, when
left alone, had the opportunity to scan the shelves in Freud's library (383).
The plot revolves around the resurgence of antisemitism in Vienna at the
time and there is the scent of foreboding. The *Anschluss,* which will force
Freud to flee Vienna, is only thirty-five years away, and, at the heart of the
mystery, is a crusading golem.

A few months later, *The Forward* carried a positive review of another
just published golem novel, *The Fifth Servant* by Kenneth Wishnia, set in
Prague in 1592 with characters such as Rabbi Loew and, of course, a golem
on a mission. Now as this book goes to press Cathy Gelbin's new scholarly
book, *The Golem Returns,* has just been announced. Her title suggests, as
does mine, the irrepressible nature of the clay man.

In *The Golem Redux* I have endeavored to read the amazing range (in
both genre and time period) of golem texts and to present to the reader
an image of these texts as a palimpsest, a layering of legend that is both
self-referential and self-renewing. Some of these texts—Gustav Meyrink's
novel *Der Golem* and Paul Wegener's film *Der Golem*—might be termed

misadaptations or misconceptions as they embody, rather than critique, antisemitism. But the contemporary Jewish American texts I have included in chapters 3, 4, and 5 both acknowledge the Shoah, implicitly or explicitly, and grapple with the interdiction against imaginative literature in the post-Holocaust era. By using the literary device of intertextuality, these novels, comics, graphic novels, and the *X-Files* episode summon for the reader the long history of Jews as a People of the Book, the long tradition of exegesis, midrash, and riffing in Jewish sacred and secular literature.

In placing a golem figure at the center of their texts, these authors intentionally choose a synecdoche of creativity, of imagination, of both the text and the intertext. By the manner in which they morph their new golem—whether it be the golems in Thane Rosenbaum's *Golems of Gotham* who return as Holocaust survivors who committed suicide or the African American baseball player who masquerades as a golem in James Sturm's graphic novel—these writers demonstrate the yearning for meaning and its evanescent quality in the postmodern age (a period often defined as co-terminus with the years since 1945). Intertextuality, then, functions like the *shem* put in the golem's mouth in some versions of the legend: it reawakens a text and transforms it into another text. The imagination serves as its elixir. Imaginative literature, we see, *is* viable—not only viable but absolutely essential to help readers ponder identity, grasp the failings and triumphs of human nature, discern what we can of divinity, and achieve social justice (and, sometimes, even laugh).

Each new golem text gestures back to its predecessors and, in doing so, creates literary memory. Such a memory for literature reminds us of the role of story in the lives of human beings, the infinite malleability of story, the expectation that each age will renew, adapt, and redeem the stories of the past. Here is what the Holocaust survivor Ivan Klima says: "If we lose our memory, we lose ourselves. Forgetting is one of the symptoms of death. Without memory, we cease to be human beings. . . . A truly literary work comes into being as its creator's cry of protest against the forgetting that looms over him, over his predecessors and his contemporaries alike, and over his time, and the language he speaks. A literary work is something that defies death" (38). Perhaps it is not just a coincidence that Ivan Klima grew up in Prague, the city most associated with the golem. His declaration acknowledges both the profound challenge of post-Holocaust literature and its equally profound necessity.

Epilogue

Golem texts are far too numerous to be treated fully in the body of this study but several deserve brief mention here because of their historical importance, their obscurity, or their idiosyncracy.

H. Leivick, "The Golem: A Dramatic Poem in Eight Scenes" (1921)

H. Leivick's early verse drama can be found in Joachim Neugroschel's collection *The Golem* (2006), which Neugroschel (perhaps hyperbolically) calls "the most famous treatment of the golem legend." Leivick, a Yiddish writer, sets his play in Prague in the 1600s, using the traditional characters of Rabbi Leyb (Loew) and his family but also introducing several new characters in the form of spirits. Leivick was born in Belarus in 1888, the oldest of nine children in an impoverished family. As a result of political activity in the Minsk Bund, he was arrested and jailed. He later reflected: "I wrote *The Golem* out of my own direct jail experience. If I had not been in prison, if I had not *lain* stretched out on a stone floor in an ever-dark cell, and if I had not seen others lie similarly, I am not sure I would have written *The Golem.* Certainly, I would not have written as I did" (Goldsmith, *Remembered,* 75). Like Isaac Bashevis Singer and Elie Wiesel, Leivick had suffered persecution as a Jew before his arrival in America in 1913. He began work on *The Golem* in his late twenties; it was published in 1921 and first performed by the Habima ensemble in Moscow in 1925. Goldsmith offers high praise indeed for this work, calling it "a remarkable, sometimes brilliant, play which combines impassioned poetry, folk legends, biblical allusions, and surrealism with philosophical and religious probing, all infused with stunning imagination" (*Remembered*, 73).

MARC ESTRIN, *THE GOLEM SONG* (2006)

Like Thane Rosenbaum's *Golems of Gotham*, the main character of Estrin's novel is himself a writer living in New York City; he concerns himself with the viability of post-Holocaust fiction, thus making this novel yet another metafiction. Estrin's book is also quite comparable to Daniel Handler's *Watch Your Mouth* in that both are romps focused on sexuality, and both have main characters who are eventually revealed as golems. Both also aspire to be comic novels with much slang, in-jokes, and plot twists. And both are printed in a variety of fonts, with texts of various kinds embedded in the narrative of the novel. Plump Alan Krieger, R.N., is the main character of *The Golem Song*, which is set from April to November 1999. Though in his mid-thirties, Alan still lives with his mother. Themes include manifestations of antisemitism; sexual relationships between Jews and non-Jews; conflict between Jews and African Americans, especially the Nation of Islam; and varieties of transformation. The novel brims with intertextual references—to the Oedipus myth, Homer, Shakespeare, Walter Benjamin, Thomas Mann, and Dostoevsky, to name just a few. There is a very funny send-up of a conversation between Alan and Martha C. Nussbaum, the eminent philosopher who holds a distinguished chair at the University of Chicago. The title of the novel notwithstanding, no mention of the golem occurs until almost page 200, more than halfway into the book. This metafiction continues the exploration of the importance of imagination we have seen in all the post-Holocaust golem texts explored here.

BERNARD OTTERMAN, *GOLEM OF AUSCHWITZ* (2001)

A curious book of short stories by Holocaust survivor Bernard Otterman, titled *Golem of Auschwitz*, has received little if any mention in the scholarly literature about the golem legend. Apparently self-published in 2001, the collection contains a brief biography of Otterman, identifying him as a "child Holocaust survivor" who has published other stories and poems "on Holocaust themes" (7). The entire text is bilingual, Russian and English; a one-page preface by the translator provides further information about the author and the text. Otterman "spent a few years in a German labor camp in Poland, survived, and ever since has been haunted by the need to find out more about the less fortunate. . . . [The book] is not really about the Holocaust—but rather about the obsession with it" (11).

The only story in the collection that includes a golem is the title story, about thirty pages long, of which half are the Russian translation. Set inside Auschwitz and narrated in the first person by an inmate who is a Jewish doctor serving in the *krankenbau* (infirmary), the story tells of eighteen-year-old Hayim, assigned to work with the narrator after he has already been in Auschwitz for six months. Hayim is a deeply pious and religious man who maintains his faith in God despite the daily depredations of the death camp. He often quotes from the Hebrew Bible to explain or distract from the actions of the Nazis. Having been assigned "to one of the most hideous kommandos (work units) in the camp—pulling teeth containing gold from the corpses before they were burned in the crematorium" (17)— Hayim begins to "organize" some of the gold for himself, thus obtaining through a bribe the more favorable assignment to the *krankenbau.* This sets the stage for the creation of a golem.

The narrator/doctor confides in Hayim a strange dream he has had in which sick inmates contribute body parts and lay them out on the operating table, and after Moses the tailor sews the parts together, the inmates urge: "Doctor Safra, make him live" (23). The doctor obliges by breathing into the figure's mouth and "on the seventh breath, his eyes opened and he started to breathe on his own" (23). The golem promptly gets up from the table, downs a bottle of peroxide (a somewhat inexplicable detail), and begins to wreak havoc in the camp, destroying a crematorium, ripping out railroad tracks, tearing down electric fence, and opening the camp gates. When Hayim hears this dream recounted, he tells Doctor Safra: "It is possible by chanting the letters and mystical names of God, to create life" (25). Though the setting in Auschwitz gives this dream a strange twist, we can nonetheless discern some similarities with the more familiar golem legend set in Prague and featuring Rabbi Loew. In many versions of Rabbi Loew's story, he begins the process of golem creation by directing a dream question to God about the troubles besetting the Jewish community and then is directed through a dream by God to create the golem; in Otterman's story, the dream certainly functions as the inspiration for creation. As we have seen, Rabbi Loew creates the golem by circling a lifeless clay humanoid shape seven times in one direction and then seven times in another direction, and we see here the use of the magic number seven. The motivation for creation of the golem in the Otterman story is also similar: the Jewish people are in danger and need a heroic savior. Just as the Prague golem "runs amok" in some stories, here the golem resorts to violence to save the community. Other aspects of the traditional legend appear here, somewhat "misplaced." While Joseph is usually the name of the golem, here it is the first name of the narrator, Doctor Safra.

When, after several days pass, Doctor Safra decides to venture into golem creation, he finds it difficult to convince Hayim to be his partner: "His concern was not whether we could make a golem, but if we *should*. He worried whether, even in the present dire circumstances, it was appropriate for a Jew to practice creation" (27). This, of course, is a dilemma central to all golem creation stories. Hayim finally agrees to try the experiment, provided the doctor can find him "phylacteries (tefillin), a tallith and the Kabbalistic book Sefer Yetzirah. This text was essential because it contains the recipe, sounds and words, for bringing a golem to life" (27). After considerable consternation about what material to use for the golem's body, Hayim and Joseph finally settle on ashes, available in Auschwitz and considered by both to be a pure substance.

Very early one Sunday morning in June, a day fewer Nazis were around the camp, Dr. Safra shapes the ashes into a human figure on a bed and Hayim wraps himself in phylacteries and tallith and begins to pray, continuing for hours. Holding the Sefer Yetzirah, Hayim paces back and forth seven times. As Hayim slumps near the bed from exhaustion, Dr. Safra pulls back the blanket to reveal the golem: "Before me lay an emaciated man, fully grown, whose skin had the color of human skin, but whose age I could not tell. His eyes were closed and his chest moved slowly up and down, typical of very sick patients in the bay. His penis was erect. With shaking hands, I examined his toes and feet, which were warm and perfectly formed" (33).

As in some versions of the legend, the golem at first is like an infant and takes some weeks to learn to walk, talk, and feed himself. Hayim demands that he be circumcised and Dr. Safra, fearing this might endanger his life, proposes a compromise: that his foreskin be pricked and allowed to bleed. "Hayim recited the appropriate blessings and we named him Tykva, which in Hebrew means 'Hope'" (35). Tykva begins to serve as a helper to the doctor, the servant role familiar in the golem legend. Meanwhile, Dr. Safra and Hayim begin to plot the destruction of the gas chambers and crematoria, using Tykva to help them. It is 1944 and the Jews from the Lodz ghetto are arriving, half of whom are immediately gassed. They smuggle Tykva into the *Sonderkommando,* hoping he will figure out a way to successfully destroy the Nazi apparatus of death. Here Otterman links the golem to the historical event of October 1944 in which the inmates rebelled and succeeded in blowing up gas chamber and crematoria IV. Hayim dies the following day of a severe strep infection and, as the killing continues in the remaining gas chambers, Dr. Safra gives up hope that Tykva will stop the slaughter.

Finally Auschwitz is liberated in January 1945, and Dr. Safra is one of the survivors, describing himself and others as "not human beings but mere shadows, golems ourselves. Ill, I was placed in a Soviet hospital. Feverish, I was assailed often by doubts as to the reality of the golem. Perhaps it had all been a dream" (43). Following his recovery, Dr. Safra immigrates to Palestine where he joins an agricultural kibbutz. There he encounters Tykva again and becomes convinced that Tykva "had helped us to win the battle and to stay in the land [that becomes Israel]" (45); further, Dr. Safra speculates that "God might have decreed that Tykva should be in His service and active in our history" (47). He declares that perhaps that is not so surprising as Tykva "was the only golem in history to have been created from human ash. Ash of innocent, righteous and observant men, women and children" (47). So, in the end, this is another story of a victorious golem who comes to the rescue of the Jewish people, not only during the Holocaust but in subsequent Jewish history.

JORGE LUIS BORGES, "THE GOLEM" (1958)

The famed Argentinean poet and fiction writer Jorge Luis Borges has also riffed on the golem legend in a poem published in his book *A Personal Anthology*. Funny and playful, the poem also raises serious philosophical questions about Kabbalah and creation. The focus of the poem is Rabbi Loew and his powerful use of letters and words:

> *Burning to know what God knew,*
> *Judah Lion gave himself up to permutations*
> *Of letters and complex variations:*
> *And at length pronounced the name which is the Key.*

Borges reveals his research on the golem in this sly verse:

> *(The cabalist who officiated as divinity*
> *Called his farfetched creature "Golem":*
> *These truths are related by Scholem*
> *In a learned passage of his volume.)*

Borges concludes the symbolically significant eighteen stanzas of the poem with Rabbi Loew questioning his wisdom in creating this "simulacrum":

At the hour of anguish and vague light
He would rest his eyes on his Golem.
Who can tell us what God felt,
As He gazed on His rabbi in Prague?

In his beautiful and moving history of himself and his family as readers and writers, "An Autobiographical Essay," Borges mentions reading Meyrink's *Der Golem* while he was learning German. He also reveals: "In 1969, when I was in Israel, I talked over the Bohemian legend of the Golem with Gershom Scholem, a leading scholar of Jewish mysticism, whose name I had twice used as the only possible rhyming word in a poem of my own on the Golem" (*The Aleph and Other Stories*, 216).

The American poet John Hollander, in an intertextual gesture, wrote back to Borges in his poem "Letter to Jorge Luis Borges: Apropos of the Golem" (1969). Adopting Borges's pattern of eighteen four-line stanzas, the poem is written in the first person, directly addressing Borges: "I've never been to Prague, and the last time / That I was there its stones sang in the rain" begins the narrator. Hollander's poem is about the power of story; translating Borges's poem has prompted memories for the narrator of his great-grandfather and his mother telling him tales of Prague and of "My ancestor, the Rabbi Loew of Prague." The narrator's family stories hold "family secrets" about the golem's sexuality, whether he can be counted in a minyan, and how he almost "stole" a child while playing hide-and-seek. "These tales jostle each other in their corner / At the eye's edge, skirting the light of day" ("Letter," 37–39). The poem closes on a melancholy note, acknowledging the loneliness of the golem as the only one of his kind.

I am grateful to Arnold Goldsmith for bringing these poems and the Borges autobiography to my attention in *The Golem Remembered* (160–68). These pages also include the full texts of both poems and a more lengthy analysis than I have provided here.

THE GOLEM OF L.A. (DIR. LEWIS SCHOENBRUN [1995])

This short (twenty-five-minute) low-budget film, produced by Ergo Media in Teaneck, New Jersey, is a touching story of a religious grandfather and his UCLA grad student grandson, David. Though his grandfather (an immigrant whose first language is Yiddish) urges him to attend services on Shabbat, David is more committed to tutoring Lucia, a young Latina who wishes to learn English. A subplot of the film involves a scheming developer who plans to tear down the synagogue in order to build luxury apartments. Ed Asner plays the role of the Rabbi Judah Lowenstein (a stand-in for Rabbi

Judah Loew of Prague). Before his sudden death, David's grandfather deploys the golem in the attic of the synagogue to protect the synagogue and gives David a medal "for mystical purposes . . . for creating a golem." The golem "runs amok" (as the rabbi recalls him doing during his earlier incarnation in the 1920s) and hacks the developer to death with an ax as well as two drug dealers who frequent the park where David tutors Lucia. Rabbi Lowenstein demands of David: "You must stop him." David knows he'll get no help from the police, as the African American detective sent to investigate the murders likens the idea of the golem to the voodoo practiced by his grandmother in Haiti and deems the supposed golem "a Jewish Frankenstein." The film ends when the golem, a tall man dressed in shabby clothing with a gray face and "EMET" inscribed on his forehead, approaches Lucia, playing alone in the park. He bends down to speak to her and she scrapes off the Hebrew letters; the golem collapses into a pile of rocks. This is very reminiscent of the conclusion of Wegener's film *Der Golem: Wie er in die Welt kam* when a young girl decommissions the golem at the end of the film by removing the *shem* from the star embedded in his chest. By this time David has accepted Rabbi Lowenstein's invitation to attend Shabbat services and say "Kaddish" for his grandfather; the theme of restoring Jewish tradition to the younger generation is thus fulfilled.

NOTES

Introduction

1. Adorno made this pronouncement in writing in 1949 and it was first published in an essay entitled "Cultural Criticism and Society" in 1951. See Adorno, *Can One Live after Auschwitz?*, 146–62. Adorno subsequently recanted this dictum, but it has remained influential in Holocaust studies.

2. Nathan Ausubel, in his *Treasury of Jewish Folklore*, gives the following explanation for the selection of the name Joseph/Yossele: "To his two disciples the Maharal said that he had named the Golem Joseph because he had implanted in him the spirit of Joseph Shida, he who was half-man and half-demon, and who had saved the sages of the Talmud from many trials and dangers" (608).

3. See, for example, Vasbinder, *Scientific Attitudes in Mary Shelley's Frankenstein,* and Glut, *The Frankenstein Legend,* 67–89.

4. See Yair and Soyer, *The Golem in German Social Theory.*

5. This film and several other golem texts not discussed in the chapters that follow are annotated briefly in the epilogue.

6. I am aware of two other recent monographs on the golem. Nicola Morris's *The Golem in Jewish American Literature* includes only one of the novels about which I write (Rosenbaum's *The Golems of Gotham*). Morris's argument focuses on the golem as a metaphor for power and powerlessness, for authorship, and ultimately for God rather than on the post-Holocaust themes emphasized in my analysis. Cathy Gelbin's *The Golem Returns* focuses on the role of popular culture in the creation of modern Jewish culture, particularly German Jewish culture.

7. See Kristeva, "Intertextuality."

8. *The Torah* (New York: Henry Holt and Company, 1996), 146.

9. For example, see Ezrahi's *By Words Alone;* "After Such Knowledge, What Laughter?" and "Dan Pagis and the Prosaics of Memory." Another scholar who has written extensively on this topic is Lawrence Langer; see his *Holocaust and the Literary Imagination.* Also notable is Susan Gubar's *Poetry after Auschwitz.* A more recent treatment of this issue can be found in Spargo and Ehrenreich,

After Representation.

10. See, for example, the work of Pascale Bos in Baer and Goldenberg, *Experience and Expression*, 23–50.

11. See Benson, "A Series of Fortunate Events for Author Daniel Handler."

Chapter 1

1. See the texts discussed in the introduction by Gershom Scholem and Moshe Idel for scholarly treatments based on original manuscripts.

2. The "blood libel," sometimes called the ritual murder accusation, was the myth circulated in the non-Jewish community that Jews sacrificed a Christian child shortly before Passover in order to use the child's blood in making matzoh for the Passover seder. For example, in 1529, half a century before Rabbi Loew's appointment in Prague, a blood libel accusation in Pösing resulted in more than thirty Jews being burned at the stake. See David, 10ff, who also recounts a similar accusation in 1505 in Budweis, also resulting in Jewish deaths (25n12). Astonishingly, Polish gentiles in Claude Lanzmann's landmark Holocaust film *Shoah* voice a continuing belief in this vicious legend.

3. The Sippurim was "a collection of Jewish folk tales, stories, myths, chronicles, recollections and biographies of famous Jews throughout the centuries, especially the Middle Ages," according to the first volume, printed in 1847 by the Prague Jewish publisher Wolf Pascheles (Sedinova and Kosakova, 18).

4. When I visited the synagogue in the summer of 2007, I struck up a conversation with one of the docents, Irena, who is a survivor of Terezin, the concentration camp located outside Prague. Curious about the attic, I asked her where the stairs to the attic were—I could not locate them. She laughed and assured me that the golem was only a legend. Then she told me that so many tourists asked about how to get to the attic that the synagogue had actually had stairs installed and she told me where to find them on the outside of the building! Sure enough, I found a series of iron rungs affixed to the exterior wall of the synagogue, leading up to a small wooden door located above the roofline. Two books I obtained in Prague have pictures of the synagogue, showing the wall that now bears the iron rungs; neither picture, one an engraving from the late 1700s (Volavkova, 19) and the other a painting from about 1890 (Sedinova and Kosakova, 39), shows the iron rungs, indicating they were installed some time in the twentieth century. See my photograph on p. 103 of this text.

5. "Of the 88,000 Jews who lived in the so-called protectorate of Bohemia-Moravia in October, 1941, fewer than 8,000 remained in April 1945" (Kieval, "Pursuing" 8). Despite the Nazi occupation, several of the original synagogues remain in Prague. Most are now museums of Jewish life in Prague before the Holocaust, but a few still hold services. Somewhat ironically, these synagogues survived because the Nazis intended to devote the buildings to a "Museum to the Extinct Jewish Race."

6. See Sherwin's discussion of arguments for the various theories (*Mystical Theology*, 196).

7. This version of Weisel's tale appears in Kieval, *Languages*, 95–96, and is described as "a modern rendition." Kieval lists the source as *Sippurim: Eine Sammlung jüdisher Volkssagen Erzählungen, Mythen, Chroniken, Denkwürdigkeiten and Biograhien berümter Juden*, ed. Wolf Pascheles, Erste Sammlung, 4th ed. (Prague: Pascheles, 1870), 51–52. Though he does not specify, my assumption is that Kieval is the translator here.

8. His book is still listed this way on Amazon.com.

9. Moldau is the German name for the Vltava River, which runs through central Prague. Both of these names appear in various versions of the tale.

10. Hsia includes a table listing twenty-three such accusations in the fifteenth century and thirty in the sixteenth, although Hsia acknowledges that these are estimates (3).

11. Regrettably, this latter edition omits the ten photographs included in the Vienna edition, except one of the statue of Rabbi Loew that still stands next to the Town Hall in Prague.

Chapter 2

1. *Die Weissen Blätter* was an expressionist journal founded in Berlin in 1913 and published by the wealthy German Erik Ernst Schwabach. When Kurt Wolff took over as manager of the journal in January 1914, it was moved to Leipzig where Wolff also published books. It was subsequently relocated to Switzerland (http://danassays.wordpress.com/encyclopedia-of-the-essay/die-weissen-blatter/).

2. All page references are to the Dover edition of the novel, edited by E. F. Bleiler.

3. Of course, the use of the term "Kafkaesque" in this context is a bit of an anachronism. When *Der Golem* was published in 1913–14, Kafka was at the very beginning of his writing career. "The Metamorphosis" had just been published and *The Trial* and *The Castle* would not appear for another decade.

4. The arrival of a stranger with a book that has a profound impact on its new owner brings to mind Borges's wonderful short story, "A Book of Sand." Though this story contains no reference to the golem, Borges did publish a poem about the golem and acknowledges that he had read Meyrink's *Der Golem*. See the epilogue for more information on the Borges poem.

5. Originally another artist—Alfred Kubin—had contracted to do the illustrations and produced several pen and ink sketches of dark, Expressionistic buildings dwarfing mysterious figures. However, Kubin became frustrated with Meyrink's meandering progress on the manuscript and instead published the illustrations in his own novel, *Die andere Seite* (Georg Müller, Munich), in 1923. Steiner-Prag's illustrations first appeared in a 1916 edition of the novel.

6. Another curious Christian twist occurs in chapter 5, "Punch," when the puppet maker recounts the old legend of Prague about the creation of the golem "to help ring the bells in the Synagogue and for all kinds of other menial work"

(26). As Arnold Goldsmith aptly points out, "Jews did not have bells in their synagogues" (99).

7. This incident in Meyrink's life, perhaps apocryphal, seems to be echoed in the arrival of the stranger at the narrator's door with the *Book of Ibbur*.

8. Another intriguing connection between Kafka and Meyrink's use of the golem legend is Kafka's attendance at Yom Kippur services at the Altneu synagogue in September 1911; it is in the attic of this synagogue that the remains of the golem are said to be stored even until the present (Gilman, 50).

9. Some sources claim that Meyrink translated as many as twenty Dickens volumes. See, for example, "Gustav Meyrink, 1868–1932," in *Twentieth Century Literary Criticism*, vol. 21, ed. Dennis Poupard (Detroit: Gale, 1986), 215.

10. See Mitchell, *Vivo*, 156–64.

11. See chapter 1 for a fuller explication of the destruction of the Josefov in the late nineteenth and early twentieth centuries. Cathleen Giustino's study, *Tearing down Prague's Jewish Town*, is the best source on this "urban renewal" project.

12. Some sources (Kracauer, Eisner) say the 1920 golem film is Wegener's second, but more recent filmographies note it is his third golem film, the second being *Der Golem und die Tänzerin* (The Golem and the Dancer), released in June 1917. Also, many sources state that the first 1914 Wegener golem film is lost to us; however, Donald Glut, who has tracked down all things Frankenstein for his comprehensive and somewhat idiosyncratic study, *The Frankenstein Legend*, claims a print exists: "For many years *Der Golem* was considered one of the many films that would never be screened again, a fate befallen the silent versions of *Frankenstein*. A print was miraculously discovered in 1958 by Paul Sauerlaender, a European film collector. The owner of a toy store in Europe was selling old 35mm movie projectors and giving his customers small lengths (from twelve to fifteen feet) of silent film which turned out to be this original [1914] Golem feature. Luckily for the sake of film history Sauerlaender was able to track down the various owners and emerge from the hunt with a complete print of *Der Golem*" (71). Glut provides no source for this information.

13. This is completely ahistorical. As we have seen, Rudolf was a supporter of the Jewish community and did not issue such a decree; however, efforts to force the Jewish community to vacate the ghetto had occurred at an earlier time.

14. See Lotte Eisner (64–74) for an extended comment by Carl Boese, co-director of the film, on how these special effects were achieved.

15. However, Ledig's article on *Der Golem* is invaluable for its careful sorting of the various prints available, its persuasive evidence that another version of Wegener's 1920 golem film existed at one time, and her analysis of Wegener's many literary and mythic sources for the film.

16. For a compelling comparison between these two films, see Bartov, 6–13.

17. Horst Wessel, born in Berlin in 1907, joined the Nazi Party in 1926 and wrote the lyrics to the song that became the Nazi anthem; it is often referred to

as the "Horst Wessel Song." He was murdered under suspicious circumstances and subsequently became a Nazi "martyr."

18. The last edict expelling Jews from Prague had been declared in 1541 after a great fire had destroyed much of Prague and a Jew "confessed" to the crime under torture (Demetz, 201).

19. For a lucid and concise summary of these laws, see Demetz, 201.

20. Six years later, Murnau used a similar circle of fire in his film *Faust* (1926) when the devil is being summoned.

21. See http://en.wikipedia.org/wiki/Astaroth and http://www.angelfire.com/empire/serpent is 666/Astoroth.html (accessed February 28, 2008).

22. See, for example, Manvell, *Masterworks.*

23. This discrepancy in the description of the film is one of the very few to be found when carefully comparing Byrne's shot analysis (1966) and Manvell's detailed summary (1973). Indeed, a close comparison reveals that Manvell has adopted much of Byrne's language and evaluation of the action in the film.

24. http://www.jewishencyclopedia.com/view.jsp?artid=967&letter=A (accessed May 21, 2008).

25. This speculation is affirmed by a footnote in Elfi Ledig's analysis of the film, in which she claims that the intertitle for this scene, "Ahasver," is missing from all prints of the film taken from the New York print. She cites Roger Manvell's identification of the figure as Moses as a mistake resulting from the omission of this intertitle (Bilski, 124).

26. Duvivier's wife was Jewish (see Crisp) and hence the flight may have been for her protection.

Chapter 3

1. See Roth, 89 for the full story of this moment in Singer's life.

2. Irving Buchen notes that this novel appeared in 1933 "under the unfortunate title of *The Sinner*" (29). Israel Joshua's most famous novel is *The Brothers Ashkenazi* (1935).

3. Curiously, biographer Janet Hadda mentions Singer's father's death only in passing and makes no mention of his mother's death.

4. Singer here connects the golem narrative with the tales of the Baal Shem Tov, the founder of Hasidism, and the wonder rabbis, who often appear in Hasidic literature. This is not surprising as Singer grew up in a Hasidic community in Poland. However, it is important to point out that Rabbi Judah Loew significantly predates both the Baal Shem Tov and the founding of Hasidism in the eighteenth century. Thus, the golem theme is not a common Hasidic motif.

5. See Goldsmith, "Singer."

6. Rosenberg, xxix.

7. Note that this is the same name as the daughter of Rabbi Loew in Wegener's film.

8. See Philip, "Fall into Flesh."

9. This confiscation of all Hebrew books actually occurred in Prague in 1560. See the *Jewish Encyclopedia* http://www.jewishencyclopedia.com/view.jsp?artid=719&letter=C (accessed January 2010).

10. Note that Yudl Rosenberg's *The Golem and the Wondrous Deeds of the Maharal of Prague* opens with a Christian carrying a dead child in a sack; he is intent upon depositing the child in the cellar of a rabbi's home, thus setting the stage for a blood libel accusation.

11. See Wiesel and De Saint-Cheron, *Evil and Exile*, 58–59, for Wiesel's explanation of why he prefers this term to "Shoah" or "Holocaust."

12. Wiesel frequently agrees to appear with political figures in the pursuit of these ideas. Note, for example, his appearance with Lech Walesa, the Polish Solidarity leader, at Auschwitz in 1988, with President Clinton at the opening of the United States Holocaust Memorial Museum in 1993, and, more recently, with President Obama at Buchenwald in June 2009.

13. See Sherwin, "Elie Wiesel and Jewish Theology" for an explanation of the significance of eighteen for Wiesel, as well as for an illuminating essay on Wiesel's spirituality.

14. For a nuanced biography of Rudolf II, which explicates his relationship with the Jewish population, see Evans, *Rudolf II and His World*. Evans notes that there is evidence of one possible suicide attempt by Rudolf in 1600 (63).

15. See Rosenberg, chapters 5–6, for an account of this debate.

16. This is an oft-repeated tale ascribing miraculous powers to the Maharal. See, for example, a small and beautifully illustrated collection of golem tales titled *The Prague Golem*, especially the chapter titled "Rabbi Loew, the Benefactor of the Jews of Prague."

17. It is intriguing to note the parallel between de Leon's authorship of the *Zohar* and Yudl Rosenberg's authorship of *The Golem and the Wondrous Deeds of the Maharal of Prague*. Both men claimed to have copied their texts from much earlier manuscripts that held the aura of authority. In both cases, contemporary scholarship has provided fairly certain evidence that these men were in fact the original authors. See Dan, *Kabbalah*, 31–33, for the story of Rabbi de Leon.

18. As Zev measures the golem he can't help but speculate: "He was a giant this man, almost seven feet, but well-formed. Did he have a member commensurate with the rest of him? Zev wondered" (172). When, later in the novel, Rochel has a miscarriage following immediately upon intercourse with the golem, the reader cannot help but wonder, too. Debate has occurred historically about whether the golem really is a man and whether he can serve in a minyan, and the response is usually no. This passage is yet another in which Sherwood creates a more human and more emotional golem than his predecessors.

19. Sherwood also alludes to the Beauty and the Beast motif in her pairing of Rochel and the golem, and to Cinderella in Rochel's role as an orphan servant girl. These are yet other intertextual appropriations made by Sherwood.

20. http://www.francessherwood.com/bookOfSplendor_author.htm (accessed July 1, 2009).

Chapter 4

1. http://www.ariekaplan.com/kingscomicspart1.htm (accessed July 2009).
2. http://www.popmatters.com/comics/monolith-1.shtml (accessed July 2009).
3. The Incredible Hulk himself is a golem-like figure. He was created by Stan Lee and Jack Kirby in 1962 and appeared in Marvel Comics off and on through the later decades of the twentieth century.
4. http://www.readyourselfraw.com/profiles/sturm/profile_sturm.htm (accessed July 2009).
5. http://cartoonstudies.org/ (accessed July 2009).
6. For an intriguing interview in which Sturm is on the defensive about his appropriation of *The Fantastic Four* characters for *Unstable Molecules* because of financial arrangements made by Marvel with him and earlier artists, see the excerpt from the *Comics Journal,* issue #251 at http://www.tcj.com/251/i_sturm.html (accessed July 2009).
7. Paul Lawrence Dunbar, *Lyrics of the Lowly Life* (New York: Dodd, Mead and Company, 1896).
8. James Sturm, *Satchel Paige: Striking Out Jim Crow* (New York: Jump at the Sun, Hyperion Books for Children, 2007). See http://www.cartoonstudies.org/books/paige/interview.html (accessed July 2009) for an interview with Sturm about this book.
9. http://www.petehamill.com/bio.html (accessed July 2009).
10. For an amusing account of his own boyhood romance with Captain Marvel, see Feiffer, *The Great Comic Book Heroes,* 20–23.
11. "Paddy McGinty's Goat" is a plaintive Irish song with many verses that Hamill's father used to sing to much acclaim in bars around Brooklyn.
12. His real name is Yossel Greenberg (109). There is something of the suggestion of a doppelgänger here.
13. The legend of the magic palace can be found in Bloch, in a chapter titled "The Wonderful Palace" (218–24); the character of the antisemitic priest, Thaddeus, can be found throughout Rosenberg's book; and the legend of Rabbi Loew turning stones into roses can be found in a chapter titled "Rabbi Loew, the Benefactor of the Jews of Prague" in the collection *The Prague Golem* (35–37). Hamill undertook some of this research while in Prague in 1989. Dispatched there as a journalist to cover the fall of communism, he found time to visit the Old-New Synagogue and the old Jewish Cemetery where Rabbi Loew is buried: "And there," writes Hamill, "something strange happened . . . I felt a shudder, a pebbling of skin, a sense of immanence, as if I had suddenly connected with all the lost centuries. The dead were not dead. The past was here, in this holy ground . . . the translator told me . . . about the Golem . . . I said: 'God, I wish I'd had a golem when I was eleven.' And uttering that wish, I knew I had my novel at last" (*Snow,* 370–71).
14. See *Snow,* 365, for Hamill's tribute to the Dodgers.
15. Such a creation of "alternate histories" is also the project of much of the

fiction of the German writer W. G. Sebald. See my "W. G. Sebald's *Austerlitz*" and Santner, *Stranded Objects*, for an in-depth study of the notion of "alternative histories."

16. See, for example, http://www.insidehighered.com/views/mclemee/mclemee23 (accessed August 2009) for a discussion of this invention by Chabon.

17. For an account of the novel as a story of "economic laws to be escaped" (299), see Daniel Punday's article about American fiction set in the comic book industry, which reveals "the corporate influence on originality and the attempt to claim ownership of artistic creations" (291).

18. Chabon has acknowledged his debt to the real-life creators of Superman, Joe Shuster and Jerry Siegel. See Binelli and Duffy, "The Amazing Story of the Comic-Book Nerd." See also the Web site for Kavalier and Clay: http://www. sugarbombs.com/kavalier/?page_id=13 (accessed August 2009).

19. This may be a nod to Mary Shelley, whose Frankenstein monster character, considered to be inspired by the golem, travels to the Antarctic near the end of that novel.

20. For an intriguing episode in Sam's growing acceptance of his sexual orientation that was eliminated from the novel, see Chabon, "An Untold Tale of Kavalier and Clay."

21. One reviewer of *The Amazing Adventures of the Escapist* complains that it is "one of the oddest comic books I have ever read"; after quoting at length from the fictional history of the Escapist comics presented by Chabon, Robert Burns muses: "I wonder what the casual reader will make of this subterfuge." This, of course, is one of the challenges of intertextuality: how much familiarity with the "original" text does the reader need in order to appreciate the intertext. This issue is often raised, for example, with the pairing of Brontë's *Jane Eyre* and Jean Rhys's *Wide Sargasso Sea*. See Burns, "Imagining the Escapist."

22. http://www.darkhorse.com/Search/Browse/Escapist/PpwNwkt8 (accessed August 2009).

23. http://www.ushmm.org/museum/exhibit/focus/antisemitism/voices/transcript/?content=20080313 (accessed August 2009).

Chapter 5

1. For a thoughtful analysis of Ozick's fiction about the Holocaust other than "The Shawl" and "Rosa," see Kremer, *Witness through the Imagination*, chapter 7.

2. For useful critical treatments of Ozick's Holocaust fiction and her concerns regarding authority to speak, see Henry Gonshak, "'A Madwoman and a Scavenger': The Toll of Holocaust Survival in Cynthia Ozick's 'Rosa,'" in *New Perspectives on the Holocaust: A Guide for Teachers and Scholars*, ed. Rochelle Millen (New York: New York University Press, 1992).

3. See Kauvar, "An Interview with Cynthia Ozick."

4. See, for example, Kremer, *Women's Holocaust Writing*, 154–55. Kremer

also comments on the intertextual relationship between Ozick's story "Usurpation" and Malamud's "The Silver Crown," and Ozick's "A Mercenary" and Jerzy Kosinski's *Painted Bird*. Kremer notes that Ozick acknowledged these influences in a personal interview.

5. Three of the chapters of the novel originally appeared in *The New Yorker*, one in the *Atlantic Monthly*, and the golem chapter, "Puttermesser and Xanthippe," in *Salmagundi*.

6. Other similarities between Ozick and Puttermesser include "a weakness for chocolate and periodontal disease" (Smith) and "the feeling of . . . being different," as well as a fondness for George Eliot (Frumkes 18).

7. Noting the silencing of women in some aspects of Jewish tradition, Ruth Bienstock Anolik provides a frankly feminist interpretation of Puttermesser in her essay "Appropriating the Golem, Possessing the Dybbuk." She sees Puttermesser's story as a birth narrative that "reveals a poignant longing for the possibility of a female presence within the line of tradition" (45). In turn, this demonstrates how "Jewish women writers open up a narrative space for the figure of the creative, powerful and vocal woman" (40).

8. See Kauvar, "Cynthia Ozick's Book of Creation." Kauvar comments on both the role of periodontal disease in the novel and the theme of utopias.

9. Ruth Bienstock Anolik notes the hidden meaning of Malachy Mavett's name: "The mayor's name is an intricate linguistic joke. Malachy Mavett is a play on the Hebrew 'malach hamavett,' the Angel of Death. The nickname Matt Mavett also recalls the Hebrew letters inscribed on the golem's forehead: 'met' means dead; 'mavet' death" ("Appropriating the Golem," 45).

10. Ozick herself was threatened with a similar lawsuit. A Jewish day school headmaster thought himself defamed in her short story "The Laughter of Akiva" (1980). The dispute was settled out of court. See Lowin, "Cynthia Ozick."

11. For a fuller account of the relationship between Bloch's and Rosenberg's texts, see chapter 1.

12. This painting was done by Jacques-Louis David and depicts the final conversation of Socrates and his students. It was painted in 1787, on the eve of the French Revolution.

13. According to Richard Bernstein's review of *The Puttermesser Papers* in the *New York Times*, the imagined journal *Shekhina* is a "thinly disguised surrogate" for the magazine *Tikkun*.

14. See http://www.jewishencyclopedia.com/view.jsp?artid=588&letter=S (accessed September 2009).

15. See, for example, Eric D. Weitz, *A Century of Genocide: Utopias of Race and Nation* (Princeton: Princeton University Press, 2003), and Zadie Smith's wonderful postcolonial novel *White Teeth* (New York: Random House, 2000), which explores efforts in three registers—science, religion, and education—to establish utopias. All three efforts fail and the novel is clearly meant to warn against the dangers of attempts to achieve utopia.

16. This essay appears in Ozick's collection of essays titled *Art and Ardor*.

17. See http://www.fordhamlawandculture.org/about/thanerosenbaum (accessed January 2010).

18. See reviews by Kim Bendheim, Steven Keeva, Harry Charles, and Vanessa Bush, all of which emphasize this aspect of the book.

19. Rosenbaum also uses the story of the lighthouse on the Hudson in the short story "The Little Blue Snowman of Washington Heights" from his collection *Elijah Visible,* another instance of intertextuality.

20. A daughter's impulse to help a needy parent is also a key theme in Nicole Krauss's wonderful post-Holocaust fiction, *The History of Love.*

21. Isaac Luria (1534–72) is the name of a great Jewish mystic and kabbalist. Alan Berger notes the comparison between Luria's beliefs and those put forward in Rosenbaum's novel, and offers this further information about Luria in his article: Luria viewed the "spiritual upheaval in the wake of the expulsion of the Jews from the Iberian peninsula . . . in terms of mission. Sparks of divine light were scattered everywhere, owing to a primal act of breaking the vessels . . . designed to contain them. Therefore the Jewish people were scattered in order to elevate these sparks by performing every act with the correct *kavvanah* [intention or meditation]. The *kavvanah* had to be for the sake of reuniting God and the *Shekinah* [female dimension of deity], which had been sundered by the breaking of the vessels" (5).

22. Quoted from *Newsday* on book cover of *Watch Your Mouth.*

23. This Daniel Handler interview can be found at http://www.sfgate.com (accessed April 15, 2005).

Bibliography

Golem Primary Texts:
Fiction and Film and Golem-Related Texts

Bloch, Chayim. *The Golem: Legends of the Ghetto of Prague.* Trans. Harry Schneiderman. Vienna: John N. Vernay, 1925.

Borges, Jorge Luis. "The Golem." In *A Personal Anthology.* New York: Grove Press, 1967.

Casken, John. *Golem.* 1989.

Chabon, Michael. *The Amazing Adventures of Kavalier and Clay.* New York: Random House, 2000.

Chatwin, Bruce. *Utz.* London: Jonathan Cape, 1988.

Duvivier, Julien, dir. *Le Golem.* Prague, A. B. Films, 1936.

Estrin, Marc. *Golem Song.* Denver: Unbridled Books, 2006.

Eve, Nomi. *The Family Orchard.* New York: Knopf, 2000.

Friedrich, Mike. "The Golem: The Thing That Walks Like a Man." #176. New York: Marvel Comics, 1974.

———. "The Golem: The Thing That Walks Like a Man." #177. New York: Marvel Comics, 1974.

Gordon, Howard. "Kaddish." *The X-Files,* Season 4, Episode 12. February 16, 1997.

Hamill, Pete. *Snow in August.* New York: Warner Books, 1997.

Handler, Daniel. *Watch Your Mouth.* New York: Perennial, 2002.

Hollander, John. "Letter to Jorge Luis Borges Apropos of the Golem." In *The Night Mirror.* New York: Atheneum, 1971.

Humphrey, Clark. "Golem at the Bat." *American Book Review* 23, no. 2 (2002): 7.

Irwin, Robert, ed. *The Golem,* by Gustav Meyrink. London: Dedalus, 1985.

Leivick, H. "The Golem: A Dramatic Poem in Eight Scenes." In *The Great Jewish Plays,* ed. Joseph C. Landis. 1921. New York: Horizon Press, 1966.

Meyrink, Gustav. *The Golem.* 1913–14. New York: Dover, 1976.

———. *Der Golem.* Bremen: Carl Schünemann Verlag, 1915.

Neugroschel, Joachim. *The Golem: A New Translation of the Classic Play and*

Selected Short Stories. New York: Norton, 2006.

Otterman, Bernard. *Golem of Auschwitz: Stories.* New York: Slovo-Word Publishing House, 2001.

Ozick, Cynthia. *The Puttermesser Papers.* New York: Knopf, 1997.

Palmiotti, Jimmy, and Justin Gray. "The Monolith." #9. New York: DC Comics, 2004.

———. "The Monolith." #11. New York: DC Comics, 2005.

———. "The Monolith." #12. New York: DC Comics, 2005.

Pechackova, Ivana. *The Legend of the Golem.* Trans. Klara Tvaruzkova. Prague: Meander Publishing House, 2004.

Peretz, I. L. "The Golem." In *The Penguin Book of Short Stories,* ed. Emanuel Litvinoff. New York: Penguin, 1979.

Petiska, Eduard. *The Golem: Old Jewish Stories from Prague.* Trans. Jana Svabova. Prague: Martin Publishing, 2001.

Piercy, Marge. *He, She and It.* New York: Knopf, 1991.

The Prague Golem: Jewish Stories of the Ghetto. Prague: Vitalis, n.d.

Rogasky, Barbara. *The Golem.* Illus. Trina Schart Hyman. New York: Holiday House, 1996.

Rosenbaum, Thane. *The Golems of Gotham.* New York: Harper Collins, 2002.

Rosenberg, Yudl. *The Golem and the Wondrous Deeds of the Maharal of Prague.* Ed. Curt Leviant. New Haven: Yale University Press, 2007.

Roth, Ina. *A Golem Walks through Prague.* Trans. Drahomira Bainbridge and Laurence Bainbridge. Prague: Baset Publishing House, 2004.

Rye, Stellan, dir. *Der Student von Prag.* Berlin: Deutsche Bioscop, 1913.

Schoenbrun, Lewis, dir. "The Golem of L.A." Teaneck, NJ: Ergo Media, 1995.

Seifert, Lucy. *The Mysterious Golem.* Trans. Anna Gustova. Prague: Petr Prchal, 2004.

Sherwood, Frances. *The Book of Splendor.* New York: Norton, 2002.

Singer, Isaac Bashevis. *The Golem.* 1969 (Yiddish). New York: Farrar, Straus and Giroux, 1982.

Stern, Steve. *Lazar Malkin Enters Heaven.* New York: Viking, 1986.

Stetinova, Dagmar. *The Golem Is Sleeping in Prague.* Trans. David Beveridge. Prague: V Raji Publishers, 2005.

Sturm, James. *The Golem's Mighty Swing.* Montreal: Drawn and Quarterly, 2001.

———. *James Sturm's America: God, Gold, and Golems.* Montreal: Drawn and Quarterly, 2007.

Tallis, Frank. *Vienna Secrets.* New York: Random House, 2009.

Thomas, Roy. "The Thing and the Golem." #11. New York: Marvel Comics, 1975.

Votruba, Jiri. *Golem: An Old Prague Tale.* Czech Republic: Fun Explosive, 2001.

Wegener, Paul, dir. *Der Golem: Wie er in die Welt kam.* Germany, 1920.

Wein, Len. "The Golem: The Thing That Walks Like a Man." #174. New York: Marvel Comics, 1974.

Wiesel, Elie. *The Golem.* New York: Summit Books, 1983.

Wishnia, Kenneth. *The Fifth Servant*. New York: William Morrow, 2010.
Wisniewski, David. *Golem*. New York: Clarion Books, 1996.

CRITICAL WORKS AND OTHER SOURCES

Adorno, Theodor W. *Can One Live after Auschwitz? A Philosophical Reader*. Stanford: Stanford University Press, 2003.
Alexander, Edward. *Isaac Bashevis Singer*. Boston: Twayne, 1980.
Allen, Graham. *Intertextuality*. New York: Routledge, 2000.
Allison, Alida. *Isaac Bashevis Singer: Children's Stories and Childhood Memoirs*. New York: Twayne, 1996.
Anolik, Ruth Bienstock. "Appropriating the Golem, Possessing the Dybbuk: Female Retellings of Jewish Tales." *Modern Language Studies* 32, no. 2 (Autumn 2001): 39–55.
———. "Reviving the Golem, Revisiting *Frankenstein*: Cultural Negotiations in Ozick's *The Puttermesser Papers* and Piercy's *He, She and It*." In *Connections and Collisions: Identities in Contemporary Jewish-American Women's Writing*, ed. Lois Rubin. Newark: University of Delaware Press, 2005.
Ausubel, Nathan, ed. *A Treasury of Jewish Folklore: Stories, Traditions, Legends, Humor, Wisdom and Folk Songs of the Jewish People*. New York: Crown, 1948.
Baer, Elizabeth. "W. G. Sebald's Austerlitz: Adaptation as Restitution." In *Reworking the German Past: Adaptations in Film, the Arts and Popular Culture*, ed. Susan Figge and Jenifer Ward. Rochester: Camden House, 2010.
Baer, Elizabeth, and Myrna Goldenberg, eds. *Experience and Expression: Women, the Nazis, and the Holocaust*. Detroit: Wayne State University Press, 2003.
Barsanti, Chris. "the graphic report. . ." *Kirkus Reviews* 72, no. 14 (July 15, 2004): 642.
Bartov, Omer. *The "Jew" in Cinema: From "The Golem" to "Don't Touch My Holocaust."* Bloomington: Indiana University Press, 2005.
Baumgarten, Murray. "Reading Cynthia Ozick: Imagining Jewish Writing." *Contemporary Literature* 37, no. 2 (Summer 1996): 307–14.
Behlman, Lee. "The Escapist: Fantasy, Folklore, and the Pleasures of the Comic Book in Recent Jewish American Holocaust Fiction." *Shofar* 22, no. 3 (Spring 2004): 56–71.
Bendheim, Kim. "Golem Dreams." *Tikkun* 17, no. 4 (July/August 2002): 80.
Bensky, Roger. "Words for an Abysmal Golem." *Substance* 20 (1978): 119–23.
Benson, Heidi. "A Series of Fortunate Events for Author Daniel Handler, a.k.a. Lemony Snicket, Including Forthcoming Film, Fatherhood." October 13, 2003. http://sfgate.com/cgi-bin/article.cgi?file=/c/a2003/10/13/DD138106. DTL (accessed June 2006).
Berger, Alan. "Myth, Mysticism, and Memory: The Holocaust in Thane Rosenbaum's *The Golems of Gotham*." *Studies in Jewish American Literature* 24 (2005): 1–21.

Bernstein, Richard. "A Passionate Idealist with a Golem and Bad Luck." *New York Times,* June 11, 1997, C17.

Bigelow, Gordon. "Michael Chabon's Unhomely Pulp." *Literature, Interpretation, Theory* 19, no. 4 (2008): 305–20.

Bilefsky, Dan. "A New Heyday (and Many Spinoffs) for a Centuries-Old Giant, the Golem." *New York Times,* May 11, 2009, A10.

Bilski, Emily D. *Golem! Danger, Deliverance, and Art.* New York: The Jewish Museum, 1988.

Binelli, Mark, and Bryce Duffy. "The Amazing Story of the Comic-Book Nerd Who Won the Pulitzer Prize for Fiction." *Rolling Stone* 878 (September 27, 2001): 58–63.

Blanchot, Maurice. "The Secret of the Golem." *Southern Humanities Review* 34, no. 2 (Spring 2000): 119–26.

Bleiler, E. F., ed. Introduction to *The Golem,* by Gustav Meyrink. New York: Dover, 1976.

Borges, Jorge Luis. *The Aleph and Other Stories.* New York: E. P. Dutton, 1970.

Bos, Pascale. "Women and the Holocaust: Analyzing Gender Difference." In *Experience and Expression: Women, the Nazis, and the Holocaust,* ed. Elizabeth Baer and Myrna Goldenberg. Detroit: Wayne State University Press, 2003.

Briggs, Kenneth A. "A Protector." *New York Times,* April 16, 1984, sec. C, p. 18.

Buchen, Irving H. *Isaac Bashevis Singer and the Eternal Past.* New York: New York University Press, 1968.

Buhle, Paul, ed. *Jews and American Comics: An Illustrated History of an American Art Form.* New York: The New Press, 2008.

Burns, Robert. "Imagining the Escapist." *Phi Kappa Phi Forum* 84, no. 3 (Summer 2004): 45–46.

Burstein, Janet. "Traumatic Memory and American Jewish Writers: One Generation after the Holocaust." *Yiddish* 11, no. 3–4 (1999): 188–97.

Bush, Vanessa. "Thane Rosenbaum." *Booklist* (April 15, 2004): 1410.

Butler, Francelia. "An Interview with Isaac Bashevis Singer." In *Sharing Literature with Children.* Prospect Heights, IL: Waveland Press, 1989.

Byrne, Richard B. *Films of Tyranny: Shot Analyses of "The Cabinet of Dr. Caligari," "The Golem," "Nosferatu."* Madison, WI: College Printing and Typing Company, 1966.

Chabon, Michael. *The Final Solution: A Story of Detection.* New York: HarperCollins, 2004.

———. *Manhood for Amateurs: The Pleasures and Regrets of a Husband, Father, and Son.* New York: Harper Collins, 2009.

———. *Maps and Legends: Reading and Writing along the Borderlands.* San Francisco: McSweeney's Books, 2008.

———. "An Untold Tale of Kavalier and Clay: Breakfast in the Wreck." *Virginia Quarterly Review* 80, no. 2 (Spring 2004): 33–38.

Charles, Harry. "Thane Rosenbaum." *Library Journal* (April 1, 2004): 109.

Chute, Hillary. "*Ragtime, Kavalier and Clay* and the Framing of Comics." *Modern Fiction Studies* 54, no. 2 (Summer 2008): 268–301.

Clayton, Jay, and Eric Rothstein. *Influence and Intertextuality in Literary History.* Madison: University of Wisconsin Press, 1991.

Coan, Peter Morton. *Ellis Island Interviews: In Their Own Words.* New York: Checkmark Books, 1997.

Coates, Paul. *The Gorgon's Gaze: German Cinema, Expressionism, and the Image of Horror.* Cambridge: Cambridge University Press, 1991.

Cohen, Sarah Blacher. "Cynthia Ozick and Her New Yiddish Golem." *Studies in American Jewish Literature* 6 (1987): 105–10.

———. *Cynthia Ozick's Comic Art: From Levity to Liturgy.* Bloomington: Indiana University Press, 1994.

Cooke, Paul. *German Expressionist Films.* Great Britain: Pocket Essentials, 2002.

Crisp, Colin. *The Classic French Cinema, 1930–1960.* Bloomington: Indiana University Press, 1993.

Dan, Joseph. *Kabbalah: A Very Short Introduction.* Oxford: Oxford University Press, 2006.

David, Abraham, ed. *A Hebrew Chronicle from Prague, c. 1615.* Trans. Leon J. Weinberger. Tuscaloosa: University of Alabama Press, 1993.

Davidowicz, Klaus Samuel. "From Myth to Film Epic: Paul Wegener's Golem." In *Jews and Film/Juden und Film,* ed. Eleanore Lappin. Vienna: Mandelbaum, 2004.

Demetz, Peter. *Prague in Black and Gold: Scenes in the Life of a European City.* New York: Hill and Wang, 1997.

Diaz, Juno. *The Brief Wondrous Life of Oscar Wao.* New York: Riverhead Books, 2007.

Eder, Richard. "Mad Emperor Meets His Match in a Rabbi with a Lifesaving Spell." *New York Times,* July 5, 2002, p. E40.

Eisner, Lotte. *The Haunted Screen: Expressionism in the German Cinema and the Influence of Max Reinhardt.* 1952. Berkeley: University of California Press, 1969

Eisner, Will. *A Contract with God.* 1978. New York: Norton, 2006.

Engberg, Gillian. "The Book of Splendor." *Booklist,* May 15, 2002, 1587–88.

Evans, R. J. W. *Rudolf II and His World: A Study in Intellectual History, 1576–1612.* Oxford: Clarendon Press, 1973.

Ezrahi, Sidra DeKoven. "After Such Knowledge, What Laughter?" *Yale Journal of Criticism* 14, no. 1 (2001): 287–317.

———. *By Words Alone: The Holocaust in Literature.* Chicago: University of Chicago Press, 1980.

———. "Dan Pagis and the Prosaics of Memory." In *Holocaust Remembrance: The Shapes of Memory,* ed. Geoffrey Hartman. New York: Blackwell, 1994.

———. "Representing Auschwitz." *History and Memory* 7, no. 2 (Fall 1996): 121–54.

Feiffer, Jules. *The Great Comic Book Heroes*. Seattle: Fantagraphic Books, 2003.

Fingeroth, Danny. *Disguised as Clark Kent: Jews, Comics, and the Creation of the Superhero*. New York: Continuum, 2007.

———. *The Rough Guide to Graphic Novels*. New York: Rough Guides Ltd., 2008.

Friedman, Lester D. "The Edge of Knowledge: Jews as Monsters/Jews as Victims." *Meleus* 11, no. 3 (Autumn 1984): 49–62.

Friedrich, Marianne M. "The Rendition of Memory in Cynthia Ozick's 'The Shawl.'" In *Jewish American and Holocaust Literature: Representation in the Postmodern World*, ed. Alan Berger and Gloria Cronin. Albany: SUNY Press, 2004.

Frumkes, Lewis Burke. "A Conversation with . . . Cynthia Ozick." *Writer* 111, no. 3 (March 1998): 18–21.

Gardner, James. "Nice Jewish Golem." *National Review*, September 1, 1997, p. 50.

Gaster, Moses. *Ma'aseh Book*. Vols. 1 and 2. Philadelphia: Jewish Publication Society of America, 1934.

Gelbin, Cathy. *The Golem Returns: From German Romantic Literature to Global Jewish Culture, 1808–2008*. Ann Arbor: University of Michigan Press, 2011.

———. "Narratives of Transgression, from Jewish Folktales to German Cinema." *Kinoeye* 3, no. 11 (October 13, 2003). http://www.kinoeye.org/03/11/gelbin//.php (accessed March 7, 2007).

Genette, Gerard. *Palimpsests: Literature in the Second Degree*. Lincoln: University of Nebraska Press, 1997.

Gilman, Sander. *Franz Kafka*. London: Reaktion Books, 2005.

Giustino, Cathleen. *Tearing down Prague's Jewish Town*. Eastern European Monographs. Boulder, CO: Columbia University Press, 2003.

Glinert, Lewis. "Golem! The Making of a Modern Myth." *Symposium* 55, no. 2 (Summer 2001): 78–95.

Glut, Donald. *The Frankenstein Legend: A Tribute to Mary Shelley and Boris Karloff*. Metuchen, NJ: Scarecrow Press, 1973.

Goldsmith, Arnold L. "Elie Wiesel, Rabbi Judah Lowe, and the Golem of Prague." *Studies in American Jewish Literature* 5 (1986): 15–28.

———. *The Golem Remembered, 1909–1980: Variations on a Jewish Legend*. Detroit: Wayne State University Press, 1981.

———. "Isaac Bashevis Singer and the Legend of the Golem of Prague." *Yiddish* 6, no. 2 (Summer 1985): 39–50.

Gottesman, Itzik. "Folk and Folklore in the Work of Bashevis." In *The Hidden Isaac Bashevis Singer*, ed. Seth L. Wolitz. Austin: University of Texas Press, 2001.

Graham, Elaine L. *Representations of the Post/Human: Monsters, Aliens, and Others in Popular Culture*. New Brunswick: Rutgers University Press, 2002.

Gubar, Susan. *Poetry after Auschwitz*. Bloomington: Indiana University Press,

2003.

Guerin, Frances. *A Culture of Light: Cinema and Technology in 1920's Germany.* Minneapolis: University of Minneapolis Press, 2005.

Haber, Gordon. "A Thoroughly Diverting Servant: Wishnia's Medieval Thriller Reads Like a 16th Century 'CSI: Prague.'" http://www.forward.com/articles/128807/ (accessed January 24, 2011).

Hadda, Janet. *Isaac Bashevis Singer: A Life.* New York: Oxford University Press, 1997.

Hamill, Pete. *A Drinking Life.* Boston: Back Bay Books, 1994.

———. "Milton Caniff." In *Masters of American Comics,* ed. John Carlin. Los Angeles: Hammer Museum and the Museum of Contemporary Art, 2005.

———. "Once We Were Kings (1999)." In *Making the Irish American: History and Heritage of the Irish in the United States,* ed. J. J. Lee and Marion R. Casey. New York: New York University Press, 2006.

———. "Pete Hamill." In *Booknotes: America's Finest Authors on Reading, Writing, and the Power of Ideas,* ed. Brian Lamb. New York: Times Books, 1997.

Harde, Roxanne. "'Give 'em Another Circumcision': Jewish Masculinities in *The Golem's Mighty Swing.*" In *The Jewish Graphic Novel: Critical Approaches,* ed. Samantha Baskind and Ranen Omer-Sherman. New Brunswick: Rutgers University Press, 2008.

Hartman, Geoffrey. "On the Jewish Imagination." *Prooftexts* 5 (1985): 210–20.

Hatfield, Charles. "The Golem's Mighty Swing." http://indyworld.com/indy/summer_2004/review_golem/index.html (accessed July 2009).

Heron, Kim. "I Required a Dawning." *New York Times,* September 10, 1989, BR39.

Hirsch, Marianne. *Family Frames: Photography, Narrative, and Postmemory.* Cambridge, MA: Harvard UP, 1997.

Hsia, R. P-chia. *The Myth of Ritual Murder: Jews and Magic in Reformation Germany.* New Haven: Yale University Press, 1988.

Hungerford, Amy. *The Holocaust of Texts: Genocide, Literature, and Personification.* Chicago: University of Chicago Press, 2003.

Hunt, Leon. "'The Student of Prague': Division and Codification of Space." In *Early Cinema: Space, Frame, Narrative,* ed. Thomas Elsaesser. London: British Film Institute, 1990.

Hutcheon, Linda. "Historiographic Metafiction: Parody and the Intertextuality of History." In *Intertextuality and Contemporary American Fiction,* ed. Patrick O'Donnell and Robert Con Davis. Baltimore: Johns Hopkins University Press, 1989.

———. *A Theory of Adaptation.* New York: Routledge, 2006.

Idel, Moshe. *Golem: Jewish Magical and Mystical Tradition on the Artificial Android.* Albany: SUNY University Press, 1990.

Irwin, Robert. Introduction to *The Golem,* by Gustav Meyrink. London: Dedalus, 1985.

Isenberg, Noah. *Between Redemption and Doom: The Strains of German-Jewish*

Modernism. Lincoln: University of Nebraska Press, 1999.

———, ed. *Weimar Cinema: An Essential Guide to the Classic Films of the Era.* New York: Columbia University Press, 2009.

Kaplan, Arie. *From Krakow to Krypton: Jews and Comic Books.* Philadelphia: Jewish Publication Society, 2008.

Katz, Adam. "Iconoclastic Commitments: Idolatry and Imagination in Cynthia Ozick and Ronald Sukenick." *Mosaic* 38, no. 3 (September 2005): 124.

Kauvar, Elaine M. "Cynthia Ozick's Book of Creation: 'Puttermesser and Xanthippe.'" *Contemporary Literature* 26, no. 1 (Spring 1985): 40–54.

———. "An Interview with Cynthia Ozick." *Contemporary Literature* 26, no. 4 (Winter 1985): 375–401.

———. "An Interview with Cynthia Ozick." *Contemporary Literature* 34, no. 3 (Autumn 1993): 359–94.

Keeva, Steven. "A Failure of Imagination." *ABA Journal* 90, no. 7 (July 2004): 74–75.

Kieval, Hillel J. *Languages of Community: The Jewish Experience in Czech Lands.* Berkeley: University of California Press, 2000.

———. "Pursuing the Golem of Prague: Jewish Culture and the Invention of Tradition." *Modern Judaism* 17, no. 1 (1997): 1–20.

Klima. Ivan. *The Spirit of Prague.* New York: Granta Books, 1994.

Knapp, Bettina. *The Prometheus Syndrome.* Troy, NY: Whitson Publishing, 1979.

Kotzin, Michael C. "Uses of Enchantment in Singer's Children's Stories." *Yiddish* 5, no. 1 (Fall 1982): 5–21.

Koven, Mikel. "'Have I Got a Monster for You!': Some Thoughts on the Golem, *The X-Files*, and the Jewish Horror Movie." *Folklore* 111 (2000): 217–30.

Kracauer, Siegfried. *From Caligari to Hitler: A Psychological History of the German Film.* Princeton: Princeton University Press, 1947.

Krause, Maureen. "Introduction: 'Bereshit bara Elohim': A Survey of the Genesis and Evolution of the Golem." *Journal of the Fantastic in the Arts* 7, no. 2 (1996): 113–36.

Krauss, Nichole. *The History of Love.* New York: Norton, 2005.

Kremer, S. Lillian. "Post-Alienation: Recent Directions in Jewish-American Literature." *Contemporary Literature* 34, no. 3 (Autumn 1993): 571–91.

———. *Witness through the Imagination: Jewish American Holocaust Literature.* Detroit: Wayne State University Press, 1989.

———. *Women's Holocaust Writing: Memory and Imagination.* Lincoln: University of Nebraska Press, 1999.

Kristeva, Julia. "Intertextuality: An Interview with Julia Kristeva." Conducted by Margaret Smallen. http://www.msu.edu/user/chrenkal/1980/INTEX-INT.HTM (accessed March 8, 2008).

———. *The Kristeva Reader.* Ed. Toril Moi. New York: Columbia University Press, 1986.

Krupnick, Mark. *Jewish Writing and the Deep Places of the Imagination.* Madison: University of Wisconsin Press, 2005.

Lang, Berel. *Writing and the Holocaust.* New York: Holmes and Meier, 1988.

Langer, Lawrence L. *The Holocaust and the Literary Imagination.* New Haven: Yale University Press, 1975.

Ledig, Elfi. "Making Movie Myths: Paul Wegener's 'The Golem.'" In *Golem! Danger, Deliverance, and Art,* ed. Emily Bilski. New York: The Jewish Museum, 1988.

Leiman, S. Z. "The Adventure of the Maharal of Prague in London: Rabbi Yudl Rosenberg and the Golem of Prague." *Tradition: A Journal of Orthodox Jewish Thought* 36, no. 1 (Spring 2002): 26–58.

Leonard, John. "Levitation: Five Fictions by Cynthia Ozick." *New York Times,* January 28, 1982, sec. C, p. 21.

Leviant, Curt, ed. *The Golem and the Wondrous Deeds of the Maharal of Prague,* by Yudl Rosenberg. New Haven: Yale University Press, 2007.

Lowin, Joseph. *Cynthia Ozick.* Boston: Twayne, 1988.

———. "Cynthia Ozick." http://jewishvirtuallibrary.org/jsource/biography/Ozick.html (accessed July 2009).

Macey, David. *The Penguin Dictionary of Critical Theory.* London: Penguin, 2000.

Madison, Charles A. *Yiddish Literature: Its Scope and Major Writers.* New York: Frederick Ungar, 1968.

Manguel, Alberto. *Into the Looking-Glass Wood: Essays on Books, Reading, and the World.* New York: Harcourt, 1998.

Manvell, Roger. *Masterworks of the German Cinema.* New York: Harper and Row, 1973.

McCloud, Scott. *Understanding Comics: The Invisible Art.* New York: Harper Perennial, 1994.

McCormick, Richard. *Gender and Sexuality in Weimar Modernity: Film, Literature, and "New Objectivity."* New York: Palgrave, 2001.

McGlothlin, Erin. "Narrative Transgression in Edgar Hilsenrath's *Der Nazi und der Friseur* and the Rhetoric of the Sacred in Holocaust Discourse." *German Quarterly* 80, no. 2 (Spring 2007): 220–39.

Mitchell, Mike. Introduction to *The Angel in the West Window,* by Gustav Meyrink. Trans. Mike Mitchell. Riverside, CA: Ariadne Press, 1991.

———. *Vivo: The Life of Gustav Meyrink.* Cambridge: Dedalus, 2008.

Morris, Nicola. "The Golem as Metaphor in Jewish American Literature." Ph.D. diss., SUNY Binghamton University, 2004.

———. *The Golem in Jewish American Literature: Risks and Responsibilities in the Fiction of Thane Rosenbaum, Nomi Eve, and Steve Stern.* Bern: Peter Lang Publishing, 2007.

Murray, Bruce. *Film and the German Left in the Weimar Republic: From Caligari to Kuhle Wampe.* Austin: University of Texas Press, 1990.

Myers, D. G. "Michael Chabon's Imaginary Jews." *Sewanee Review* 116, no. 4 (2008): 572–88.

Newfield, Jack. "An Interview with Pete Hamill." *Tikkun* 13, no. 2 (March–April 1998): 24–28.

Noerr, F. A. Schmid. *"Der Dichter Gustav Meyrink."* In Gustav Meyrink, *Des Deutchen Spiessers Wunderhorn: Gesammelte Novellen.* München-Leipzig: Paul List-Verlag, 1948.

Noiville, Florence. *Isaac B. Singer: A Life.* Trans. Catherine Temerson. New York: Farrar, Straus and Giroux, 2006.

Norton, James. Review of *The Golem's Mighty Swing,* by James Stern. *Flakmagazine.* November 2, 2001. http://www.flakmag.com/books/golem.html (accessed July 2009).

Novak, Barbara. "Lonely Monster." *New York Times,* November 14, 1982, BR48.

Nussbaum, Emily. "The Long Con." *New York Magazine,* June 25, 2007, 38–41, 114.

Olshan, Joseph. "Interview with Frances Sherwood." *People Weekly,* June 28, 1993, pp. 22–23.

Orr, Mary. *Intertextuality: Debates and Contexts.* Cambridge: Polity Press, 2003.

Ozick, Cynthia. "Innovation and Redemption: What Literature Means." In *Art and Ardor.* New York: Knopf, 1983.

———. "The Rights of History and the Rights of the Imagination." *Commentary* 107, no. 3 (March 1999): 22.

Peacock, Scot. "Thane Rosenbaum." *Contemporary Authors.* Vol. 214, pp. 302–4. Detroit: Gale, 2004.

Philip, Neil. "Fall into Flesh." *Times Educational Supplement,* February 25, 1983, p. 34.

Powers, Peter Kerry. "Disruptive Memories: Cynthia Ozick, Assimilation and the Invented Past." *Meleus* 20, no. 3 (Autumn 1995): 79–97.

Prenatt, Diane. "Interview: Frances Sherwood." *Belles Lettres* 10, no. 2 (April 1995): 22–26.

Punday, Daniel. "Kavalier & Clay, the Comic-Book Novel, and Authorship in a Corporate World." *Critique* 49, no. 3 (Spring 2008): 291–302.

Rosenbaum, Thane. "Art and Atrocity in a Post-9/11 World." In *Jewish American and Holocaust Literature: Representations of the Postmodern World,* ed. Alan Berger and Gloria Cronin. Albany: SUNY Press, 2004.

———. *Elijah Visible: Stories.* New York: St Martin's, 1996.

———. "The Holocaust Survivor Who Can Let Death Go." *New York Times,* July 11, 1999, AR8, 16.

———. "Imagining a Life after the Unimaginable." *New York Times,* April 19, 1998, AR15–16.

———. *Law Lit, from Atticus Finch to "The Practice": A Collection of Great Writing about the Law.* New York: New Press, 2007.

———. *The Myth of Moral Justice: What Our Legal System Fails to Do Right.* New York: Harper Collins, 2004.

Rosenfeld, Alvin, and Irving Greenberg. *Confronting the Holocaust: The Impact of Elie Wiesel.* Bloomington: Indiana University Press, 1978.

Roth, Philip. *Shop Talk: A Writer and His Colleagues and Their Work.* Boston: Houghton Mifflin, 2001.

Rothstein, Edward. "A Legendary Protector Formed from a Lump of Clay and a Mound of Terror." *New York Times,* September 11, 2006, B3.

Rottensteiner, Franz. Afterword to *The Green Face,* by Gustav Meyrink. Trans. Mike Mitchell. Riverside, CA: Ariadne Press, 1992.

Royal, Derek Parker. "An Interview with Thane Rosenbaum." *Contemporary Literature* 48, no. 1 (2007): 1–28.

Rubenstein, Bilhah. "Narrative Construction in the Works of Yitskhok Bashevis-Zinger and Their Relationship to Kabbalah." In *Isaac Bashevis Singer: His Work and His World,* ed. Hugh Denman. Boston: Brill, 2002.

Rybar, Ctibor. *Jewish Prague.* Trans. Joy Turner-Kadeckova. Prague: Akropolis Publishers, 1991.

Sanders, Julie. *Adaptation and Appropriation.* New York: Routledge, 2006.

Santner, Eric. *Stranded Objects: Mourning, Memory, and Film in Postwar Germany.* Ithaca: Cornell University Press, 1990.

Scheunemann, Dietrich, ed. *Expressionist Film: New Perspectives.* Rochester: Camden House, 2003.

Schlüpmann, Heide. "The First German Art Film: Rye's *The Student of Prague.*" In *German Film and Literature: Adaptations and Transformations,* ed. Eric Rentschler. New York: Methuen, 1986.

Scholem, Gershom. *From Berlin to Jerusalem: Memories of My Youth.* New York: Schocken Books, 1980.

———. *On the Kabbalah and Its Symbolism.* Trans. Ralph Mannheim. 1960. New York: Schocken Books, 1965.

———. *The Messianic Idea in Judaism and Other Essays in Jewish Spirituality.* New York: Schocken, 1995.

———. *Zohar, The Book of Splendor: Basic Readings from the Kabbalah.* New York: Schocken Books, 1949.

Schutz, Diana, ed. *The Amazing Adventures of the Escapist.* Vol. 2. Milwaukie, OR: Dark Horse Books, 2004.

———. *The Amazing Adventures of the Escapist.* Vol. 3. Milwaukie, OR: Dark Horse Books, 2004.

Schutz, Diana, and Dave Land, eds. *The Amazing Adventures of the Escapist.* Vol. 1. Milwaukie, OR: Dark Horse Books, 2004.

Sedinova, Jirina, and Eva Kosakova. *The Golem Walks through Jewish Town.* Trans. Joy Moss Kohoutova. Prague: The Jewish Museum, 1994.

Sherwin, Byron. "Elie Wiesel and Jewish Theology." In *Responses to Elie Wiesel,* ed. Harry James Cargas. New York: Persea Books, 1978.

———. *The Golem Legend: Origins and Implications.* Lanham, MD: University Press of America, 1985.

———. *Golems among Us: How a Jewish Legend Can Help Us Navigate the Biotech Century.* Chicago: Ivan R. Dee, 2004.

Sherwood, Francis. "Autobiographical Essay." In *Contemporary Authors*. Vol. 220. Detroit: Gale, 2004.

Sibelman, Simon. "Jewish Myths and Stereotypes in the Cinema of Julien Duvivier." In *France in Focus: Film and National Identity*, ed. Elizabeth Ezra and Sue Harris. Oxford: Berg, 2000.

Silberman, Marc. *German Cinema: Texts in Context*. Detroit: Wayne State University Press, 1995.

Singer, Isaac Bashevis. "The Golem Is a Myth for Our Time." *New York Times*, August 12, 1984, sec. 2, p. 1.

———. *In My Father's Court*. New York: Farrar, Straus and Giroux, 1966.

———. *Love and Exile*. Garden City, NY: Doubleday, 1984.

———. *Nobel Lecture*. New York: Farrar, Straus and Giroux, 1978.

Singer, Isaac Bashevis, and Richard Burgin. *Conversations with Isaac Bashevis Singer*. Garden City, NY: Doubleday, 1985.

Singer, Marc. "Embodiments of the Real: The Counterlinguistic Turn in the Comic-Book Novel." *Critique* 49, no. 3 (Spring 2008): 273–89.

Sivan, Miriam. *Belonging Too Well: Portraits of Identity in Cynthia Ozick's Fiction*. Albany: SUNY Press, 2009.

Smith, Dinitia. "She May Offer Cookies, But She Still Wields a Ferocious Golem." *New York Times*, July 5, 1997, sec. 1, p. 11.

Spargo, R. Clifton, and Robert Ehrenreich. *After Representation: The Holocaust, Literature and Culture*. New Brunswick: Rutgers University Press, 2009.

Spiegelman, Art. *Maus I: A Survivor's Tale: My Father Bleeds History*. New York: Pantheon, 1986.

———. *Maus II: A Survivor's Tale and Here My Troubles Began*. New York: Pantheon, 1991.

Spiro, Mia. "Re-Animating the Golem: Artificial Anthropoids and the American Jewish Woman Writer." Unpublished essay, 2005.

Stavans, Ilan, ed. *Isaac Bashevis Singer: An Album*. New York: Library of America, 2004.

Steiner-Prag, Hugo. "Einführung." In *Der Golem*, by Gustav Meyrink. Bremen: Carl Schünemann Verlag, 1915.

Strauss, Walter A. "The Golem on the Operatic Stage: Nature's Warning." *Journal of the Fantastic in the Arts* 7, no. 2 (1996): 191–200.

Strysik, John. "The Schizophrenic Scenario of Lemony Snicket." *Creative Screenwriting* 11, no. 6 (2004): 26–27.

Sturm, James. "The Golem's Mighty Swing." *Elysian Fields Quarterly*. http://www.efqreview.com/NewFiles/v18n2/offthewall.html (accessed July 2009).

Suomala, Karla. "Healing the World and Mending the Soul: Understanding *Tikkun Olam*." In *Covenantal Conversations: Christians in Dialogue with Jews and Judaism*, ed. Darrell Jodock. Minneapolis: Fortress Press, 2008.

Templin, Charlotte. "An Interview with Frances Sherwood." *Indiana Review* 20, no. 1 (April 1997): 119–25.

Tytell, Frances Wilke. "The Golem Speaks: A Study of Four Modern Jewish

American Novels." Master's thesis, Wake Forest University, 2005.

Vasbinder, Samuel Holmes. *Scientific Attitudes in Mary Shelley's "Frankenstein."* Ann Arbor: UMI Research Press, 1984.

Versaci, Rocco. *This Book Contains Graphic Language: Comics as Literature.* New York: Continuum, 2007.

Vice, Sue. *Holocaust Fiction.* New York: Routledge, 2000.

Volavkova, Hana, and Pavel Belina. *The Lost Jewish Town of Prague.* Trans. Gita Zbavitelova. Prague: Paseka, 2004.

Walton, David. "PW Talks with Michael Chabon." *Publishers Weekly* 242, no. 15 (August 21, 2000): 45.

Watson, Tracey. "Pete Hamill, 1935–." In *Contemporary Authors: New Revision Series.* Vol. 127. Farmington Hills, MI: Gale, 2004.

Weich, Dave. "Michael Chabon's Amazing Adventures." http://www.powells.com/authors/chabon.html (accessed August 6, 2009).

Wiesel, Elie. *From the Kingdom of Memory: Reminiscences.* New York: Summit Books, 1990.

Wiesel, Elie, and Philippe-Michael de Saint Cheron. *Evil and Exile.* Notre Dame, IN: University of Notre Dame Press, 1990.

Wiesel, Elie, et al. "The Holocaust as Literary Inspiration." In *Dimensions of the Holocaust.* Evanston, IL: Northwestern University Press, 1977.

Winkler, Gershon. *The Golem of Prague.* New York: Judaica Press, 1980.

Witek, Joseph. *Comic Books as History: The Narrative Art of Jack Jackson, Art Spiegelman, and Harvey Pekar.* Jackson: University Press of Mississippi, 1989.

Wolitz, Seth L., ed. *The Hidden Isaac Bashevis Singer.* Austin: University of Texas Press, 2001.

Yair, Gad, and Michaela Soyer. *The Golem in German Social Theory.* Lanham, MD: Lexington Books, 2008.

Zaleski, Jeff. "The Book of Splendor." *Publisher's Weekly* 249, no. 20 (May 20, 2002).

Index

Bloch, Chayim (*continued*)
golem in, 78; magic palace in,
199n13; Ozick's use of, 160–61;
purpose of, 35; Rabbi Loew in,
61
blood libel: in *The Book of Splendor,* 94;
Christian belief in, 35, 194n2; Loew
and, 26, 35; in nineteenth century,
32–33; pogroms based on, 4; in
Pösing, 194n2; in Prague, 32, 45;
protection from, 22; role in golem
creation, 3, 75, 83, 161; in Rosenberg,
29, 30, 94, 198n10; in Russia, 165
Bloom, Harold, 137
Bohemia-Moravia: Holocaust in, 194n5;
Jewish communities of, 23; Statuta
Judaeorum (1262), 32
Book Yetsirah (Book of Creation), 5, 19,
161; golem creation in, 20; in *Golem
of Auschwitz,* 188; in *The X-Files,* 178
Borges, Jorge Luis: "An Autobiographical
Essay," 190; "A Book of Sand," 195n3;
"The Golem," 189–90; knowledge of
Meyrink, 190, 195n4
Borowski, Tadeusz, 11; in *The Golems of
Gotham,* 169
Briggs, Kenneth, 86–87
Brod, Max, 42
Brontë, Charlotte: intertextual
adaptations of, 38, 200n21
Buchen, Irving, 197n2
Burns, Robert, 200n21
Buscema, John, 113
Byrne, Richard, 61, 197n23

Campbell, Joseph, 48
Captain Marvel comics, 129, 131,
199n10
Captain Midnight (radio program), 133
Carrey, Jim, 181
cartoonists, Jewish: name changes by,
111, 126, 140
Casken, John, 4
Celan, Paul, 11; in *The Golems of
Gotham,* 169, 176
Chabon, Michael, 10; genre fiction of,

137–38; influences on, 140, 200n18;
interest in golems, 138, 139; love of
comics, 143–44; truth and lies in,
138–39, 147
*The Amazing Adventures of
Kavalier and Clay,* 13, 137–47,
149–50; comics in, 144,
145–48; comics industry in,
141–43; dichotomies of, 145;
doppelgängers in, 140; escape
in, 141–43, 144, 145–48;
imagination in, 144, 147;
metamorphoses in, 141–43,
144; readers of, 146; setting
of, 140; superhero golem in,
141–42; transformation in, 144
"Golems I have Known," 138–40
Manhood for Amateurs, 149
Maps and Legends, 139, 146
"The Revenge of Captain Nemo,"
140
The Yiddish Policemen's Union,
148
Chagall, Marc, 172
Chomiak, Bohdan, 116
Cohen, Sarah Blacher, 153
Colby, C. B., 139
comics: magic potions in, 130; power
fantasies in, 129; underground, 119;
valorization of, 141, 143, 145
Comics Code Authority, 119
comics industry, American, 13, 14; in
*The Amazing Adventures of Kavalier
and Clay,* 141–43; American fiction
in, 200n17; development of, 141;
Golden Age of, 112, 144; Jewish
founders of, 111–12, 139; superhero
craze in, 141
Cooke, Paul, 57, 58
creation: biblical story of, 4; ritual
representation of, 20. *See also* golem
creation
creativity: golem's links to, 6, 35, 74; link
to Hebrew language, 157; and love of
God, 75; in post-Holocaust literature,
12, 183; as reinvention, 173; of saintly

golem legend, German, 5, 20, 36; in German philosophy, 4; Romantics' use of, 21
golem mosaic (Jewish Quarter, Prague), *ii*
The Golem of L. A. (film), 4, 190–91
golem texts: for children, 4; creation of literary memory, 183; disrespect for Judaism in, 36, 49, 52, 70; of early twentieth century, 2; homage to Judaism in, 70; of Jewish American writers, 15; of late twentieth century, 2; metafictional commentary in, 12; in *Oesterreichischen Wochenschrift*, 35; as palimpsests, 21, 111, 126, 165, 182; post-Holocaust, 2, 4, 8–10, 13–15, 17, 88–89, 100, 120, 127–29, 132–37; and September 11 attacks, 2
Gottesman, Itzik, 80
Gray, Justin, 118
Grimm, Jacob: golem legend of, 5, 21
Grossman, David: *See, Under Love*, 11
Gubar, Susan: *Poetry after Auschwitz*, 193n9
Guedemann, Moritz, 35
Guerin, Frances: *A Culture of Light*, 55–56

Hadda, Janet, 71, 197n3
Hallote, Bernard, 155
Hamill, Billy, 129
Hamill, Pete, 19; comics collection of, 130; contact with Jews, 131; knowledge of Holocaust, 131; knowledge of immigrant experience, 127; life and work of, 128; in Prague, 199n13; as *Shabbos goy*, 131
  A Drinking Life, 129–32
  Snow in August, 14, 50, 127–29, 132–37; autobiography in, 129; baseball in, 129, 134; as *bildungsroman*, 137; comics in, 135; depiction of antisemitism, 132–33, 134, 137; golem creation in, 134, 135, 136; Holocaust in, 137; Holocaust

survivors in, 128, 134, 136; imagination in, 136–37; Jackie Robinson in, 134, 135, 136; Kabbalah in, 133, 135, 137; popularity of, 128; Prague in, 132, 133; Rabbi Loew in, 132, 133–34; setting of, 140
Handler, Daniel: influence of Holocaust on, 181–82
  Watch Your Mouth, 14, 152, 186; doppelgänger motif of, 181; intertextuality of, 180–82; *shem* in, 181
Hans Westmar (film), 57
Hart, Ferdinand, 66
Hartman, Geoffrey, 2–3, 9–10, 88; on the written word, 17
Hasidism, 197n4
Held, Hans Ludwig, 33
Hess, Johannes, 74
Hilsenrath, Edgar: *The Nazi and the Barber*, 12
Hilsner, Leopold, 33
Hirsch, Marianne, 179
histories, alternate, 11, 199n15
Hitler, Adolf, 47, 57, 66; Americans' awareness of, 143, 155; Beer Hall Putsch, 64; Duvivier's representation of, 67
Holitscher, Arthur, 74
Hollander, John: "Letter to Jorge Luis Borges," 190
Holocaust: in Bohemia-Moravia, 194n5; disruption of meaning, 8, 9; imaginative works about, 2, 138–39, 153–54, 176; impact on families, 151–52; impact on Second Generation, 170; misrepresentation of, 154; Ozick's writings on, 152–54; postmodern perceptions of, 100; representation, 2, 9, 10–11, 12, 143, 153; Singer on, 70; in *Snow in August*, 137. *See also* literature, Holocaust
Holocaust survivors: in *The Golems of Gotham*, 169; in *Snow in August*, 128, 136; suicides, 169

Hsia, R. P-chia, 33, 195n10
Hutcheon, Linda, 9; *A Theory of Adaptation*, 8
Hyman, Trina Schart, 4

Idel, Moshe: *Golem*, 4, 7
imagination: as agent of meaning, 11; autonomy of, 154; distrust of, 88; failure of, 170; golem's symbolization of, 137; history and, 161; liberating role of, 144; moral, 137; in *The Puttermesser Papers*, 167; in *Snow in August*, 136–37; and traumatic memory, 151
imagination, Jewish, 9; ambivalence concerning, 10; golem in, 3, 35, 74, 100, 137; honoring by golem legend, 35; intertextuality of, 2, 10, 15, 25, 100; in medieval philosophy, 10; Nazi attack on, 12; in post-Holocaust literature, 2, 3, 12, 88, 140–41, 142, 148–49, 168, 170, 183, 186; as redemption, 85; role in survival, 99; written word in, 17
immigrants, Jewish: assimilation of, 111, 127; into Germany, 64; in graphic novels, 120–21; from Russia, 165
The Incredible Hulk, 199n3
influence, anxiety of, 137
intertextuality: in *The Book of Splendor*, 99, 198n19; in creation of Superman, 112; familiarity with originals in, 200n21; in golem legends, 9, 37; of *The Golem's Mighty Swing*, 49–50, 123; of *The Golems of Gotham*, 173; of *The Golem Song*, 186; of Jewish imagination, 2, 10, 15, 25, 100; literary memory in, 15, 25, 100; as metafiction, 8, 99; in Meyrink's *Golem*, 49, 69; Ozick's use of, 156, 201n4; and post-Holocaust literature, 8–10, 183; of *The Puttermesser Papers*, 164–65, 166; as *shem*, 183; of Singer's *Golem*, 79; of *Der Student von Prag*, 56–57; as transgressive, 12; of Wegener's *Golem*, 51, 52, 65, 68

Irish Americans, immigrant experience of, 127
Isenberg, Noah, 50; on Wegener, 64

Jewish Daily Forward, 70, 81
Jewish Quarter (Prague), *103;* Cemetery of, 136, 199n13; confiscation of books from, 84, 198n9; decadent atmosphere of, 45–46; destruction of, 24, 196n11; golem legends of, 12, 18, 22–28; golem souvenirs from, 2; history of, 23–24; illustrations of, 45; in Meyrink, 25, 41–46, 49, 50; pogrom of 1389, 23; population of, 23; threats to, 3; tourists to, 2; in twenty-first century, 24. *See also* Old-New Synagogue; Prague
Jewish question (Germany): Final Solution to, 68; technological solution for, 55
Jews: association with usury, 57; of Bohemia-Moravia, 23; emancipation of, 23; European images of, 63; immigration into Germany, 64; medieval merchants, 22–23; as outsiders, 63; as People of the Book, 3, 10; post-Holocaust identity of, 177; relations with gentiles, 37; stereotypes of, 40, 44–45, 46
Jews, American: assimilation of, 111; in comics industry, 111–12, 126, 139; male identity of, 126–27; women writers, 201n7
Jews, Polish: culture of, 70–72; expulsion from Prague, 23, 58, 94, 196n13, 197n18; golem legends of, 5, 21; under Holy Roman Emperors, 58; of Warsaw, 72–73
Jews, Russian: immigration to U.S., 165
Josefov. *See* Jewish Quarter (Prague)
Joyce, James: intertexts of, 38
Jud Süss (Nazi propaganda film), 45, 52, 125
Jung, Carl, 48

Kaballa (comic monster), 114, 116–17

Prague (*continued*)
  Puttermesser Papers, 161; Sherwood's
  experience of, 90; in *Snow in August*,
  132, 133; synagogues of, 96, 194n5.
  See also Jewish Quarter (Prague);
  Old-New Synagogue
propaganda films, Nazi, 45, 46, 52, 57,
  63, 125, 126
Psalm 139, golem in, 5, 12, 17, 74
Pseudo-Saadya, 5
Punday, Daniel, 200n17

rabbis: creation of life, 18–19; wonder,
  74, 197n4
racism, American, 125–26
Rava, Rabbi, 161
Rawicz, Piotr: in *The Golems of Gotham*,
  169
representation: of creation, 20; effect of
  trauma on, 143; of Holocaust, 2, 9,
  10–11, 12, 143, 153; realist, 9
Rhys, Jean: *Wide Sargasso Sea*, 38,
  200n21
Rich, Adrienne, 38
ritual murder. *See* blood libel
Robinson, Jackie: in *Snow in August*, 134,
  135, 136
Rogasky, Barbara: *The Golem*, 4
Rosenbaum, Thane, 19; on Holocaust
  narratives, 171; life and work of,
  169–70; post-Holocaust writings
  of, 176, 177; in Second Generation
  writers, 151, 169, 170
  Elijah Visible, 174
  The Golems of Gotham, 14, 151,
    168, 170, 171–77, 180; critical
    reception of, 177; destructive
    golems in, 176; golem creation
    in, 174–75; Holocaust in, 172,
    174–75; Holocaust survivors
    in, 169, 175, 183; identity in,
    177; intertextuality of, 173;
    magical realism of, 172, 176,
    177; narration in, 174, 175;
    setting of, 171; suicide in, 172,
    173; themes of, 177

"The Little Blue Snowman of
  Washington Heights," 202n19
  The Myth of Moral Justice, 170
Rosenberg, Yudl, 5, 12, 18; experience
  of blood libel, 32, 33; Singer's use of,
  75, 76
  *The Golem and the Wondrous
    Deeds of the Maharal of
    Prague*, 8, 28–33; Bloch's
    use of, 28, 33–35, 160;
    blood libel in, 29, 30, 94,
    198n10; destructive golem
    in, 78; editions of, 29; golem
    decommissioning in, 30–31;
    Hebrew versions of, 29, 34;
    intextual references from, 29;
    Loew in, 28–32; protector
    golem in, 29–30, 31; Rudolf
    II in, 30; Sherwood's use of,
    89; sources of, 28, 30, 189n17;
    Thaddeus in, 29, 30, 199n13;
    Yiddish version of, 29, 34
Rothberg, Abraham: *Sword of the Golem*,
  6
Rothstein, Edward: "A Legendary
  Protector Formed from a Lump of
  Clay," 2
Rudolf II (Holy Roman Emperor),
  198n14; in *The Book of Splendor*, 13,
  93, 94, 95, 97, 98; death of, 94; in
  Duvivier's *Golem*, 66, 67; as Hitler
  figure, 67; interest in the occult, 26,
  94; meeting with Loew, 26, 30, 77;
  relations with Jewish community,
  37, 58, 196n13; in Rosenberg, 30;
  in Singer's *Golem*, 77; in Wegener's
  Golem, 51–52, 54, 58–59, 62, 64
Russia: blood libel in, 165; immigrants
  from, 165; pogroms in, 33
Rye, Stellan: *Der Student von Prag*, 56

Salmonova, Lyda, 59
Saloun, Ladislav Jan, 65
Sanders, Julie: *Adaptation and
  Appropriation*, 8
Sauerlaender, Paul, 196n12